Southern Fried Fiction

How The Insidious Onset Of Depression Derailed A Successful Man's Life

A MEMOIR

Stuart Hotchkiss

ISBN: 1507665806
ISBN: 9781507665800
Library of Congress Control Number: 2015901198
CreateSpace Independent Publishing Platform
North Charleston, South Carolina

Front cover illustration of Halsnoch by E. J. Pettinger

Printed in the USA

For the Rt. Rev. John Stuart Thornton,
Retired Bishop, Episcopal Diocese of Idaho

A beloved friend on the Way

Table of Contents

Prologue

My man had told me he could get his hands on a basic model Glock handgun for three hundred bucks. His assurance that it would be clean and untraceable didn't matter to me. You can't put a dead man in jail.

And that's what I planned to be in a few days—dead and gone.

My career in publishing had been cut short by senseless litigation. I'd accumulated debt the size of Texas. My mother had just drawn her last breath. I was estranged from my only son and about to go to jail for failing to pay his private college tuition. Worst of all, my wife had told me to find another place to live. She wanted me off her payroll and out of her life.

My heart was shattered, and I was trapped in the maelstrom of depression. What was the point of living?

I scrambled to come up with the money. A ten-volume collector's set of American Civil War books was all I had left to unload. Thank goodness for eBay. Some zealous guy in Maryland won my auction, and I drove the books to his house the next day. He paid me in cash and made me flush.

The stage was now set for the biggest score of my life.

As I sat alone at the bar of a Washington, DC, tavern, waiting for my benefactor to return, the moment felt utterly surreal. East was west; hot was cold; day was night. But tomorrow everything would change. To mark the occasion, I downed what I believed would be my very last beer, a seasonal brew made by Magic Hat in Vermont and appropriately called Wacko. I'd always found drinking beer invigorating. As it flowed down my throat, the taste of this liquid song of summer refreshed me. This was one thing I'd miss once I was gone, but not much else.

Suddenly, there *he* was, toting a black gym bag. He played it very cool, waiting what seemed like a dog's age to remove the Glock. I held the gun briefly under the bar and then stashed it away. *Christ, the thing weighs a ton!* I realized. He quickly explained how to use it, and I gave him the money. He didn't pry into my business, and I didn't volunteer anything. He'd probably read about me soon enough in the *Washington Post*, I figured.

I planned to drive south to Richmond, Virginia, in the morning. My destination was Hollywood Cemetery, where I was going to sit beneath a granite angel on the family plot overlooking the James River and pull the trigger. Courtesy of those old books I'd been lugging around my entire adult life, I'd be doing the deed in a cemetery that was the resting place of twenty-five Confederate generals. I'd lost all my possessions, my pride, and my dignity, but not my sense of irony.

Before my rendezvous with death, I wanted to fulfill a commitment I'd made to my primary care physician, Dr. Jennifer Beach. I'd spilled my guts to her two weeks earlier about wanting to commit suicide. I'd promised her I wouldn't do anything until I returned to see her this day. I didn't owe Dr. Beach a thing, but she'd certainly earned my respect. She seemed like the only person who gave a damn about me, even if it was in her job description.

I entered the medical center and took a seat in the packed waiting room. Dr. Beach emerged, a mere seven minutes behind schedule. I rose and met her, one foot inside the "Patients Only" area. "Thank you so much for coming back to see me," she said in a caring, compassionate voice. I forced a token smile.

She was proud of me for standing there in front of her—alive.

"Do you still feel suicidal?"

I nodded. She had a room full of patients in her outer office waiting to be processed, but my gesture froze time. I was the center of her universe.

As she looked at me, there was a powerful message in her eyes. So powerful, in fact, that it was epiphanic, and I continued to listen.

"If you're set on this, then I'm obliged to help," she confessed, foremost as a legal disclaimer but also as an act of compassion.

I could have lied about being suicidal and walked away, but I was tired of pretending. That's all I'd done my entire life.

"Perhaps we can make a difference," she continued. "What do you have to lose?"

Dr. Beach had a point. I had absolutely nothing to lose but time, and I was already willing to throw away whatever days, months, or years I had left on earth. Something in her argument was convincing, because I'd forgotten all about that loaded gun. I'd become so accustomed to feeling like people wanted to destroy me that I'd forgotten what it felt like for someone to care about me.

Over and over, she kept asserting, "I want to help you."

And hearing her pleas, I started to see possibilities. I could voluntarily check myself into Georgetown University's psychiatric ward for observation and treatment. There was no shame in that, I thought to myself, but first I had some questions.

"What exactly are they going to do?" I asked.

"They'll evaluate your overall health. They'll use therapy to try and increase your sense of well-being and talk about what's been happening in your life, what's brought you to this point. They'll also take a look at medication alternatives to help you feel more stable. Most of all, they'll offer you a completely safe and healthy environment."

I was all too familiar with the medication part; the real question was, did I have the stomach to explore my life? Along with periods of fun and adventure, the majority of my time on earth had been shaped by tragedy, misfortune, betrayal, and bad choices. Was I prepared to revisit all this? Was I strong enough to stick with the process?

Dr. Beach was right. Maybe, just maybe, if I faced my demons head on, I could turn myself around. I might yet find my happy side again. While I was by no means convinced, my plan to kill myself later that day was neutralized. I was willing to live at least another day.

"How does this all work? I mean, my life is so chaotic, where do I even begin telling someone the mess that I'm in?"

"Most people," the doctor told me, "just start from the beginning."

CHAPTER 1

To the Cottage Born

ON A TYPICAL Wednesday afternoon in the spring of 1966, you'd find me in the rear seat of Mrs. Kimbrough's station wagon with her son and three other fifth-grade classmates. This was her day for carpool duty.

After picking us up from school, she'd chauffeur us home, one after another. We traveled through some of the nicer middle-class neighborhoods in Richmond, Virginia. She'd pull off the main road into short and narrow driveways and wait until her charges were safely inside their houses before driving on.

Her penultimate stop was 6709 River Road, a coveted address just west of the city limits and north of the James River. It was right past the Hayes and Hunton estates. You couldn't miss it if you tried.

Once through the gated entrance, she moseyed up a long driveway past a dozen tall oaks that were planted there in 1917—the year the estate was built. The main dwelling, the manor house, was an architectural marvel, with its formal living and dining rooms, breakfast room, sunroom, and not just one but two kitchens on the first floor. Up the grand center-hall staircase, there were five bedrooms and a study on the second floor and full servants' quarters up on the third floor.

It was one of several structures sitting on a combined four acres of prime property called Halsnoch, a fictional estate name conceived by its owner. He had wanted it to sound Scottish and told us it was a translation of "Henry's Hill."

As Mrs. Kimbrough's vehicle approached the circular part of the driveway at six o'clock, the entrance to the manor house was halfway around at twelve o'clock. She would always ooh and aah when she faced it head on, even though she'd seen it a hundred times before.

"Stuart, you sure are one lucky little boy living here," she observed one day.

I paused to reflect on her compliment and didn't immediately answer. Perhaps it wasn't the first time she'd said this, but it *was* the first time it had hit me as being untrue.

I saw her eyes creep into the rearview mirror, getting more and more inquisitive as the five or ten seconds of silence passed.

"Yes, ma'am, I certainly am," I replied.

As an eleven-year-old boy, I was already a conflicted soul.

It wasn't just the framed exterior of the mansion that caught Mrs. Kimbrough's eye; she was equally impressed with the red-brick steps and sidewalks, holly trees, and English boxwood that were part of the sumptuous landscaping.

But she didn't drive to twelve o'clock that day or any other day she had carpool duty. No, she'd stop after driving counterclockwise to three o'clock on the circle. That's where I got out. I didn't live in the "big house." My paternal grandfather, his second wife, and his eldest son, a confirmed bachelor—that's right, three adults—lived there, and very comfortably, I might add. My parents, my older brother, and I lived fifty paces down a slate walkway in a small two-bedroom cottage. I never heard Mrs. Kimbrough or any other carpool mother call it anything. Not even quaint or cozy. Compared with the big house, it looked more like the servants' quarters.

This was a mix of affluence and welfare that didn't belong in the same picture. I knew that anyone directing a compliment toward Halsnoch meant it for the lord of the manor, and they presumed he "had money." Indeed, Henry Starke Hotchkiss, one of my namesakes, looked every bit the part. His bourbon-soaked accent and captivating manners charmed men and women alike. He wore high-street bespoke suits and diamond-point bow ties to complete the look of a landed gentleman.

He was my master and a formidable man. He spoke his mind and had his way. When he barked out an order, I answered back, "Yes, sir, Papa," drawling the last word in Southernese as "Paw-paw." I rarely dared to cross him—out of fear and respect.

He was determined for people to think he was a self-made man. The truth, now that I'm allowed to speak it, was his mother gave him the money to buy Halsnoch. Her family, the Starkes, had held prominent positions in neighboring Hanover County. This head start—along with a career that included three veep-level jobs in bonded warehousing, shoe manufacturing, and banking—allowed him to raise his three sons and a daughter in style, and to keep his family front and center in Richmond society.

By the time the Great Depression hit, Papa was, according to family lore, on the brink of financial ruin. Be that fact or fiction, he was indeed fortified—in 1934, at the age of fifty-three—by inheritance from yet another Starke, his mother's brother, Ashton. Why this well-to-do socialite—described in the press as one of the "Makers of Richmond"—chose to leave most, if not all, of his estate to his nephew and not to his widow was simply not discussed—ever. I marveled at how a secret *this* big was never the subject of gossip. Kudos to those involved in the cover-up, because Halsnoch and Papa's standing were preserved.

Furthermore, it enabled my grandfather—this master of the dance of distraction—to retire and lead a modest yet comfortable life as a gentleman farmer. Like his uncle Ashton, Papa became civic minded. He campaigned tirelessly for Southern Democrats who refused to bend to any party lash. He was a vigorous speaker—his unrivaled loquacity wore down opponents and earned him the nickname Honey Boy. He was the ideal of an informed citizen and, as such, became Richmond's unofficial ombudsman. Important people—politicians, business leaders, police chiefs, and entertainers—graced the front door of Halsnoch to seek Papa's counsel. They never left dissatisfied. Or sober.

By the 1960s, this *paterfamilias*—now in his eighties—found himself running the business of family. Papa's discretionary income had become my nuclear family's disposable income. He raised my older brother, Nicky, and me like his own children, because my father, Nelson, was not able to do so. Consequently, Big Daddy—a nickname given to Papa by some of his cronies after the debut of *Cat on a Hot Tin Roof*—kept a tight grip on our emotions, motivations, and aspirations. If we thought we were ever going to leave this life of Riley, then we had another think coming.

I have to admit, Halsnoch was a captivating place. Nicky and I took full advantage of its acreage and natural splendor. There were orchards, vegetable and flower gardens, hunting dogs, goats, and lots of nooks and crannies. We were able to design a miniature par-three golf course that included some pretty tricky shots over those spreading oak trees that lined the driveway. River Road was out-of-bounds, yet hitting a moving car, accidentally or not, was never a worry. Papa was our commander in chief. He had our backs and made no apologies for wielding power.

We'd collect fallen Rome apples and Bartlett pears from the soggy leach fields in the orchard, in part to keep them from getting chopped up by the Jacobsen high-wheel lawn mower and making our backyard smell even worse. We'd pile the overripe nuisance fruit at the base of the trees and hurl the hardest, most unripe pieces like baseballs forty yards or so across the goat yard, over the heads of a pair of floppy-eared Nubians. It was a rare feat when a pome cleared both the yard and the snake-infested maintenance shed that bordered the Hayes's property.

Papa was enamored with baseball and loved to showcase to his guests any talent we had. He would gather his rota of contemporaries for stiff libations not on the fancy sun porch but rather on a small and uneven piece of lawn adjacent to the big house—closer to the action. One could feel tipsy just sitting there, even before the first whiff of Smith Bowman's Virginia Gentleman. After the host finished crushing ice in a canvas cotton bag—the Lewis brand, naturally—for his signature mint juleps, we were allowed to borrow the foot-long wooden club, using it as a miniature bat to blast tennis balls into the outfield of our very own Field of Dreams.

This was as good as things got for me at Halsnoch. The more mundane chores of yard work—mowing the upper and lower lawns, pulling a Heinz variety of weeds, pruning nine-foot-tall forsythia, and barbering each blade of grass that covered the circle of stones in the driveway—was far more the norm...and expectation. Unlike most kids, whose chores maintained one household, Nicky and I found ourselves more often than not serving at the pleasure of Papa as well as our own parents. Never once did I forget that my clan was squatting.

Hard work did have one huge reward. From the time Nicky was nine and I was six, we sponged off of Papa's membership to the Country Club of Virginia as junior members and became, time permitting, golf rats during the summer. Someone in the family would drop us off in the morning and pick us up in the evening. When we needed something to eat or drink, we went to what was then called Ollie's snack bar and gave the server Papa's membership number—H221. That's all there was to it. The irony was not lost on me that we belonged to a country club that served the bastions of Richmond society and my parents were poorer than the help.

Without trying to sound like a brat, the life I was living then didn't completely seem like mine; it seemed like one chosen for me by Papa. It was an uncomfortable notion, and the older I got, the more I became depressed. There was no one else to whom I could turn.

Papa's sister, Lizzie, my great aunt, was equally controlling. She doled out the tuition to send Nicky and me to the same exclusive, private boys' school, St. Christopher's, that my father and his brothers had attended. To her, it was a family tradition that couldn't be broken. To make her point, she told us she'd rather live in the po' house than have us attend public school.

My great aunt never worked for wages, choosing instead to volunteer her time and talent and live a simple, yet comfortable, life from the inheritance she had received from her parents. Fiercely independent, she was adamantly opposed to public handouts. Lizzie battled the Social Security Administration every month to return her benefit checks. She told them she didn't deserve the money, but they refused to oblige her and kept on sending checks. So she deposited the funds into a savings account and never touched a dime of it. Suffice it to say, Lizzie lived well within her means.

There was no getting around the fact I came from good stock. Ever since Samuel Hotchkiss first emigrated from England to New Haven, Connecticut, in 1638, it was common for each generation of Hotchkiss men to be leaders in their communities, own land, and marry into equally fine families. My mother Margaret's family—the Grants—was never talked about at home, but they were one-time players in Richmond, too. In the early 1900s, they had held title to Grantland, over six hundred acres of real estate a few miles west of Halsnoch. Mix these two bloodlines together, add more than a jiggerful of Southern gentility, and you have a pretty good recipe for WASP soup.

Problem was, my father had let the soup get cold, and Nicky and I were the only ones left to reheat it. It was the sort of pressure we never asked for or handled well. There had never been a lawyer in the family, but by golly, Mr. Hunton, our dear friend and neighbor, would certainly arrange a job for me. He was, after all, the managing partner of Hunton & Williams, one of the most highly respected law firms in the South.

"I've never met a poor lawyer," my mother liked to preach from her bottomless supply of maxims.

She had married a man who graduated—with distinction—from St. Christopher's and then Virginia Military Institute. He'd served in World War II then taught at two military high schools in Virginia before deciding to open up a gift shop—called The Playroom—in Richmond. Her expectations were never fulfilled—he never made more than grocery money as a businessman, *and* the Hotchkisses weren't wealthy.

Despite proof that life is a crapshoot, she couldn't wait for the day Nicky and I went out into the world with a St. Christopher's education. At the heart of the school lay a passion and commitment to prepare each student to excel in life. They didn't necessarily build souls, but they did build successful men. We'd have a life full of wealth and opportunity, not the one she'd been living vicariously through her friends.

Along with a rigorous academic program, St. Christopher's had a long-standing tradition of assigning its Lower School students to one of two literary societies, the Lees or the Jacksons. This helped boys develop public-speaking skills, a sense of teamwork, creativity, and self-esteem. In fifth grade I was chosen by my peers to be president of the Jackson Society. I wasn't the most brilliant or well-read student, but I was really good at memorizing. And, like Papa, I could deliver a good speech.

Three times a year, the school held "open" meetings, to which the public was invited. Proud families would fill the Lower School auditorium and strain neck and shoulder muscles to catch a glimpse of their little "saints" on stage. Afterward, the attendees spilled out onto the school lawn to gloat over their prodigies. Papa and Lizzie came mainly as substitutes for my parents, one or both of whom were always stuck at the gift shop my father owned. Not surprisingly, my elders stood out in the much-younger crowd.

"Who the heck is the lady with Stuart's grandfather?" said the ignorant and uninitiated as Papa and Lizzie hovered over me during the post-meeting brag fests.

Papa, who could have been mistaken for a retired headmaster, cut a fine figure and fit right into the picture. Lizzie's physical appearance, however, was an entirely different matter. Her short, slicked-back hair, flat chest, and round tortoise-shell eyeglasses made her look more like a male city lawyer than a society belle.

And so the chitchat continued.

Civil rights and antiwar activist Dr. Martin Luther King Jr. was assassinated on March 4, 1968. It was a real eye-opener for me, a time to reflect on what was wrong with white America, especially in the South. The reaction to the shooting from students and teachers at St. Christopher's was so venomously racist and hateful I can't bear to acknowledge what was said then—or by whom.

Papa's reaction befuddled me. Normally quite progressive in racial matters, he switched gears once James Earl Ray was arrested at London's Heathrow Airport and charged with Dr. King's murder. Papa believed Ray was an unwitting pawn, used by the anti-King faction of the National Baptist Convention—not the Hoover-led FBI or any other part of the government—to stir up civil unrest. Rather than let off some steam from a soapbox, he chose instead to validate those who made crude and meritless remarks about Negroes.

That summer, matters went from bad to worse. Papa found himself forced to hire a second yardman, a black man much younger and stronger than the elderly black gentleman who'd worked at Halsnoch since its inception. To Papa's credit, he let the old "grinder" keep his job and dignity. But he never gave the new hire a chance to prove himself. He kept comparing him to the incumbent, knowing full well that, as a product of the times, he'd never find another man so loyal, hardworking, and trustworthy. "You can't trust these new *nigras*," Papa would say. "They just want too much."

And he didn't stop there. He claimed the new yardman had been stealing lawn equipment from the garage, a large detached building in plain view of the big house, with several stalls used to safeguard lawn mowers and a variety of yard implements. If the suspect had been white, my grandfather would have settled the matter quickly with words—and a shot of whiskey. But since the man was black, Papa wanted to catch him in the act and teach him a lesson he'd never forget. I was made to sit sentry at the bedroom window with a loaded Winchester pointed at a key point of entry to the garage. I'd never shot a thing in my life, not even a tin can, but there I was in hot pursuit of a fellow human being. Papa had replaced the buckshot in the shells with rice, and I was instructed to shoot the man in the ass, on sight. Mercifully, I sat there with my eyes closed until the end of my shift, and nothing went missing.

This exposure to Papa's racism became the catalyst for my newfound support of the civil rights movement. I wore "Free Bobby Seale" buttons to school, advocating the release of the jailed Black Panther. I traveled by bus to the slums of East Richmond and bought my vinyl 45-RPM records from the Churchill Record Shop—paying at least a 40-percent premium over the price charged at Gary's, where white Richmond shopped.

I also started adding more "color" to my schoolwork. After all, St. Christopher's was an Episcopal school and preached racial diversity—or so I thought.

Every eighth grade student at St. Christopher's was required to complete a year-long research project and present it orally to the student body before graduating middle school. The typical project focused on a notable colonial man or woman whose portrait hung in the school hallway. But I chose the path *never* traveled and researched a group of local radio personalities who were very much alive and making a difference in the poorer half of our community.

The idea popped into my head like the refrain of a hit song. These local soul legends had founded the seminal black radio station, WANT, in 1951. I tuned in regularly to its 990-AM frequency and bought most of my records based on the music I heard there. That got me in the door. When I went to the station for my first interview with veteran disc jockey John "Tiger Tom" Mitchell, he asked if I knew the derivation of the station's call letters. I had no clue and became worried that he might terminate the interview due to my lack of homework.

"With All Negro Talent," he cackled, exactly the way he did on air.

We clicked from that moment on. My presentation at school concluded with a recorded message from Tiger Tom instructing the judges to award me an A for my creativity and innovation. That's exactly what I received, along with a standing ovation from half of the faculty and students.

The other half didn't take kindly to my presentation. Aside from overlooking true Southern patriots like Thomas Jefferson, Patrick Henry, and Robert E. Lee, I had also crossed the color barrier. I received a barrage of "nigger lover" comments that fortified my resolve to open people's minds.

This former society president quickly became an outsider at St. Christopher's. Unlike Nicky, I had veered off the straight and narrow, and I started being perceived as an anomaly, an enigma, and a rebel.

One snowy December day, some classmates and I were burning off some steam during recess. We made snowballs and took them inside the classroom to throw at one another. One of mine sailed out of the strike zone and hit a two-foot placard above the blackboard. Maroon ink had been printed on gray cardboard to produce the words of the school's honor code. Some of that ink started to bleed from the melting snow.

A witness to this seemingly harmless incident reported it to the honor council. I had not lied, cheated, or stolen a thing. But I had "defaced" school property, a sign that symbolized personal integrity and community responsibility. I was tried before nine elected peers. I suppose the charge was "dishonorable behavior." Had I been found guilty, the council would likely have recommended to the headmaster that I be expelled from school. Although cooler heads prevailed and I was acquitted, the damage had been done. I wanted out.

And I wanted to expose a blatant cover-up. One of our teachers, a well-known sexual predator within the student community, was able to fly under the radar because no one came forward. We were too afraid of embarrassing our families. My parents had given their consent for me to travel during freshman year with the teacher to Baltimore and stay over-night with him and two other boys in one motel room. I told them that we drew straws to determine sleeping arrangements. The poor kid who drew the short straw was awakened by the perv in the middle of the night and forced to "wrestle." My parents were utterly unfazed.

"The poor man is a bit shell-shocked from the war," they offered as an excuse—a response that left me feeling that his welfare was more im-portant than mine.

I begged my parents to let me transfer to public school. The burdens of keeping up appearances all those years had steadily become unsus-tainable. My father heard me out, but he was caught between a rock and a hard place. He couldn't cross Lizzie. There'd certainly be hell to pay, and she might even disinherit him.

My mother flat-out refused to discuss the matter. She was the poster child for not getting a college education. Abandoned by her father at the age of five, she was raised by her mother and a bunch of other hard-done-by fe-male relatives. After high school, she was accepted to the College of William and Mary but, due to a purported lack of money, couldn't attend. She chose to get married instead—a secret she kept from me for over thirty years. That union, derailed in part by the couple's move to Bayonne, New Jersey, lasted less than two years. Based on her own past, the thought of *my* looking a gift horse like St. Christopher's in the mouth made her sick to her stomach.

Meanwhile, brother Nicky kept a low profile. He was not a boat rock-er; in fact he loathed calling any sort of attention to himself. Most of his teenage years had been awkward, exacerbated by painful shyness and a pimply face only a mother could love. He focused entirely on sports. With no interest in girls or drinking with the guys, he developed a reputation around school as a loner, which made him an easy target for teasers. In typically brutal teen fashion, they branded him Nasty Nick.

In truth, Nicky was a great brother. His affection for me was never more on display than the summer of 1968, during one of our family pilgrimages to the resort city of Virginia Beach. We stayed at a cottage offered to our family by kind Richmond families who enjoyed sharing their comforts. After breakfast, we'd generally all walk together to the beach. Then Nicky and I would go off and either do things together or pal around with schoolmates who were also there from Richmond.

Our slice of heaven was enjoyed by hundreds of people and was seemingly safe and well patrolled by lifeguards. Certainly safe enough for a thirteen-year-old like me. At one point, I went into the water by myself and swam a bit too far out from shore. No big deal, usually. But not paying proper attention to the current, I began drifting farther and farther away from the beach without anyone noticing.

When I realized I was in danger and cried out for help, no one could hear me. I was steadily losing the fight to keep my head above water when, out of nowhere, came big brother, swimming toward me the way that young Spitz fella did a few months later down in Mexico City. He reached me not a moment too soon. I was breathless and weak. He lifted my head above water, held me in his arms, calmed me down, and figured out a way to swim us both safely back to shore. This was my kind, loving brother at his best.

I wondered how I would ever be able to repay him. I owed Nicky my life.

But I was a selfish little prick. Rather than accept Nicky for the type of person he was and support him through periods of bashfulness and dilemma, I basked in my own achievements and poked fun at his failures. I tried pushing his buttons every day to make his blood boil. His temper ranged from mild verbal outbursts to violent physical assault. When he absolutely couldn't stand me anymore, given the chance, he'd pin me to the ground and beat my upper arms with his fists until he saw bruises.

"Stop it. Stop it. If you keep hitting me, I'll get cancer!" I screamed in a feeble attempt to get the monster I'd created off me.

"Listen to me, you little runt," Nicky countered. "Stop. Giving. Me. Such. A. Hard. Time," came his words, one at a time, between punches.

When I complained to our parents, all they did was tell me that I deserved to get hit because I teased Nicky too much. They were right. Even though I felt the need to lash out at Nicky—and he was the easiest target—it was a horrible way to treat my best friend, the one who'd actually saved my life.

Since he was older and stronger, the only way I could escape injury was to outrun him and keep running until he gave up the chase. One night, Nicky's temper erupted like a volcano, and we ran a race for the ages through a neighboring tract of land that was part of the University of Richmond campus. I got out in front of Nicky and stayed ahead of him—by no more than a nose—by zigging while he zagged. Beyond the field, we continued our race along a private road that encircled the women's dormitories. That's when we drew the attention of campus security. The two of us retraced our steps and ran back home, with me outrunning Nicky and both of us outrunning the security officers.

These sorts of nights were becoming much too regular, much too dysfunctional.

We both had far too many negative emotions—yes, depression, that unspoken *d* word—and took it out on each other. That's how awkwardly codependent we'd become. Sharing a small bedroom in the cottage, sleeping in the same twin beds that we'd had as young boys, only exacerbated the situation. One of us had to find another place to sleep. If not, with Nicky having two more years of high school, I'm certain one of us would have ended up killing the other.

To add some urgency to the situation, I had developed a hands-on interest in girls. I needed some privacy.

Directly behind the big house sat a building, about half the size of the cottage, which looked like it had once been lived in, perhaps used as a home by a servant or the yardman in his younger days. Yet it sat there, apparently abandoned, and I had never inquired about it until now.

I asked Papa to explain its history, praying it might, somehow, resolve the awkward sleeping arrangement. My grandfather was most cooperative, inviting me inside for a tour. Full of spider webs and crickets, it looked like it hadn't been visited in a decade.

"Stukey boy," he said, "this place used to be my office." Whenever he called me Stukey rather than Stuart, it usually predicted another tick in the win column.

It was a comfortable space with a separate bathroom and shower, and a functional kerosene stove built into the fireplace. Papa waxed nostalgic over a number of vintage publications, caked in decades-old dust but still arranged neatly on bookshelves. He picked up one of a ten-volume collection of hardbound and illustrated American Civil War books published in 1911 to look for his great uncle Jedediah, a famous cartographer of that era. I didn't care much about war, past or present, so I tuned him out and started to arrange the room in my mind as a studio apartment.

Papa was in a giddy mood, and giddy usually meant generous. So I turned to him and asked, "Has anyone ever lived here?"

He shot me a surprised and intrigued look. That very moment, his mind started to wander back at least forty years in time. I let him enjoy his fantasy and, before he had a chance to answer my question, I got right down to business.

"I'd like to clean this place up and use it as my sleeping quarters," I declared.

Start out slow, I reasoned. Ask for a piece of the moon, not the whole thing. Papa didn't ask me to expound on my reasons for wanting it, nor did he ask if I'd run the idea past my parents. He simply agreed that if I scrubbed the place down and made it livable, it was all mine. *What an easy sell*, I thought.

So in short order, after cleaning the cobwebs and exterminating the centipedes and spiders, I became arguably the only fifteen-year-old in West End Richmond to have his own bachelor pad. Perhaps Papa had somehow gotten inside my head, and I hadn't felt it. Regardless, it was a great inducement for me to stay at Halsnoch.

Or so I wanted him to think.

The office also had a small, unused space partitioned off from the main room by a locked door and barricaded with a large and heavy oak desk. What could possibly be inside? Papa told me the room had originally been designed for storage but never used. *What has he been hiding in there?* I wondered. This was one family secret I was determined to unlock. It didn't take long to find the key to the door, but when I opened it, there was a second metal door—much like the door to a bank vault—with a combination lock. Unlocking that required the skill of a safecracker.

I invited a buddy or two over nearly every weekend to try their luck. For months, no one succeeded, but word spread quickly, and I soon had a waiting list. One night, we finally heard that magic click, and it left us all a bit spooked. What if we opened the door only to find a heap of dead bodies? Chicken me, I was the last to cross the threshold. Once inside and aided by the meager beam from a cheap flashlight, we felt like we had stepped into our own Emerald City. And the only thing behind the wizard's curtain at that moment was Jack Daniels.

Papa had not just stockpiled whiskey during the 1920s and 1930s; he had prepared for the apocalypse. There were hundreds, perhaps even a couple thousand, of amber-colored bottles stacked one on top of the other—all full of whiskey and unopened since the end of Prohibition. More than enough hooch for all of Richmond to have gotten "tight" that night.

We lads celebrated our feat by drinking a random bottle of a long-in-the-cask, and even-longer-on-the-shelf, Canadian rye whiskey. I'm told I had a blast until I passed out, covered in my own vomit. The next morning, my guests managed to walk to the cottage, eat breakfast with my parents, and offer them a plausible explanation for my absence. To this day, I can't tolerate even the faintest smell of brown whiskeys.

When Nicky entered his senior year in high school, he had received no guidance regarding college, other than the unforgettable prognosis that no one in the family could pay the tuition. No one at home or school had spent time with him to try and do some creative math. Instead, he was manipulated by a propaganda machine and made to believe that his love of sports would translate into an athletic scholarship.

Yes, St. Christopher's had been a good fit for Nicky. Its small size and lack of marquee athletes allowed him to showcase his better-than-average talent. But he was no all-star. No college tried to recruit him.

Thus, in normal academic fashion, Nicky applied to two small colleges in North Carolina—Elon and Catawba—and was accepted at both. These were fine schools by anyone's definition. But they each cost a small fortune to attend.

Rather than immediately matriculate to college and find a way to pay for it himself, Nicky asked the family if he could do a postgraduate year at St. Christopher's. He was certain that one more year of football and basketball would produce head-turning results and attract recruiters. Naturally, Lizzie was consulted on the matter.

"The best thing for that boy right now is college," she advocated.

Lizzie was dead right, but without her support or a scholarship, Nicky wasn't going to college. She was the only family member who had the financial ability to set Nicky free. I was perplexed. Why couldn't she pay for a first year of college just as easily as a fifth year of high school?

Negotiations between the elders ensued, and Lizzie ultimately stroked another check to St. Christopher's. As most of us had predicted, Nicky's extra year at St. Christopher's didn't change a thing. His numbers on the football field and basketball court were embarrassingly flat. I had certainly been a distraction, too, by being the only sophomore on the football team, and a starter at that. But he kept the faith and summoned the energy to apply even to stretch schools like Wake Forest University. His dreams were out of line with reality, but his inner circle couldn't summon up the courage to tell him so.

All of the colleges to which he applied made it quite clear during the interview process that his acceptance would be based entirely upon academic achievement. He would not receive any scholarship money. So, like his mother, Nicky never went to college, but for very different reasons.

Those of us who cared for Nicky could see the hurt in his eyes. But no one knew, or could even begin to imagine, that he'd been keeping his own secret from the family. He had another passion besides sports. One day, while cleaning up *his* room, the room I'd vacated for *my* privacy, our mother found, quite accidentally, an unfinished letter to a younger male student at St. Christopher's. A love letter.

She was utterly gobsmacked.

There had never been any speculation about Nicky's sexual orientation. Lizzie's, yes, but the discussion of her lifestyle was off limits. And, unlike my brother, she wasn't in distress.

How many letters had he written prior to this one? we wondered. We started digging and found out there had been several others.

The recipient of Nicky's affection wasn't moved in the slightest. In fact, he wasn't even gay. He certainly didn't deserve to get caught up in something that most people thought at the time to be downright immoral. Nicky had embarrassed the underclassman and put him in a sticky situation. Justifiably, the boy filed a complaint with the school.

A few carefully chosen faculty members at St. Christopher's were brought in quickly to avert a crisis. They helped Nicky construct an apology and an agreement to cease and desist from further contact. The storm ended peacefully, and Nicky's faux pas was buried with all the other family secrets in the deepest part of the James River.

I didn't care one way or another about Nicky's sexuality. Even if he was the *only* closeted student at St. Christopher's, then so be it. Needless to say, my parents were mortified, but this was not the first, or last, time that they would shift smoothly and quickly into denial mode.

I desperately tried to engage my parents in a dialogue—not just about Nicky, but about all of the problems facing our family. They were holding back tears and keeping stiff upper lips, but I really thought I could find a chink in their armor if I tried hard enough. They *had* to see this past year of rejection letters as a warning of bigger things to come. A storm was heading our way.

Nicky was feeling at loose ends. His glory days as an athlete were over. He had few, if any, true friends and a virtually nonexistent support group. Maybe he'd build one if he ended up attending community college or working down at the local sporting goods store. I was more afraid that if he stayed in Richmond, he might rot from a bad case of social stigma.

I started walking around on eggshells. One frigid Saturday evening, no more than a week or two after things had quieted down, I strolled over from the office to the cottage for dinner—as I did every night. I found everyone and everything to be eerily quiet. Even the furnace appeared to have taken the night off. Nicky was at home but behind closed doors. As soon as I entered the house, my parents asked me to step into their bedroom. Their news—that Nicky had tried to run away from home that afternoon but got cold feet and called them to come down to the bus station to get him—made me proud of my brother. *Good on ya, Nicky*, I thought. Then the other shoe fell. They'd also found a suicide note, which they had torn up and thrown in a wastebasket.

Their instructions to me were unmistakably clear: I was not to talk about this to anyone. Not to Nicky, not to Papa, not to Aunt Lizzie, not to anyone at school. Not even to them! Just forget it ever happened. This was simply a momentary lapse in judgment on Nicky's part and nothing more. He did not have a problem. Families like ours didn't have these kinds of problems.

In an effort to better understand Nicky's pain, I went to every wastebasket in the house until I found enough scraps of paper to piece the original suicide note back together. It read pretty much as follows:

Dear Mom and Pop,

I love you both very much and Stuart, too. And Papa and Aunt Lizzie. I've tried really hard to make you proud of me, but I'm not good at anything and everyone makes fun of me at school. I don't want to be any more trouble to you, and I don't want to hurt inside anymore either. I'm better off dead than alive. I hope you won't be [embarrassed].

Your devoted son, Nicky

I couldn't find the one piece of paper that would have made the note whole, so I added the word *embarrassed*, but I had no doubt it was the word Nicky used. Such a submissive young man, he never wanted to let his family down.

I went back to my parents and waved this shocking, yet unspeakable, piece of paper in their faces and cried out, "Can't you assholes read? Nicky needs help!"

But even now, with Nicky perched precariously on the edge of life, my parents continued to turn a blind eye.

I wanted so desperately to march up to the big house and show the note to Papa. He'd always fixed our problems. Surely he could fix this, too. But I didn't.

Despite my love for Nicky and concern about his well-being, I wasn't prepared to stand up to my parents. A month shy of my sixteenth birthday, I was too well trained in perpetuating secrets and keeping up appearances. But things were going to change. That transcendent moment of surrender was about to happen. Somehow, someway, I was going to let go of all fear and enter a world of total freedom.

CHAPTER 2

Mardi Gras

THAT FEARLESS VERSION of Nicky who saved his insubordinate younger brother from drowning in the Atlantic Ocean was seared in my memory. It was adding fuel to the fire inside me. It was the perfect time for me to repay him. He was suffering under the weight of his own expectations, and our family's paralysis was just dragging him down deeper.

The solution was simple: I would show him how to make a clean break from Halsnoch.

I waited to make my move on February third—on a Wednesday and in broad daylight. It was just another run-of-the-mill weekday as far as any of my contacts were concerned. The night before, I had packed a large, green duffel bag full of clothes and my complete eight-track stereo system—yes, speakers and all. I crammed in my favorite tapes like The Beatles' *Let It Be* and Cream's *Goodbye*—the appeal of R&B artists like Kool & the Gang and The Chi-Lites had waned. Before bedtime, I stashed the bag in the trunk of our mother's white 1966 Oldsmobile Delta 88 four-door hardtop.

Misery is when you can't leave the party, but now that I had a driver's license, I was, in that moment, happy—I had my own emotional and physical transportation. Nicky and I had been taking turns driving this beast of a car to and from school. When our mother needed it during the day, she'd take us to school in the morning and pick us up after sports practice in the late afternoon. But being the evening chef, she often preferred for us to drive back and forth to school on our own.

Wednesday had already been designated as one of those days. I drove what would soon become the getaway car, and Nicky rode shotgun. I had not shared a thing with him. We went to morning chapel as required, took our respective seats, and went our separate ways after the service concluded. I tracked down my classmate Scott Ellett in the courtyard outside Chamberlayne Hall, the main building on campus. I said very little as I handed him a piece of paper with a message. He looked baffled as he opened up my note and read,

Don't worry. I'm heading out of town for a while, but I'll call as soon as I get settled. Please find Nicky and tell him he'll need to catch a ride home with someone else today.

Scott's gut reaction was part "Run that by me again" and part "Coming from Stuart Hotchkiss, I'm not surprised by anything." Unfortunately, I'd put Scott in an awkward position; he was a member of the honor council, and I was clearly about to break a sacrosanct rule at St. Christopher's by committing truancy.

I needed to look no further than my own family to realize that people who appear confident in what they're doing are the ones who create the best illusions. When I walked away from Scott toward the parking lot, I was shaking like a leaf but maintaining a most confident look. I got into the car and drove straight to the First & Merchants Bank on Libbie Avenue. I handed my savings passbook to the teller and told her that I wanted to drain my account—$500 or so of Christmas and birthday money that had accumulated over the years. Oddly, she didn't seem the least bit fazed. I took my money, said, "Thank you," and walked proudly out the lobby doors.

I drove on to Richmond's Byrd Airport. During the days before airline deregulation, there were fixed airfares to places both near and far. Shopping for an airline ticket required no advanced planning or comparison pricing. Byrd serviced only two carriers at the time, so I walked up to the nearest counter. I was going as far as my money would take me.

"How far from Richmond does your airline fly?" I asked the agent, concentrating on keeping my voice at full adult pitch in an attempt to display authority.

He turned around to look at a giant route map behind him. I could see the answer to my own question over his left shoulder.

"Our outermost points are Portland, Oregon, and Phoenix, Arizona," he responded as he turned back around to face me.

I knew Phoenix would be warm in February, but I wasn't sure about Portland. Although I loved cold weather, I hadn't packed a lot of winter clothes. So I asked him the price of a one-way ticket to Phoenix. What's the point of a round-trip ticket when you're running away? The fare was only $150, so I paid it.

The route to Phoenix required a connection in Washington, DC, via Piedmont Airlines, a regional carrier. It was the first time I'd ever been on an airplane and, even though it was a puddle jumper, I'll never forget the ride. I was expecting some sort of "zoom zoom" sensation, but the plane hardly felt like it was moving. It might as well have been tethered to a giant rubber band that kept stretching in flight.

I could easily have remained preoccupied with this surreal feeling the entire flight, but a familiar face startled me. The father of a classmate was onboard the plane, and I did everything I could to keep him from noticing me. I removed my wool and leather St. Christopher's monogram jacket. I curled up into my seat to make myself less visible. I didn't ask the stewardess any questions, fearing the father might recognize my voice. After the plane landed, I made sure to be the last passenger to exit. Fortunately, he didn't see me during the flight or in the airport as I hustled to make my connection.

The DC to Phoenix leg was uneventful. The thrill of flying at low altitude to Washington was negated by the monotony of cruising above the clouds to Phoenix. We landed at dusk, and I headed straight for the taxi queue. I entrusted my driver to choose an inexpensive motel in a safe part of town. He asked me a fair number of questions in order to deposit me in the best spot, and his choice of a cabin at the back of the

Kon Tiki Lodge was right on the money. I liked the prospect of living in a place that sounded like an old Thor Heyerdahl hangout.

I hurried to the motel lobby to call my friend Scott back in Richmond—as promised—before his family turned in for the night. Of course, this was an era before cell phones and calling cards. Since the motel clerk couldn't make enough coin change for me to feed the pay phone, I had no choice but to call Scott collect. His father answered the phone, and the operator said to him, "I have a collect call from Stuart Hotchkiss. Will you accept the charges?"

"Who did you say was calling?" he challenged the operator. When she repeated my name, Mr. Ellett yelled upstairs to his son, "Scotty, come down here right now and tell me what in blazes is going on!"

He always called his son Scotty—not Scott—when he was upset. Covering the mouthpiece, he spoke with Scott privately for a moment, and then he came back on the line and told the operator that he would accept the charges. Scott's reaction was truly one of relief—he hadn't seen me around the school campus since early morning and had probably told half the school by now. How embarrassing for him if I'd showed up at school the next morning. I confirmed that I was in Phoenix and doing just fine.

I would love to have been a fly on the wall in Scott's house after our call ended. One thing I was sure of was that his father would call my parents right after we hung up. I was down with that—my parents deserved to know where I was and that I was safe. At the same time, this would blow a Hotchkiss secret wide open.

After a good first night's sleep—aided, no doubt, by having my sound system—I ventured out onto Van Buren Street in the morning. Perhaps more than any other street in Phoenix, this one was known for prostitutes, pimps, porn, police, and poverty. All I remember seeing in daylight were heaps of fallen oranges scattered along the sidewalks. *Oranges, not cacti, in Arizona?* I asked myself again and again. *Are they fake or real?* Sure enough, by nightfall, the cops were out in disproportionate numbers. I couldn't help but wonder if they were looking for me.

I intended to stay in Phoenix long enough to land a job and stabilize myself. The first order of business was to purchase a cheap but reliable used car to get around town. I was wet behind the ears, but heck, I'd just made it to the urban desert all on my own. I laid eyes on a 1963 Oldsmobile Super 88—the predecessor to my mother's Delta 88—and it looked plenty roadworthy. Not asking a lot of questions and figuring that a hundred-dollar price tag wouldn't break the bank, I sealed the deal when the salesman told me I could have it for ninety-nine dollars. Hey, a buck saved was worth three gallons of gas back in 1971.

The job market in Phoenix was impossible, at least for a teenager who looked his age. I hauled my ass from one end of this already-sprawling city to the other, visiting nearly two dozen businesses of all shapes and sizes and delivering the same phony rap: "My family has fallen on hard times, and I've been forced to defer my high school education in order to help make ends meet."

No one bought it, nor did anyone make any suggestions about where else I might look. After three or four days in Phoenix, I was starting to run low on money and decided to move on. I planned to head east and sleep in the car a few nights until I found a job.

I had a long stretch of road ahead and miles of confidence inside me. I settled in for the perfect ride, just the desert and me. I'd barely gone thirty miles southeast on Interstate 10 when my hoopty started wheezing and coughing. I had to slow it way down, barely able to keep up with the *minimum* speed limit. Cutting the engine off for any reason—even a job— seemed like a big mistake. I was overcome with a fear of being stranded.

Trudging along past Tucson and crossing into New Mexico was touch and go, and I would soon have to stop for gas. There wasn't a lot of action in the desert, and as many as fifty miles separated interstate exits. When I got to Luna County—a great name for a place that felt as desolate as the moon—the car made up its mind that we'd be exiting at Deming, the county seat. The 88 was now showing signs of full-blown gastritis. Crawling into a Texaco gas station made me think of Papa—the stock he owned in this oil company represented his largest chunk of wealth—and made me feel like I could trust the man behind the "great big star." I instinctively asked the attendant to fill the car with gas and clean the desert grunge off the windows.

Why had I believed that a tankful of gas would cure my car's problems, much like feeding a hungry, cranky child? This car was clearly in need of CPR, not food. As the price dial on the gas pump approached three dollars, I asked the attendant if there might be someplace in town to have the car serviced. He asked where I'd come from. When I told him, he said, "It wouldn't be worth your money to fix this car. I can't believe you made it this far from Phoenix."

I was stumped. If I were home, Papa would've known what to do. But I'd run away from the security of Halsnoch, and now I had to make my own decisions. Maybe someone would buy the car and pay my original purchase price, or something close to it. I ran that idea past the attendant. Well, this guy was no kid; in fact, he owned the gas station. He walked around the car, checked under the hood, examined the body, and yes, kicked the tires, too. He made up his mind in less than a minute.

"I'll give ya twenty bucks for it and take it off ya hands."

I'm the one who hesitated. An eighty-dollar loss was a tough pill to swallow. So I tried to rationalize his offer by confirming, "And you'll give me back the three bucks I just paid for gas, right?"

"No, I'm buying the car as is—ya shoulda offered to sell the darn thing before ya bought the gas."

Why don't they teach negotiation skills to sophomores in prep school? Wouldn't they be more useful in the long run than a third or fourth year of Latin?

The man had me. I sold the car and threw the duffel bag over my shoulder like an army recruit. I'd never hitchhiked before, but it was an essential part of books I'd read, like Jack Kerouac's *On the Road*. I couldn't remember how the novelist's alter ego, "Sal" Paradise, solicited rides, but that made no difference. I wanted to invent my own hand gesture anyway. I assumed it would take a few hours of practice before getting my first lift and lots of short rides from different people to make some headway east.

Well, lady luck smiled on me that day. A clean-cut, thirty-something, good-looking man driving a sports car stopped to pick me up within two-to-three minutes.

"Where ya headed?" he asked me.

"El Paso," I said.

I had no idea where I was headed, but I felt giving him a clear-cut answer would make his decision to offer me a ride easier.

"That's a cinch," he shot back. "I'm going to Fort Rucker. Come on and jump in."

I had no clue what or where Fort Rucker was. It could have been in New Mexico or Timbuktu. But since the guy looked like he could have been one of my teachers, I eagerly accepted the lift. Fort Rucker, it turns out, was in Alabama, some fifteen-hundred miles to the east and past lots of big city options for me, like El Paso, San Antonio, Houston, Baton Rouge, and New Orleans. And once at Fort Rucker, I'd have even more options like Montgomery and Tallahassee. So I settled in for the long ride, one that I could choose would last a few hours or a couple of days.

My driver's name was Ernie; polite and well spoken, he didn't ask a lot of questions and drove really fast. He accepted no money from me for gas, required very little sleep, and played some great music on the radio. He referred to his army post by the pseudohomonym, Mother Rucker. He raised the allure of hitchhiking beyond that of a classic novel.

"If you're not particular about where you're headed, why not go to New Orleans?" Ernie suggested. "Mardi Gras should be startin' up any day now."

Mardi Gras is an annual festival held around the world on Shrove Tuesday, the day before Ash Wednesday. In New Orleans, the term Mardi Gras has come to mean an extended period of celebrations and parades that reaches its bacchanalian crescendo on "Fat Tuesday." Think of one St. Patrick's Day parade in New York City. Now think of fifty parades in New Orleans over a ten-day period. My timing couldn't have been better. I would arrive two days prior to the official start of the parades, just ahead of the throngs of tourists, and right when the city started to hop.

"You won't believe the parades," Ernie said with a smirk. "There'll be lots and lots of floats, and all the people on them throw coins and beads to the crowds."

Then he told me about the nubile young women standing on hotel balconies in the city's French Quarter neighborhood, flashing their boobs at passersby below. I admitted to Ernie that I was a virgin; he promised that this wouldn't be the case after a visit to New Orleans. He didn't have to say another word to sell me on The Big Easy.

Some thirty hours after getting picked up in Deming, I arrived in New Orleans. Ernie and I had just driven across the entire states of Texas and Louisiana together—twelve hundred miles—and bonded on a number of levels. We both tried to make light of our impending separation, but as a downside to hitchhiking, the last five minutes together would have to last a lifetime. Ernie followed the road signs to Vieux Carré and found a busy intersection in the quarter where he could pull over and turn me loose.

"Good luck, my friend. I wish I could join you. But I got to get back to Mother Rucker."

I proceeded to explore the old square until I came upon a group of people huddled around some street performers. I seized an opportunity to start a conversation, one that eventually got around to "Where are you from?" and all that. Fortunately, the people I met were Cajuns and embraced the fact that I'd arrived in time for Mardi Gras. When I told them I needed a free place to stay, they directed me to a building at 515 Decatur Street. Locals would certainly recognize this address if they had heard of the Head Clinic, an outpatient service center that treated men and women with suspected venereal disease. The floor above the clinic also served as a safe haven for a small number of juvenile runaways like me. Fortunately, one of the six beds was unclaimed when I arrived.

In exchange for free lodging, I was expected to volunteer a few hours a day at the clinic. They had me man the switchboard in the evenings and perform a little triage over the phone to help callers determine whether or not the pain from peeing or the amount of discharge from a genital sore warranted a visit to the clinic. After working and living there a few days, I discovered that the clinic was supported by Earling Carothers Garrison, known since the early '60s as Jim Garrison, the district attorney of Orleans Parish best known for his investigation into the assassination of President Kennedy.

Jim Garrison was physically impressive at six feet six inches tall, handsome, and well built except for an age-appropriate paunch. He was always well dressed. Few called him Mr. Garrison. His voice was deep and beautifully modulated, and no one mistook him for anyone else when he spoke. His manner was casual and unhurried, and he exhibited a great sense of humor. Although much younger than Papa, his larger-than-life personality made me feel like I hadn't skipped a beat since leaving Halsnoch. He knew we needed more than just a free place to call home, so he offered us a number of small handyman jobs at his personal residence in the city and paid us rather well. I installed new screens on his porch during my sojourn, even though the old ones looked to be in far better condition than the ones we had at the cottage in Richmond.

Local companies were also encouraged to offer clinic dwellers part-time work during Mardi Gras. I'm not sure who did the prodding, but I sensed that Mr. Garrison had a hand in that, too. I caught magic in a bottle once again when I showed up at Antoine's, a legendary restaurant in the quarter specializing in French-Creole cuisine, and was offered a job on the spot as a dishwasher. And I mean hands-in-the-suds dishwasher, not someone who loaded and unloaded a Hobart that did the washing for you. Every evening, I scrubbed mountains of dirty plates still sticky from the rich and buttery sauce of an appetizer of Oysters Rockefeller or entrées like Chateaubriand and Trout Pontchartrain.

I wasn't allowed inside the main dining room at Antoine's, but I could tell the restaurant served hundreds and hundreds of customers each day during Mardi Gras. I heard the constant rise and fall of crowd noise as the kitchen doors swung open and shut. *How can patrons have a normal conversation in a place this loud?* I pondered. They couldn't, and it didn't matter—food this splendiferous trumped resonance.

Most of the kitchen staff were older black women who couldn't bear to see a young white boy like me get skinny in New Orleans, of all places. These ladies weren't born yesterday and knew I missed my mother's Southern cooking. They made sure that I ate well while at work, one bowl of Creole gumbo after another.

Combining my free room and board along with my wages from Antoine's and Mr. Garrison, I soon had more than the original five hundred dollars I had withdrawn from the bank back in Richmond. Living at the clinic was both practical and euphoric. I had unlimited access to Jax beer, a local product that fell off trucks leaving the brewery in the quarter and into our hands. Rolled cannabis lay in ashtrays waiting for someone to light it and pass it around. I didn't inhale the first one properly, but a saucy teenage girl corrected my form and, after we smoked an entire joint together, helped me lose something I didn't need to go looking for.

Throughout this adventure, common courtesy compelled me to call home and update my parents about my safety and whereabouts. I demanded—and received—the freedom to stay in New Orleans in return for this modest consideration. I thought about the possible public relations storm in Richmond and how they would be handling it, not whether my parents actually missed me or feared for my safety. They knew it would take a village to get me home, so they gave others permission to call me at the clinic and apply pressure—people like my track coach at St. Christopher's and my minister at church. Finally, my parents themselves called twelve days into my stay, on Fat Tuesday.

"Stuart, we hope by now you've been able to sort things out in your mind," my father said. "But I want to make myself very clear. I want you home in two days. Either come back on your own, or I'll come down to New Orleans and get you. You decide."

For my father to put his foot down like that was a sign that he was all business. I took him at his word and promised to go home. Before hanging up, I asked, "Did Papa put you up to this?"

"Young man," he barked back, "I wouldn't push your luck."

I was actually elated by his response. I had waited all these years for my father to show some backbone, always certain that familial seniority would prevent that from happening. Seeing my father change for the better made it easy for me to give him—and the rest of my family—a second chance. Tit for tat.

Although the parades had ended, it wasn't easy leaving the party. I treasured the experiences of attending Mardi Gras, working at Antoine's, meeting Jim Garrison, and crashing at the Head Clinic. I'd made my exclamation point. Somehow, after all the memories faded, I would try to regress back to the life of a high-school sophomore.

The road home to Richmond wasn't easy. I crawled out of New Orleans, one short ride after another. During one stretch, I had been stranded on a state road in Alabama for hours when a harmless-looking, middle-aged man finally came along in a pickup truck and offered me a ride. I was in desperate need of a ride, but I didn't act out of sheer impulse. I sized him up pretty good in the brief time I had, then looked again to study his face. There appeared to be nothing sinister about him.

Experience had taught me to never judge a book by its cover. Unfortunately, the St. Christopher's teacher who abused my classmates and me in Baltimore was just the first of four men I'd already suffered in silence. Never did I dare complain about the other assaults from an older relative, a sleep-away-camp counselor, and a VMI alumnus. Despite these dreadful experiences, ones I never wanted to repeat, my inner antenna told me to accept the ride. I didn't hesitate to open the passenger door and, once inside and moving again, subject myself to fate.

"How long you been out here?" he asked.

I didn't want to tell him the truth. No sense in advertising the fact that we were very much alone.

"Just an hour or so," I said.

It was midafternoon, and I hadn't eaten a thing all day. I was fatigued and disoriented, and I didn't want to talk. All I wanted was a ride to a more traveled highway.

After he'd driven a few minutes, he pulled over to the shoulder of the road and completely unfolded a state road map. It covered both of our laps and, without any foreplay, his index finger quickly moved south from Alabama to somewhere in the Gulf of Mexico—and my crotch. I knew what he wanted. I also knew that between his size and the rifle he had hanging behind us, he would definitely get it if I didn't skedaddle.

This was no time to ponder my predicament, but shit, how did I not see this coming?

Enter the soul of my maternal grandfather and other namesake, Stuart Strange Grant. Nice to finally make your acquaintance! I'd only been fed a few stale crumbs about his life. After leaving my grandmother and five-year-old mother behind in Richmond in the early '20s, my "good-looking" grandfather first traveled to Los Angeles and worked as a stuntman in Hollywood. From what I was told, there were no letters home and no child support. Then, completely out of the blue, he reunited with and housed my mother for one year in Sacramento, California—her senior year in high school—and never saw her again. He died at a young age and seven years before I was born. And he took whatever secrets there were to that story to his grave.

I tried to imitate what I imagined to be one of his signature moves by opening the passenger door of the now-moving vehicle and jumping out. It wasn't a smooth move—in fact, it could best be described as an ungainly belly flop—but the landing spot was soft, and my only damage was a bruised ego.

A full day later, I found myself no farther than Sumter, South Carolina, and, once there, put my thumb away for good. A state trooper heading south on a divided highway turned around after he noticed me on the side of the road. *What now?* I wondered. He asked me all kinds of questions about the state of Minnesota, for which I had no answers. He thought I was being insolent and took me to a nearby police station. After being peppered with more questions, I finally figured out that he had me confused with another runaway. I offered that I lived in the Commonwealth of Virginia and volunteered my driver's license as proof.

"Then I'm gonna call one of your parents," he promised. I prayed my mother wouldn't be out on the golf course or playing bridge that day. If she was, I was willing to stay a night in Sumter rather than give him Papa's number.

He instructed the operator to place a long distance call to Atlantic 8-1820 in Richmond, that being the only way he could reach the outside world without direct dialing equipment back then. It took what seemed to be an eternity for my mother to answer the phone, but she eventually did. The trooper spoke with her, and after the call ended, he stared me down like a drill sergeant and said, "Young man, you should be very grateful she wants you back."

He escorted me to the nearest bus depot and stayed with me until a Greyhound bus destined for Richmond left its appointed bay. His compassion for both my parents made me stop and realize that I should, in fact, be grateful. The kid from Minnesota probably didn't have it so good.

The bus pulled into the station in Richmond on a Friday evening, twenty-three days after I had departed from Byrd Airport. I was met by one very relieved and merciful father. It was a touching reunion. He was more forgiving than I expected. The bark I heard in his ultimatum phone call days earlier had been replaced with an onomatopoeic "ruff." There would be plenty of time for my father to display an angry side when we both got in front of Papa, but for now, absolute love ruled the moment.

I knew he'd already started to think about how we could put this whole episode behind us. He didn't want a confrontation. In the most genuine way possible, he shook my hand and pulled me in toward his body for an unabashed man hug. I wish I had looked him in the eye right then and there and said, "I love you," if for no other reason than for his showing up at the station. But I was a typical self-centered teenager and still living off the fumes from the past month. I just forced a smile. Yes, I was relieved in some ways to be at a place called home, but at that particular moment, I didn't want to hang out at the cottage and play a live version of Twenty Questions with my parents. I wanted to see a long list of classmates and regale them with tales from my adventure.

Nicky was playing in the semifinal game of a basketball tournament that night as well, and I debated whether my presence there would be a good thing or a distraction. My parents politely asked that I go to the game before seeing my friends. If I did, I had their blessing to stay out as long as I wished. I could tell they were walking on eggshells, and I had them eating out of my hand. But I did as they asked.

The following morning, I slept in past noon. Nicky was preparing for the final game of the tournament that Saturday night, so the two of us didn't find time for a good heart-to-heart conversation. During our brief encounters that day, he showed more deference to me than ever before. It was like plastic surgery had been performed on the face of our sibling rivalry. We were finally at peace with each other. This night, no one had to negotiate with me to go to the game and cheer Nicky on. Unfortunately, it was a miserable team performance and the first and only time I can re-member Nicky not scoring any points in a basketball game. By the end of the contest, Nicky looked like he'd had the life sucked out of him.

I wish I had said something to try and comfort Nicky that evening, but he just wanted to be left alone. I wanted to praise him for all that he'd done as a brother, things I'd come to realize and appreciate while away. And I wanted to tell him how leaving Halsnoch and coming back with a fresh set of eyes made a world of difference for me. He didn't have to run away after all. He just needed to ride out the last three months at St. Christopher's, and then he'd be a free agent. The world would be his oyster.

CHAPTER 3

The Fall of Richmond

THE NEXT NIGHT was Sunday and a school night. I can't remember the exact time, but it was late enough to be listening to some soft acoustic stuff in my room—still in Papa's old office. I thought I heard a soft knock on the door, but I ignored it because I wasn't expecting anyone. Then I definitely heard a second and louder knock along with my name being called out. I opened the door, and standing there opposite me was my father's sister, Alice. She had never come to visit me at the office before, so why now? The look of panic on her face told me that something was terribly wrong.

"I'm so sorry, Stuart," she said in a weak and unsteady voice, "but there's been an accident."

She didn't have to say anything more; I intuited the rest of the news.

Nicky had placed one of Papa's pistols in his left hand and shot himself in the temple. The site of his final act was sacred to him—the St. Christopher's football field. The bullet proved fatal, but his death wasn't instant. A passing jogger apparently found him lying on the ground in agony, his cries for help barely audible. The police arrived and an ambulance followed, but taking Nicky to the emergency room at St. Mary's Hospital was fruitless.

Damn it. I had known something bad was going to happen after the horrific basketball game he'd had the night before. But why did he have to resort to this? I wanted to rush over to the hospital right away. Aunt Alice told me that my father was already on his way and I could do more good by going to the cottage and trying to calm my mother.

When I arrived, my mother looked like someone I didn't know. Her hair wasn't neat and lustrous as usual, but frizzy and flyaway—think Phyllis Diller on steroids. She paced around the living room, ranting, "Why? Why? Why?" Alice was frightened and staying out of her way. My experience working at the Head Clinic certainly hadn't prepared me for a situation like this, but I took charge anyway. I first called a classmate's father who was a former chaplain of St. Christopher's. He rushed right over and tried his best to calm my mother, but she didn't respond to his prayers. She tuned out everyone and everything but the thought of her dying son. The only way to bring her back to earth was to call for paramedics and have them sedate her. They arrived quickly and made certain she got a good night's sleep.

I was able to see Nicky the next day. I'll never get out of my mind the sight of my brother in the hospital bed that Monday morning. To my horror, the left side of his head had become so swollen he looked like the Elephant Man. He was also hooked up to a ventilator that snored in a perfectly dreadful four-part discord. The torture of being in the room with Nicky for even five minutes was more than I could bear.

From that point forward in my life, I never feared dying. It was living that scared me to death.

After nearly four days of praying for a miracle, my parents finally allowed the doctors to convince them to pull the plug. As part of the process, doctors appealed for some of his organs: "Did you know that as many as twenty-five people could receive Nicky's gift and be kept alive?" the doctors said with a sense of urgency.

My parents were not accustomed to making fast decisions on a normal day and especially not in a time of crisis like this. They—as well as much of the country—were not enlightened about organ donation in those days. The doctors had to act quickly, and my parents were in no mood to make such a momentous decision.

"We don't think that would be fair to Nicky," they decided. They were conventional parents and quick to deliver their verdict. Nicky would be having an intact, full-body burial.

As we passed through the gates of Hollywood Cemetery for Nicky's graveside service, the eyes of Richmond's elite zoomed in on my parents and me. The past month—my running away and now Nicky's suicide—had produced a family meltdown of unparalleled proportions that was quite the news and gossip around town. How my parents—especially my mother—were going to compose themselves in the next few minutes was a mystery to me.

I had underestimated them. Being true members of Richmond's genteel society, they remained uncharacteristically stoic until the service ended and the funeral director whisked us away. Then my mother fell apart again. She cried every day and remained in shock and denial for weeks on end. To those who tried to say the right thing to ease her pain, she kept repeating, "What did we do to deserve this?" and "Why us?"

I could have told everyone the truth. I knew every detail of Nicky's depression and the family cover-up. My mother was stuck in self-pity mode and needed to snap out of it. It made her quite unattractive, a quality she detested in other people. I wanted to shake her and hug her at the same time. I also wanted her to consult a psychiatrist.

I knew it was an idea that would never float. My family viewed therapy as a complete waste of time and money, not to mention a sign of weakness. They were toe-the-line Richmonders who would only discuss pleasant topics like the debutante Bal du Bois, the Camptown horse races, and the parties at Berkeley Plantation down in Charles City. They would never sit in a room with a stranger to analyze a tragic event like Nicky's suicide. It just wasn't the way they were raised.

My father had done a marvelous job of balancing the dual roles of grieving parent and host. He greeted a multitude of visitors who had gone to the hospital to pay their respects as Nicky was clinging to life and then to Halsnoch after the funeral. But he made a faux pas he'd never live down. In dressing for the hospital Monday morning—yes, a Southern gentleman dresses even for emergencies—he mistakenly threw on a novelty necktie decorated with a hardware screw sitting inside the letter U. He unwittingly continued to wear it for three days until his bachelor brother pulled him aside and berated him for such poor taste.

My father's pain was visceral; eight years in a military environment must have conditioned him for emotionally charged moments like this. Yet the evidence of his guilt was undeniable. He admitted, if only to himself, that his failure to force Nicky to go to college rather than do a postgraduate year at St. Christopher's had led to this tragedy. Sadly, my father realized too late how important it was for Nicky to get away from Halsnoch. He wished he could see Nicky living in a college dorm room somewhere in North Carolina, happier than ever. The reality of Nicky lying six feet under ground seemed too harsh a punishment for my father's parental imperfection.

Papa felt his grandson's death was my father's fault, too. He told my father that he hadn't kept a tight enough rein on either one of us. His disapproval—occasionally escalating to the level of disgust—rained down on my father like a mighty waterfall. As much as I always loved Papa, I think he had an ulterior motive for wanting my father to feel the brunt of guilt for Nicky's suicide. After all, the loaded gun negligently left in the top drawer of his bedside table and within reach of a teenager like Nicky had deadly ramifications.

As for me, I was suffering from a bad case of survivor's guilt. My running away and high times in New Orleans hadn't helped Nicky at all. It just seemed to make matters worse. Lots of people—coaches, teachers, family friends, and priests—counseled me not to feel that way, but I couldn't shake how I felt. I put on a brave face, but inside I was shattered.

I carried on with my classes at St. Christopher's as best I could despite being a double enigma. Curiosity seekers eagerly plied me with questions about my trip ("Is New Orleans as wild as people say?") as well as Nicky's suicide ("Why was he so depressed?"). I had to balance two completely different emotions as I tried to engage in polite conversation.

Maintaining relationships became increasingly uncomfortable and more difficult. I wasn't feeling affectionate, sharing, or honest. In fact, I never wanted to have a best friend again. Best friends die.

After giving us time to grieve, the school headmaster, Warren Elmer, called my father and me to his office. He was truly concerned for our welfare at this horrible time in our lives, but his position also required him to cast judgment upon my recent transgression. Tragic figure or not, I had been a truant from school when I ran away. Now I had to face the music.

Mr. Elmer was a rare scholar and academic. He was the first imported headmaster in St. Christopher's history; his predecessors had all been native Richmonders as well as "saintly" scholars. Richmond outsider he may have been, but Mr. Elmer was both a fair and impartial judge and jury. I don't think he knew too much about the Hotchkiss family business, but he was wise enough to figure out that if one of the school's top scholars and athletes ran away from home in his sophomore year, something deep and meaningful must have triggered it. Add to this Nicky's suicide, and even a blind man could see that something was terribly wrong at Halsnoch.

Mr. Elmer couldn't have been fairer with his punishment. He didn't want to interrupt my studies with a lengthy suspension or an expulsion. I'd been through too much already. He also didn't want me to feel like the school pariah or humiliate me in front of my peers. He thought he'd found an acceptable middle ground by having me serve weekend detention until the end of the semester. This way, I would be out of sight of prying eyes and vicious tongues.

My father thanked Mr. Elmer and looked at me with a broad and winning smile as if to say, "You lucky dog—in my day you would've been expelled."

My father stood up to leave, thinking our meeting was over and a deal had been struck. But he'd underestimated my renewed desire to leave St. Christopher's. I asked to speak with Mr. Elmer alone, and both men agreed to let me do so. After my father left the room, I unloaded on poor Mr. Elmer as if I were in therapy.

"I don't belong here," I practically shouted in desperation. "I'm not like the other students. None of *them* live with their grandfathers! I just want to go to public school like regular people. Why doesn't anyone understand?"

Mr. Elmer just listened patiently and puffed away at his ubiquitous Dunhill pipe.

"My Aunt Lizzie doesn't get it either," I continued. "She makes me practically beg her for the tuition, and I tell her not to bother. I don't want it. She's not listening to me. Nobody is listening to me. My family and I keep going round and round on this issue every year, and they won't let me leave. Please, Mr. Elmer. I just want out!"

St. Christopher's was a damn fine school, but I'd gotten off the bus to maturity a few stops too soon. I could not bring myself to appreciate or respect what Lizzie's gift truly meant. I resented being the odd boy out demographically and its broader ramifications. The day I left for Phoenix, someone had stolen cash from the school bookstore, and I became the immediate suspect. I recognize that my timing may have contributed to my presumption of guilt, but being condemned without first being heard made me feel like the new *nigra* yardman.

Sometimes it's good for partners who continually quarrel with each other to take a break. That's how I felt about St. Christopher's. And it gave Mr. Elmer the perfect out: Why not just let me go to public school for the rest of the semester? We'd see how things went and leave the door open regarding my junior and senior years. So we cut our own deal. When my father came back into Mr. Elmer's office, the decision was announced as a *fait accompli*. My father handled things much better this way. The matter was settled.

Mr. Elmer himself called the principal of Douglas Freeman High School and set the transfer in motion. I was attending classes at my new school within days. I went through a fair amount of culture shock as the new kid at Freeman. There were girls everywhere, and they flirted; there were black students; there was no dress code; there was no morning chapel; classrooms were overloaded with students; and the tenth-grade curriculum at Freeman was the same as my eighth grade at St. Christopher's.

It was an eye-opening experience to say the least, especially not knowing a soul and arriving so late in the school year. My transition suffered a significant setback a week or so into my tenure when another

Freeman student came up to me and asked, "You're new here, aren't you? What school did you come from?"

It was an innocent, and appropriate, question. When I answered, he was eager to volunteer some information he'd read in the local paper. "Oh, wow, isn't that the place where the guy just blew his brains out?"

I didn't want to be known around Freeman as the brother of the guy who had just killed himself. Nicky's actions were much more complicated than that. Unwilling to risk getting hurt any more than I already had been, I simply kept to myself.

It was also a bizarre time in my life because sports played no role at all. Track season was already in progress, and the coach politely declined my request to join in late. I'd also left a hole in the St. Christopher's team. It left the editor of the school yearbook *Raps and Taps* to conclude, even if he did have his facts turned around, "The outlook for this year's team is uncertain due to the status of Stuart Hotchkiss, a runaway from Phoenix, Arizona."

So, for the first time in my life, I took pleasure in reading, even though my attention span was limited. I did acrostics and other puzzles to keep my mind fit. I combed through the *World Book Encyclopedia* like a walk through the woods.

Then the divine hand of fate intervened—at Freeman, no less—and I was converted from clueless to cruciverbalist.

I really do mean *constructing* crossword puzzles and not merely solving them. My biology teacher at Freeman offered her class a chance to earn extra credit in exchange for working on a project outside the normal curriculum. For most students, that meant doing lab experiments or other research. For me, it meant combing through a large assortment of textbooks at both the Freeman library and Richmond Public Library. I documented as many biology words and definitions as possible and sorted them by broad categories: anatomy, cell structure, ecology, molecules, physiology, plants, etc.

I decided to construct a puzzle on a single topic—anatomy—because some of the clues could legitimately be racy. I turned it in to my teacher and challenged her to solve it. She was amazed—actually, I wouldn't be exaggerating if I used the expression *blown away*. She made a huge fuss about the puzzle to the class, to other teachers in the science department, and most important, to the head of the science curriculum for the Virginia Public School System (VPSS), Scott Rodgers.

Mr. Rodgers visited Freeman one day and invited me to share my methodology. When he realized how much research I'd done and that I had the capacity to do an entire book of puzzles, he offered me his full support and cooperation, including access to a drafting table and typewriter. All of a sudden, I had an after-school routine again, and this spring's sprint was not on a cinder running track but rather to meet a publication deadline.

Mr. Rodgers convinced the school system to distribute my puzzles for beta testing to every biology teacher across the state during the 1971–1972 school year. The VPSS would pay all costs of printing and distribution in exchange for free use of the puzzles as a supplemental teaching tool. Word about the puzzles soon spread to members of the St. Christopher's community. My stock started to rise again. I received dozens of supportive letters from people earnestly imploring me to return to private school.

I had fleeting thoughts about returning to St. Christopher's for only one reason—I was bored to tears academically at Freeman. I liked being challenged in a classroom. I couldn't imagine faking an interest in learning for two more years. I had certainly underestimated the value of a St. Christopher's education.

I sat down and composed a proposal letter to Mr. Elmer—one that I didn't share with my family—explaining that while I appreciated the normal track to graduation, what I wanted and needed was a fast finish to my high school education. I came up with a plan that I thought would satisfy St. Christopher's minimum graduation requirements: summer school prior to fall matriculation, followed by an overloaded junior year, and then summer school again. This accelerated pace would buy me a year to work my way across the country and save some money for college.

Mr. Elmer was never one to fiddle-faddle, and he replied immediately with a thoughtful, yet unequivocal answer:

It simply cannot be done, Stuart, and I hope you can accept that. Your senior year can be full of extracurricular activities such as the school newspaper and yearbook...

Papa was livid when he learned that I was negotiating with St. Christopher's. He was still bitter about my leaving the school in the first place. He rode my father incessantly about having more control over me. One evening my soft-spoken and obedient father wasn't having it anymore, and he finally stood up to his own father, the one who'd controlled him his entire life.

"Nelson, get a grip on your family. You're letting this boy get away with murder!" commanded Papa.

"Father," he shot back, "for once in my life, let me handle this on my own!"

It was a defining moment in my relationship with my father. He was standing up for compassion and reason, and the fact that he gave Papa a dose of his own bad whiskey made me very proud of him. And this time, I added a long overdue "Thank you."

Though dissatisfied with Mr. Elmer's response, I didn't reply immediately. I wasn't interested in a protracted stalemate, but I wanted to think long and hard before eating crow. This wasn't like buying and selling a piece-of-crap used car in the desert. And furthermore, I was busy at the time composing a poem to present to my grandfather on his ninetieth birthday.

So soon after Nicky's death, it was hard to think about celebrating anything, even a milestone event such as this. But Papa was too popular and too sociable—let's just say "too familiar"—in West End Richmond to be ignored. John and Isabel Hayes hosted a lavish party at their stately residence and invited a veritable Who's Who of the Richmond elite to join in the festivities.

On such a special occasion, I was allowed to drink beer at the party, and I chose to drink it out of a bottle rather than a glass. That choice didn't sit well with my bachelor uncle, Junior, who had never hosted a single event his entire life. What did he know about party etiquette? I'd never had much respect for Junior, never liked the way he, too, mooched off his father. He made a good living as a tobacco buyer, didn't have a wife or children to support, and felt it was his prerogative to come and go from Halsnoch as he pleased. So when he told me to act like a gentleman and drink out of a glass, I basically told him to go fuck himself.

Our commotion got Papa's attention. "What's all the fuss about?" Papa asked as he approached us going at it. He listened to both sides, then snarled at Junior and told him to go fuck himself in politically correct ways I didn't know existed.

"Come on, Stukey Boy," he said to me. "Let's go back to the party so you can read me that piece you've been working on."

I was always uncomfortable with the notion that Papa made more of a fuss over me than Nicky, especially when I'd notched a hole in one at the age of ten and on his eighty-fourth birthday. That night in 1965, he took the entire family to "The Club" for dinner—the only place we dined away from Halsnoch—and told anyone he could about my "ace" and my being the youngest club member to ever accomplish such a feat. Nicky, I'm sure, dreaded the entire evening.

By the time I was sixteen, I was no longer playing or receiving plaudits for my golf, so I tried my hand at poetry. I was certainly no prodigy, but I strived to pay tribute to Papa in a memorable way. And I had asked to read my handiwork aloud. The crowd was hushed and told to listen. I recited each line slowly and distinctly, like I'd been trained to do as a Jackson at St. Christopher's. I nailed all the inflections. I bragged about his legacies, praised his good looks, and closed with an ad lib of how he and his second wife had met and married two years after my nana died.

Papa received an adoring look from Elise, a woman young enough to be his daughter. In fact, my step grandmother was even younger than Junior! Papa first encountered her by accident while mowing a patch of ornery dandelions between the gates of Halsnoch and River Road. She was driving by in her car and pulled over when she spotted Papa. She asked him in the most respectful way possible if he might be able to take care of her lawn, too. Elise had mistaken Papa for the groundskeeper, and he played right along.

"Yes, I most certainly would," Papa replied.

"Shouldn't you ask 'Muh-*dam*' first?" Elise insisted.

This was the South after all, and, although her native Washingtonian mannerisms were noticeably more progressive than most Richmonders, she considered his unvetted answer a bit forward for a mere day laborer.

He grinned, and out came his cheeky response, in his own accent: "That won't be necessary—I happen to sleep with '*Mad*-um.'"

The crowd burst out in laughter and applause, and Papa's day was made. He held out both hands for me to grab and pulled me into his chest for an appropriate hug. Then he went over to Junior and, as if to add insult to injury, pointed out, "You'd better learn to drink beer from a bottle if you ever expect to deliver a damn fine speech like that."

Yes, I was still Papa's boy. Despite my running away from home and the weird new ways I was expressing myself, he had my back. It wasn't lost on either one of us that now that Nicky was gone, I was the lone, great Hotchkiss hope.

Shortly after the party, I went to work at the historic Chalfonte Hotel in Cape May as a combined bellhop and waiter. The hotel was owned by a classmate's grandmother and was visited each summer by fine families from Richmond, Philadelphia, and Pittsburgh. The hotel was old and Victorian, and so were its ways—no air conditioning in the rooms and family-style dining. Guests were treated to the splendors of "soul food with its Sunday clothes on" prepared by fifty-year Chalfonte veteran and head chef Helen Dickerson and her two daughters.

Working at the hotel that summer, I met the old-line McConnon family from Pittsburgh. Their son, Wicky, was the hotel night watchman and a rising senior at Clark University in Worcester, Massachusetts. He'd chosen Clark because it had a liberal academic program that included taking classes on a pass/fail basis and designing one's own major. On the outside, Wicky seemed like a pretty conservative and buttoned-down guy, but I soon came to realize that he was a lot like me—a wolf in sheep's clothing. The seed had been planted.

Just before the end of summer, I learned that Papa had badly sprained his ankle tripping across the threshold from one room to another in the big house. It was the simplest of accidents, yet its consequences were profound. The initial order was for Papa to stay off his feet for a few weeks and avoid normal activities like yard work. Telling Papa to rest was like telling a hyperactive kid to sit and read. His body and his mind had been eternally programmed for exercise.

While his convalescence helped heal his ankle, Papa's overall health took a turn for the worse. He was admitted to Stuart Circle Hospital to treat some secondary illnesses that cropped up from his inactivity. As soon as I got home, I went to visit Papa in the hospital, and he asked me if I'd made my decision regarding high school. I hadn't done so, not officially. He didn't advise, nor in typical Papa fashion did he demand. Instead he asked me to return to St. Christopher's as a *favor* to him. Papa asking for a favor? Could this be his final wish for me because he knew that he was dying?

I wasn't going to disappoint my grandfather any more than I already had. I ate a giant helping of humble pie, contacted Warren Elmer, and re-entered St. Christopher's.

Papa's organs started to break down by late September. Even though he was a nonagenarian, watching a robust and brilliant man like my grandfather waste away like that—from a measly sprained ankle—was a painful experience for everyone. He'd become physically and mentally worn-out. He never left the hospital, and on October 20, he was dead. It caught us all off guard—we had been certain Papa would live to be a hundred years old.

Losing the two most important people in my life in the same year—and at such a young age—was numbing. *I must have caused this to happen!* I kept telling myself. The same dapper man who had been the picture of health and had spoken so eloquently four months earlier at his birthday party was now pale and mute. It was a real awakening for me to think I'd never hear that commanding Southern voice again.

After Papa's funeral, the impending demise of Halsnoch became real. While three of his four heirs could have easily afforded to keep the estate as their home or an investment, none of them could be bothered with its upkeep. My father felt differently, but, for all practical purposes, he had no vote—only seat and voice. The decision to sell the property was reached unanimously and without debate. In hindsight, it was a dreadful financial decision. Halsnoch was practically stolen for the price of $107,000!

Before the heirs closed on the property, the business of divvying up Papa's personal possessions took place. The family silver, antique furniture, oriental rugs—these all went quickly. Personal mementoes—like pictures from Freeman Gosden, who voiced the characters Amos, Kingfish, and Lightning in the *Amos 'n' Andy* show; handwritten letters from Virginia governor and senator Harry F. Byrd; and an old stringless banjo given to Papa by the famous tap dancer and Richmond native Bill "Bojangles" Robinson—were all junked because they were deemed not to have any financial value.

And when his heirs discovered Papa's stash of booze, they simply poured out all the liquid and threw away the bottles. They said it was worthless and possibly illegal—albeit some forty years after the repeal of the Twentieth Amendment. Didn't they know that whiskey gets better with time? Hadn't they ever heard anyone talk about the smoothness of aged whiskey? How could a family who lived for the perfect highball at five o'clock have gotten it so fundamentally wrong?

I had one prize in sight that the family failed to haggle over: the 1963 Ford Galaxie 500 hardtop sedan that Papa had so proudly driven around Richmond. The car bore the license plate number 19. This was a special tag—one ordinarily given to a high-ranking public official—that Papa had received as a political favor. I had driven the car locally a few times while Papa was alive and enjoyed getting such special attention from the tags. When I pulled into a gas station, the attendant not only gave me full service, he would also wash the car windows a second time for good measure.

The estate kept the title to the car but, for all practical purposes, it was now mine. It had silver leather upholstery, with front reclining bucket seats and a rear bench seat wide enough to sleep on. I took it on the road for the first time in January 1972 to visit Wicky in Worcester and interview with the Clark admission office. It drove like a top.

The first edition of my puzzles, *The Biological Crosswords*, debuted on schedule in September 1971 and was well received by teachers as a concept. But as more critical feedback came in, quite a few teachers admitted that they couldn't actually teach with it. The problem was it didn't follow any single textbook in subject order and chapter sequence, which is how most other supplemental materials were formatted. As far as what I told Clark admissions, it was a published work by a mere sixteen-year-old kid. No more, no less. They were impressed.

Mr. Rodgers had remained bullish and encouraged me to send my handiwork to a few educational publishers like Lippincott, Scott Foresman, and Macmillan to get their reactions. I followed his advice. Unfortunately, they were unsettled as well by its failure to mirror any of their own textbooks. Would one of them have signed me on if I revised the puzzles to align with their backlist? Perhaps, and even likely, but I no longer had the same passion as when I had started. I was much-too focused on getting on with other parts of my life. So I let it all go into the vast wasteland called experience. Paradoxically, had I not created the puzzles in the first place, I may never have attended college.

St. Christopher's knew nothing about my interest in Clark or my application until they received the university's transcript request. Mr. Elmer and other school officials thought I was foolhardy for chasing such an impossible dream. The moment of truth arrived in April 1972, when a thin envelope from Clark arrived in the family mailbox. I was sure it was a rejection letter. Many good things come in small packages, but not college acceptance letters. They were usually stuffed with a multitude of inserts needing immediate attention, but the letter I opened was short and to the point: I'd been accepted as a member of the Class of 1976. There it was, typewritten and signed by Clark's director of admissions. I couldn't help feeling a little smug.

George McVey, the new incoming headmaster at St. Christopher's for the 1972–1973 academic year and Mr. Elmer's successor, pulled me aside one day and said, "Hotchkiss, you won. Congratulations!"

We were both smiling.

Mr. McVey reached out to me with more than just words; he also offered an olive branch. He was willing to do me a huge favor—but we'd have to keep it on the down low for the time being. If I were to enroll in summer school at our rival private school, Collegiate, and successfully complete two core classes, Mr. McVey would slip me a backdated diploma under the table.

"You never know when you might need it one day," Mr. McVey prodded.

I thanked him and accepted his offer. Perhaps he felt I might not officially earn a college degree either.

The stint in summer school lasted only six short weeks, and it was not dull by any means. My teachers—yes indeed, both—acted far outside the norm. One was a woman in her early thirties who quite often conducted classes outside on the school lawn. She liked to sit directly opposite me with her legs akimbo, wearing nothing at all under her short skirt but a grin! As hard as she tried to cajole me into a quickie, I never obliged. I wanted that diploma a whole lot more than I wanted her.

The other teacher was a corpulent and tweedy man in his fifties who liked a stiff drink. He invited another student and me over to his wee abode on a friend's estate—a supersized Halsnoch—one evening after school, ostensibly for dinner. We accepted, much too impulsively as it turned out. He plied us with enough Dewar's White Label Scotch to get us drunk and then tried to force his hands down our pants. Fortunately, we double-teamed the old bastard and escaped. Rather than awaken his landlord—recently ranked by *Forbes* as the eighty-seventh richest family in America—we walked four miles in complete darkness back to the safety of our homes. Nothing more was ever said between the parties.

My parents had been busy in the late spring and early summer nailing down a new place to live. Fresh with inheritance, they were able to buy their very first home. They didn't really want to move too far from the old homestead, and luckily they didn't have to. They found a spacious rambler built in 1950 that sat on a double corner lot in the residential neighborhood called Westham. Two people could finally live in a four-bedroom house, rather than the other way around.

Between the end of summer school and the beginning of college, I had to move my belongings from Halsnoch to my parents' new house. Only one item required some ingenuity—a tree I had acquired while working part-time in late spring and early summer as a groundskeeper at Chatham Square, the gated enclave where my Aunt Alice lived. One of her neighbors had specially ordered the tree but, for some reason, changed her mind when it arrived. Rather than turn the orphaned tree into compost, I volunteered to take it home and plant it in rich soil. The tree had unusual leaves, much like a marijuana plant, but no one on the job site knew its species. The crew foreman thought for a moment, then volunteered, "Moonlight over the Mountain tree," with such conviction, I believed him.

I took the tree to Halsnoch and planted it outside the office. Thankfully, it took root and adapted very nicely. Ordinarily, it would've made sense to leave the tree behind and let it convey to the new owners, but I had a more sinister plan.

In late April, my friend Scott Ellett and I planted a few marijuana seedlings on the lower forty of his family's property. By moving day, in mid-June, I had one beauty about to flower and almost the same size and shape as my tree. Neither a trained eye nor a vivid imagination would be able to tell the difference. Inspiration hit me, and I decided to dig up the plant and move it to Westham. In order to complete the circle of deceit, I dug up the real tree and turned it into compost after all.

My marijuana plant immediately took root and thrived in my parents' new yard. I was headed back to Cape May to work a couple of weeks in August at the Chalfonte before college started and, ordinarily, my parents would have gladly watered it in my absence. However, they had a trip planned to Virginia Beach and would be away the same time as I was. So I turned to my new next-door neighbor, the administrative chief of Henrico County, for a favor. When I asked if he could possibly care for the tree those two weeks, he was happy to oblige.

When I returned from Cape May, I found that my plant had produced big fat buds, so big they *had* to be picked before I left for college. I thanked my neighbor for his assistance and asked him if taking care of the tree had posed any problems.

"Not in the least," he answered. "I'm going to look into getting some for the county—it's one of the hardiest species I've ever seen."

No sooner had I succeeded in gaining a fan of the tree than I chose to harvest it, whether it was ready or not. After picking the buds, I removed the stalk, too, leaving a rather noticeable bald spot in the yard.

"It sure looked healthy to us," offered my parents when I tried to explain its sudden demise and mysterious disappearance.

I asked them to do me a huge favor and break the news to our neighbor after I left. He had such a green thumb and had grown very fond of the "tree." There was no possible way I could look him straight in the eye and tell him myself.

So there I was, committed and on my way to Clark for one semester. I didn't have any idea what I'd be doing in six months, but that didn't matter. I was confident that I'd made the right decision to plow forward. *How could things get any worse?* I argued.

CHAPTER 4

Woolly Adventure

TWO MONTHS INTO my first semester at Clark University, I was already realizing I'd made a colossal mistake in choosing to enroll there. Clark was a good fit in terms of my need for independence. That being said, I was a gefilte fish out of water. Seventy percent of its student body hailed from the more comfortable suburbs of New York City and Long Island. It was an easy place for students to defer life.

Being Southern, Protestant, and financially challenged, I had to work overtime to fit in. The school's most popular major, psychology, was always the conversation starter. Freud this and Freud that. I thought it was all a bunch of psychobabble—and crap.

Drugs were ubiquitous on campus. I'd gone from a self-sufficient pot grower to a consumer of hallucinogens, including blotter paper LSD, mescaline, and horse tranquilizers. They all produced disturbing "trips," especially unnecessary anxiety and, sometimes, unrelieved terror. Things a fragile mind like mine clearly didn't need.

My safety net became Professor Roy Andersen's astronomy class. He gave great lectures, but I particularly loved going outside on cold, clear nights to stargaze and learn many of the constellations. The more I witnessed the enormity of the heavens, the more I believed in extraterrestrial life. When then-governor Jimmy Carter first filed his report in 1973 about a UFO sighting in Georgia, it didn't garner a lot of national attention, but it sure got mine.

Just as the clear January skies made stargazing seem supernatural, the first semester came to an abrupt close. I wasn't willing to go into debt to stay at Clark, but I hadn't made any other plans, either. Fortunately, Dr. Andersen encouraged me to stay an extra month in January—known as winter term—to participate in his one-month independent study. I could do so tuition free. The assignment was to build my own six-inch reflector telescope. Each day was a grind—literally and figuratively—using my hands to carve out a smooth, parabolic mirror. Listening to the good professor talk about our shared passion kept me engaged.

I turned eighteen a few days before the term ended, on January 23, 1973. I was not planning to celebrate that Tuesday in any special way. I had no gifts to open—not even from home—and no idea what I would be doing or where I'd be living in a week. I was totally skint. So I just settled into the dorm lounge that night to watch President Nixon appear on national television and give his "Peace with Honor" speech. He announced that the Vietnam-era draft was ending. That particular cloud of uncertainty about my future had been lifted.

After the speech, the news cut away to another story developing elsewhere in the world. Earlier that day, a volcanic eruption had occurred on the island of Heimaey off the southern coast of Iceland. Reports were coming in showing the spray of lava and volcanic ash. It was causing a major crisis for the five thousand inhabitants of the island and nearly led to a permanent evacuation. Many houses had already been destroyed, and the lava flow threatened to close off the harbor. Without a harbor, the island's fishing fleet would be brought to its knees. For a nation of Iceland's size, this was an all-hands-on-deck international crisis.

When I was a kid, my parents had subscribed to the *Around the World* travel series, featuring photograph stamps that had to be applied throughout each booklet. My favorite installment combined Iceland and Greenland and explained, among other things, why they were both misnomers. But something else in the description about Iceland—perhaps its gorgeous women—had held me spellbound. Someday, I was going to see this place with my own eyes.

The volcano was the perfect excuse. It would be a priceless eighteenth birthday gift to myself. I'd done volunteer work before, but something this challenging and on the world stage would rock. I couldn't get to Iceland without first earning some money, but the eruption was forecast to continue until July, so time was on my side. Keeping my options open, I took an official one-year leave of absence from Clark.

I returned to my parents' home in Richmond to work and finance my trip. In short order, I found a job as a Yellow Cab driver. My first day on the streets, I was held up. I couldn't tell what the perp had concealed in his coat pocket, but this was no time to play guessing games. I fully cooperated and wasn't harmed. Turns out all the guy wanted was a free joy ride. Once he finally left the cab and I filed my police report, I was back on the job. I was not going to let anyone ruin my date with the volcano.

I was too kind to be a successful cab driver, and my wages suffered as a result. I got really annoyed walking heavy bags of groceries up several flights of stairs and receiving nary a penny for my trouble. After all, I was only doing this job for the money. So some of the older cabbies took pity on me and taught me the art of "high flagging." Rather than engaging the meter when transporting a passenger, I quoted a flat fare in advance, like a gypsy cab. It was an illegal practice, but my daily earnings doubled.

The streak didn't last long. I called it quits two months into the job—the night I lost complete sight of a passenger due to a burned-out light in the rear of the cab. I was driving him to a destination in Richmond's Churchill neighborhood, then a crime-ridden part of town with a high murder rate. We didn't talk. I tried to observe him through the rearview mirror, but it was useless. The only thing he said the entire trip was, "Stop looking at me, man."

I prayed to God that if He let me drop this guy off without getting harmed, I'd take my cab straight back to the station before my shift ended and quit the next day, which I did. My belief in God had been shaken after Nicky died, but that night He answered my prayers, and I most definitely felt His presence.

By the time I got everything together for my trip to Iceland, it was early May. I purchased a backpack, tent, and sleeping bag and a few other camping accessories. I was going to get there on the cheap by hitchhiking as far north and east as the Canadian province of Newfoundland and then sail the rest of the way across the North Atlantic Ocean. I planned to work my way over on a fishing boat or a freighter to add to the experience. I was eighteen going on thirty, and I had the world by the balls.

There were no long farewells or tears shed the day I left Richmond. Not visible ones anyway. As much as my parents must have worried about my safety, I think they were also proud of me. After all these years of our living together at Halsnoch under Papa's rule, they now had their own life and I had mine. Change had done us all a world of good.

The first part of my journey from Richmond up the East Coast to Bar Harbor, Maine, was aided in part by bus service. Then the fun began. I sailed by ferry to the town of Yarmouth on the southern tip of the Canadian province of Nova Scotia and started hitchhiking full-time. I still had a long way to go to get to Iceland, but it felt so liberating to cross my first foreign border.

As I wound my way up the entire length of this beautiful province, I found the inland parts beaming with yellow and lilac wildflowers and its abundant coastline beaches waiting patiently for hardy swimmers to arrive. Along the way, I made a detour to a neighboring province, Prince Edward Island, and stayed there on a bucolic farm owned by a couple who had picked me up in Nova Scotia. Life was good, but I hadn't forgotten about the road ahead of me. To get to Iceland, I needed to get to and travel across the "rock" of Newfoundland.

They say half the fun is getting there; they lie. The ferry ride across the Cabot Strait—from North Sydney, Nova Scotia, to Port aux Basques, Newfoundland—was six straight hours of choppy seas and zero visibility. It was too unstable to walk the decks. I got up only to vomit over the rails. When I stepped off the ferry in Port aux Basques, a sudden gust of wind blew my hat straight into the air like a kite. And even though it was spring, I now felt colder in Newfoundland than I had the entire winter in Massachusetts.

Almost six hundred miles due east was the capital city of St. John's, a port city where I'd have my only shot at picking up ship's passage to

Iceland. The city was dotted with colorful Victorian row houses cascading down to the harbor, fusing bold color with some of the oldest streets in North America. Although nearly frozen stiff by the time I arrived in St. John's, I was pleased to find myself surrounded by inviting pubs and pretty women. The docks were also easily accessible, so I could walk right onto ships and speak with "yer man" about forthcoming voyages.

To my dismay, no ships were making a move anytime soon. Newfoundland was still feeling the effects of an unusually harsh winter, and most of the vessels in the harbor had been stuck there since the last thaw. New ships wouldn't be getting into port for a while either. Only one determined, or perhaps demented, fisherman had his trawler prepared for departure back to his native Faeroes, an isolated group of small North Atlantic islands between Scotland and Iceland.

"It's only seven hundred kilometers from your destination," he said like an overanxious travel agent in perfect English.

I knew little about world geography those days and feared he was conning me into some shenanigans. Yet he spoke with such self-confidence that I actually thought about taking the plunge, despite my bad experiences on the way home from New Orleans. In a strange way, his free spirit made me feel grounded. And I was certainly a gamer in terms of going mano a mano with the cod.

In the end, even though it would have been easier to say yes, I found the courage to say no. Two or three times, as I recall. After taking stock of my situation, I decided to abandon my idea of crossing the Atlantic by sea. Instead, I turned around and started hitchhiking to Kennedy Airport in New York City.

Two days later, I arrived unscathed at the Icelandic Airlines terminal at Kennedy, and it was a mob scene. The mass of travelers there looked like they'd been stranded by a cancelled flight, not about to board one that was on time. They were all about my age and kitted out with the same checked luggage—JanSport backpack, North Face sleeping bag, and Kelty tent. This was only my third time on an airplane and a wake-up call to the reality of bargain travel. I wondered how the airline could get all these people and all this stuff on the same plane. Somehow, they managed.

The air onboard the plane was hot and humid, and the strong smell of body odor could have choked a horse. Conversations among passengers were lively and in many languages. Forget trying to sleep. Fortunately, the flight was short, and we landed safely at the international airport in Keflavík, thirty miles southwest of the capital city of Reykjavík and home to the NATO military base.

It was popular and inexpensive back then for Americans to fly to Europe on Icelandic Airlines. These flights included that initial stopover in Iceland, and some travelers would stay for a day or two to visit waterfalls or go pony trekking before continuing on to Luxembourg. Although I had planned to only visit Iceland, it was nice to have what amounted to a free trip to the continent in my hip pocket if I should choose to use it later. After all, I wasn't planning to stay in Iceland once my work on Heimaey was finished.

I noticed that most of the passengers deplaning with me at Keflavík headed straight to the duty-free shop to buy handmade Icelandic sweaters as souvenirs. Sweater making was a major cottage industry in Iceland, dominated by cash-strapped housewives. They knit with a soft unspun yarn, called *lopi*, using what's known as the Continental technique. I didn't purchase anything at the shop that day, but as I witnessed the buying frenzy, I mused that spinning wool into a business might be a golden opportunity. That could wait, but getting to Heimaey couldn't.

I was looking for the motor coach—known as the *Flybus*—to get to Reykjavík and catch a direct flight to Heimaey. As I made my way to the ticket queue, some kind soul—an Icelander, my guess—offered to drive me to the port town of Þorlákshöfn, where I could catch a ferry to the island instead. I was compelled to accept his invitation whether disposed to it or not. It was made in broad daylight in front of plenty of witnesses. And given that the Icelandic population is remarkably homogenous, most of those witnesses were likely relatives.

As we drove along, mostly in polite silence, I concluded that the jagged landscapes, at least in this part of the country, were far less memorable than that of Newfoundland. We proceeded mostly through grand lava fields that were covered in wet and spongy moss. Nasty headwinds tossed the Land Rover like a crispy kale salad. The road was rutted and potholed, yet the driver never took his foot off the gas pedal. He knew the sailing schedule, and there was no time for slowing down.

As I'd done many times in the past, I said a quick good-bye to one more stranger and caught the last ferry of the day by an eyelash. And to end my up-and-down journey on a high note, the ride over was as smooth as a punt on an English river.

Once I disembarked at Vestmannaeyjar—the only town on Heimaey—I was surrounded by hundreds of other foreigners and volunteers. It was now five months since the eruption, but you could have just as easily believed it had happened only a week ago. What had once been a typically colorful Icelandic town was now gray and barren. Virtually all of the homes with the once-alternating red, yellow, blue, and green roofs were now under volcanic ash.

Volunteers gathered at the local secondary school. We were put to work immediately and given a place to stay on the gymnasium floor. We toiled two six-hour shifts a day, using wide shovels to remove the ash from the roofs. I worked up a tremendous appetite and ate like I was on a cruise ship, even though the selection was limited to fish, lamb, and potatoes. In the mornings, I would perk up my taste buds with copious amounts of strong coffee and creamy pastries.

During my time off, I'd venture as close as possible to the hole of the new mountain—Eldfell—that had formed from the eruption. I would look at the multiple colors of the cooling lava above ground and peer down at the even brighter shades in the earth's furnace below. Thanks to a kind stranger who applied hair spray to the rock samples I'd collected, I can still see these colors today.

About three weeks into volunteering, a number of us were offered free passage back to the mainland and paying jobs as longshoremen on the docks in Reykjavík. My new employer would be Eimskip, Iceland's largest shipping company. I would be responsible for loading frozen cargo bound for Europe and America and unloading a variety of consumer durables that had landed in Iceland. There was so much buzz about Reykjavík's night scene—some of the volunteers had already passed through on the way to Heimaey—that I couldn't pass up such an opportunity.

What I did forgo—out of necessity—were cigarettes. In a tobacco-friendly state like Virginia, I seem to recall paying three dollars or so for an entire carton of cigarettes. I couldn't afford *not* to smoke. But in an import-dependent country like Iceland, one *pack* of smokes cost nearly eight dollars! That got me to kick the habit for nearly fifteen years.

The longshoreman job was perfectly fine until the cold weather and darkness of winter approached. Just like in Newfoundland, the wind is what makes you feel cold in Iceland. There are a lot of wide-open vistas throughout the country and no trees to block the winds. I was eager to learn the Icelandic language so I could shout back at this *helvítis rok*—literally translated, "damned gale"—which I did quite often.

Now that I was earning a few *kronur*—and not smoking—I could afford to go out on Saturday nights to nightclubs. Seems like half the population of Reykjavík did the same thing. One night, I ordered myself and a lovely Icelandic blonde—quite an oxymoron—sitting next to me a cocktail. I preferred a beer but, sadly, this beverage was then illegal in Iceland. The young lady thanked me and promptly took the drink with her to a table to join some friends. When she was done, she brought the empty glass back and placed it on the bar in front of me.

"What just happened here?" I asked the bartender.

"Icelandic women are very independent, and she thought you were trying to buy her affection," he explained.

It was a good lesson learned early in my stay, because at twelve bucks a drink, a guy like me couldn't afford to flirt.

By November, I landed an indoor job with Eimskip, and even though it was monotonous—unloading large vehicle tires as they came into the warehouse by truck—it was a cozier job in terms of the weather and a fast way for me to learn the Icelandic language. My mates were working class and didn't speak English. They wore industrial clothes and wool hooligan caps as a matter of working-class pride. They'd kill some long periods of idleness by playing a card game called *Olsen Olsen,* quite similar to Crazy Eights. I longed for a seat at the table.

I could learn enough vocabulary on my own, but I needed and received lots of help with the hardest part of the language—the grammar—from my landlady, Ásta Jónsdóttir. She'd often invite me upstairs to her living quarters and sit with me over coffee and snacks to tutor me on verb conjugations and noun declensions. She was a refined lady and detested all the slang I was picking up at work. I hung in there, as much for her company as the lessons, and ended up kicking some serious butt back at the warehouse playing *Olsen Olsen.*

Living and working in Iceland during the winter months aggravated what I didn't realize at the time were my formative years of depression, but I soldiered through the darkness. I got up in the morning and commuted to work in the dark. I took my morning and afternoon coffee breaks in the dark. Lunch hour was the only time of day when darkness cleared, but it never gave way to pure, unadulterated sunshine. Streetlights and car headlights were never turned off. This almost total lack of sunlight is lethal to the emotionally fragile. One could try to distract oneself with work—most people had two jobs to finance their capitalist lifestyles—but the only sure remedy for me was romance.

I lumbered over to the University of Iceland student cafeteria one night in a blinding snowstorm to check out their dinner buffet. I sat by myself but paid careful attention to the coeds. They were more refined than the girls I'd met at bars and clubs, and some weren't even speaking Icelandic. I had to find a way to keep coming back to this venue and looking like I belonged there.

I discovered that the university offered a class called Icelandic for Foreigners and got permission to audit the class. I instantly fit in on campus. Maybe it was that confidence thing again. One night at the cafeteria, I was invited to sit with a beautiful Norwegian girl named Lise and some of her countrymen, who were enrolled as full-time premed students. She spoke English well enough, and with a decidedly foreign and sexy accent.

I looked forward to sitting and speaking with Lise again, preferably alone, if I were so lucky. Perhaps Norwegian women treated aggressive men the same way as their Icelandic counterparts. I didn't want to repeat my earlier mistake at the nightclub.

We were both strangers in a strange land, and it provided us with a reason to keep meeting. Between her school and my work schedule, Lise and I didn't have any free time to spend with each other during the day. But our nightly meetings at the cafeteria became a greatly anticipated part of our daily grind. One weekend, after exams, we were able to go out on a real date to a club, have some drinks, and let our hair down. That night, the clothes came off and a strange sort of romance began.

My going over to her dorm room to spend the night and keep her warm became the mainstay of our existence for nearly four months. I knew she'd be returning home to Norway one day to do her residency and practice pediatric medicine, but what the hell did she know about me? How could I begin to try and explain that, despite my current appearance as a warehouse clerk—Sears work boots and all—I had a high school diploma from St. Christopher's? What in God's name would that mean to her?

Lise didn't seem to care about my status, nor was she embarrassed to be seen with me in front of her countrymen. I didn't question her motives, nor did I object to the role of body warmer if, in fact, that's how she really viewed me. I could only surmise that as long as I was asked to keep my appointed rounds, I was making her quite happy.

I was certainly comfortable being Lise's friend with benefits, but by the end of 1974, I was ready to return home. After all, my parents had not seen me for a year and a half. Lise's commitment to her education had started to make me feel a bit anxious about returning to college myself. My official leave of absence from Clark had long ago expired, but I was certain that I could find other options.

Somewhat to my surprise, Lise didn't want me to leave, not then anyway. She was in tears. That made my decision tougher for sure, but at the end of the day, I said my good-byes to her and flew home to America in time for Christmas. I detached myself from this relationship without regret or fear of retribution. It was just one of those rite-of-passage things.

Due to archaic foreign-exchange regulations, I could only covert Icelandic *kronur* back into American dollars at the rate of a hundred dollars a day. I'd just have to leave the bulk of my savings in the bank and come back later to exchange it. Hoping that I would return, Ásta let me leave my camping gear and golf clubs at her house. This act of kindness guaranteed another stay in Reykjavík, but for reasons I never imagined.

I arrived in Richmond safely and spent a delightful Christmas with my parents and friends. I made it very clear to everyone that my journey to Iceland had ended and I was looking forward to resuming college. I found it easier than ever to reconnect with family and old pals, and I presumed that they saw a positive change in me, too.

I suddenly reversed my decision two days after Christmas and announced that I would be returning to Iceland immediately. A short telegram had arrived from Lise: "Stuart, I'm pregnant. I need you. Please, please, please come back to Reykjavík."

Today, I'm sure I would have taken the news somewhat in stride, texted or e-mailed Lise with a host of questions, trusted my innate ability to discern the truth, and then made a decision. Yes, even me, the forever-spontaneous and crazy one.

But these were days like World War II, when "shocking" news was dispatched via letter or telegram and so people came to dread them. Lise's thirteen words weren't the least bit ambiguous. To have responded with questions and started a who-knows-how-long telegram volley would have been pointless and expensive.

I kept the news to myself and started to panic. I didn't want to be a father. I was only nineteen years old, and in so many ways, I didn't even know Lise. I certainly didn't want to set up house with her. That was never part of my attraction to her. I thought about it for a few hours—max—and realized there was no other choice, at least not one that I could live with. I needed to go back to Iceland.

So began my fatal attraction to women.

I called in a favor with my old employer, Eimskip, and pleaded for free passage to Reykjavík aboard one of their freighters. I would happily work onboard as barter. God knows I would need something to do during an eleven-day voyage across the North Atlantic to Iceland in the dead of winter other than try to figure out fatherhood. Eimskip came through for me, and I wired Lise to let her know that I was on my way and would be back in Reykjavík by the middle of January.

My parents drove me to Norfolk, Virginia, to board the freighter. They didn't ask a lot of questions en route. I wish I could have had a dialogue with them about my predicament, but we could still only talk about pleasant things. For the rest of their lives, they never asked and I never offered the truth surrounding this return trip to Iceland.

The eleven days at sea were challenging, to say the least. I spent most nights strapped into my bed to prevent being injured from a sudden ejection. The weight of the ship would violently shift from one side to the other as the huge swells tossed us around like ragdolls. I had managed to send Lise one update while I was sailing, and I'm sure the words sounded morbid to her because I was scared shitless. As soon as the ship pulled into Reykjavík Harbour, I called Lise to tell her I was on my way to her dorm room.

Something didn't sound right in her voice. I prayed that she and the fetus were OK. I prayed that she would divulge any earth-shattering news on the phone—I was already suffering more than my fair share of anxiety.

She paused momentarily, fiercely trying to translate her innermost thoughts from Norwegian into English. Unable to do so, she had no choice but to be curt. "When you get here, we need to talk."

I was greeted in a manner totally inconsistent with the way I had left her in tears nearly a month before. I was expecting to get mauled, but instead I got a peck on the cheek. She seemed impassive; something was obviously amiss. The words didn't come easily for Lise. I thought for sure that she had miscarried. I was wrong. She claimed to have experienced a pseudocyesis—an hysterical pregnancy. She wanted so desperately to get pregnant that she had developed many of the signs and symptoms of a real pregnancy.

More news followed. It explained why she had sounded so detached and so distant on the phone. Since she'd sent me the telegram, she and another med student from Norway had hooked up. The two of them were now an item. She had no room for me in her life—or under her duvet—anymore.

I was at a complete loss for words. There were so many emotions running through my mind that I couldn't decide what to dwell on first.

As one would expect, it took me several long winter nights in the Arctic to come out of my funk. I was depressed and in a very lonely place. I was extremely embarrassed. And my future was now completely uncertain.

I was, nevertheless, back in my beloved Iceland. This was home to me in many ways. I knew my way around, and I could speak the language. I went to the local Eimskip office to find and chat with my old bosses about employment opportunities. If I could find something right away, I was prepared to lick my wounds and stay here indefinitely.

Within a few days, I received a call from a man named Adalsteinn Þorbergsson, a licensed plumber in town and a friend of my last Eimskip boss. "Steini" said that he might have a job for me. I told him I had no plumbing experience, but he said that he could teach me. So we met, and he described the contract he had just received from the City of Reykjavík. Steini was hired to install the plumbing system inside a new day-care center being built adjacent to the city hospital. He needed an assistant to help him measure, cut, and thread the pipes—nothing more complicated than that.

I soon found out that Steini had a different motive for hiring me. He wanted to immigrate to San Francisco in the worst kind of way. A year or so earlier, he had fallen in love with the city and a captivating woman. He wanted to learn enough English by the time the day-care center project was completed in order to make a smooth transition to America. As long as I could teach him English, he'd be a happy camper.

I decided to accept Steini's offer and remain in Iceland four more months or so. There was no existing building to protect us from the elements as we worked, so we drank lots of coffee and *brennevín*—the local firewater—to stay warm. We were a match made in heaven. We both wanted to learn something new, and we were excellent teachers and students. Some days, Steini and I were forced to huddle very close together on a slab of concrete and lift our caps away from our ears to hear each other talk because of *helvítis rok*. But we persevered, and eventually the walls of the new building rose up around us. We could finally see light at the end of the tunnel.

I knew by the end of the project that I'd have an even bigger foreign currency dilemma than the one I had faced back in December. And I certainly didn't want to leave anything behind this time.

I remembered the cash-strapped housewives of the Eimskip workers. The guys had pestered me to buy woolen goods from their wives to send back to the states, but I had had no interest at the time. Now it made sense to revisit that opportunity. Perhaps I could buy a large enough quantity of sweaters and hats and scarves to "cash out" my savings and potentially profit from the investment as well. I'd run this by a guy who really knew the business of Icelandic woolens.

Steini introduced me to Tom Holden, an American who had met an Icelander—now his wife—in Colorado and moved with her to Iceland to start a family and a business. Hilda Hlutafélag (Hilda Inc.) had quickly become the second largest exporter of Icelandic woolen products and was still expanding. Tom and I spoke freely about my short-term dilemma and his long-term goals.

"Buy as many woolens as you can now directly from the wives; you'll save a lot of money. Once you get settled and determine there's a real business opportunity for you, we'll be there to supply you," Tom offered.

I appreciated his candor. Tom's largest market was the United States, even though at the time there were only three merchants carrying his line: catalog retailers L.L. Bean and Carroll Reed and brick-and-mortar retailer Landau's in Princeton, New Jersey. I asked Tom to suggest another untapped market, and he immediately mentioned the five-college mecca in the Connecticut River Valley of western Massachusetts: "You've got four private colleges right there in the same place, and tons of parents come every weekend to visit their kids and bring lots of money."

Throw in the University of Massachusetts and its sheer volume of students, and the master seemed to know exactly what he was preaching.

Retail merchandising? Was I nuts? This was my father's occupation and one that nearly put us in the poorhouse. He had worked six days a week and would have worked seven if it had been customary in the '50s and '60s for businesses to be open on Sundays.

Because of—and perhaps in spite of—these bittersweet memories, I longed to experience the world of retail for myself. Perhaps it would help me understand my father better. Whatever it was about the retail trade, it made him tick. So what if I got bored when no one came to shop, or peeved when I overheard a supercilious comment about my prices or the wares themselves? I was twenty years old, for crying out loud. When would my skin ever be this thick again?

I spent my last three days in Reykjavík rounding up woolen goods. My haul netted about five hundred pieces from thirty different sources. The last two hundred dollars I converted from *kronur* and stashed in my wallet. My bank account was finally closed. I felt so pleased that my affairs were in order. I gathered my things from Ásta's house and bade her a heartfelt farewell.

My voyage home in May 1975 originated in Reykjavík aboard the *Brúarfoss*, a freighter in the Eimskip fleet. We circumnavigated the entire island of Iceland to collect frozen fish at a dozen or so ports and then headed across the North Atlantic. Our destination was the small city of Cambridge on Maryland's Eastern Shore. A production facility there processed our cargo into breaded and battered fish products.

On the early leg of the voyage, I was able to visit a few remote towns in the eastern part of Iceland that I would never have been able to reach by car. Places like Neskaupstaður, Eskifjörður, and Fáskrúðsfjöður—all brief stops—but full of residents fathered and grandfathered by Russians and other Eastern Europeans who had spent some cold winter nights there. These Eastern Icelanders were much darker in hair color and complexion than their brethren to the north, south, and west.

The May sailing felt like a cruise compared with the winter trip, and this time we also had a female Icelandic passenger on board. Passengers could pay a small fare to travel aboard the freighter without having to work and were offered their own cabins. Generally, people working on the ship like me would have to double up, but since I had brought so many over-sized boxes on board, the captain of the *Brúarfoss* thoughtfully gave me a private cabin. It was adjacent to the one occupied by the female passenger.

The captain showed more than a mild curiosity as to my excessive consumption. He came right out and asked me what I had inside those boxes. Fair question.

When I told the captain about my buying spree, he related to my story and the opportunity that lay ahead for me. But he needed to know two things. First, had I labeled the goods with tags indicating content and country of origin? Second, had I enough money to pay the customs duty upon our entry into the United States? Honestly, I didn't know what he was talking about. I was young and carefree, and Tom Holden had failed to mention these not-so-small details. But now, halfway across the North Atlantic, I was going to have to sort this matter out and fast. The captain offered to get the ball rolling.

Icelandic tradition would not allow the captain to get jiggy with the female passenger in either his or her quarters. He merely suggested that I facilitate an afternoon tryst between the two of them in my cabin—à la Jack Lemmon's character in *The Apartment*—which I quickly agreed to. Playing matchmaker paid dividends. It gained me entrée to the first engineer, who was the real pirate of the ship.

"Captain says you are a nice man and I should help you with a problem," mentioned this short, overbuilt Icelander, dressed in oil-stained coveralls.

I thought the engineer meant he was going to offer an instant solution, but he didn't. He expected to be compensated in some manner for his services. In addition to being an able seaman, the engineer was a farmer in southeast Iceland, where he raised horses. They were raised for their meat, not for work or for racing. As repulsive as the idea of slaughter was to me, there was a ready market for horsemeat in Iceland because it was significantly less expensive than beef.

The engineer wanted me to buy me a horsehide he'd taken with him on the voyage. Or, if I preferred, a bunch of Danish pornography. The magazines looked so crude and used I wanted to vomit. The poor horse had already been killed, so what difference would it make if I bought the hide?

I forked over a hundred dollars for the hide but asked him to keep it until we finished our journey. He counted the number of boxes and measured their sizes, like a moving estimator would. He didn't ask a thing about their contents. He simply assured me that once we got to Cambridge, he would get everything—including the horsehide—into the country without any hassles or cost. I think the word for this is *smuggling*.

As the *Brúarfoss* approached the Chesapeake Bay, I intuited that Cambridge was not far to the northeast. I became nervous about the time and how the engineer and his crew would pull off this escapade. They obviously knew better. There was a Panamanian banana boat offloading at the single dock in Cambridge, so we had to anchor the ship and wait overnight for our turn. That gave everyone working under the engineer's orders plenty of time to place my goods in rowboats and transfer them, moonlight and all, from the ship to a safe house on land.

The next day we docked in Cambridge, where I was greeted by a US Customs officer and asked to show what I planned to remove from the ship. We went to my cabin, and he saw my golf clubs, my camping gear, a few clothes I'd purchased and worn while in Iceland, and one partially filled box of woolens I was truly bringing home as souvenirs. He asked over and over again if there was *anything* else, which made me paranoid. So a crewmember, who knew that the customs officer had a weakness for *hangikjöt*—Icelandic smoked lamb—took the gluttonous bureaucrat downstairs to the ship's galley for a sumptuous lunch.

Word was sent back upstairs about fifteen minutes later that the American was free to leave the ship. The customs officer had no time to waste with me. I was skipping down the ramp and off the *Brúarfoss*. My parents had driven up from Richmond to meet me, and I'm sure they thought the smile on my face was due to their presence. In part, it was. Just to celebrate a bit more, I took them onboard the *Brúarfoss* and let them meet the captain and the engineer. My parents were impressed by how friendly we all seemed to be with one another. They especially liked the gift of smoked lamb presented to them by the ship's cook.

When my parents and I drove away from the dock, I told them we'd have to make a stop to rent a U-Haul trailer. "For what?" they asked. I told them I had done a little business while in Iceland and had to pick up some merchandise in town. The engineer had handed me a piece of paper with a street address in Cambridge and told me to go there straightaway. We pulled up in front of a decent-looking house, where a young, busty, blond American woman greeted my knock. As I ogled this woman, I couldn't help but think about the crew's upcoming shore leave.

"Wasn't it nice of this lady to store these boxes for me over the winter?" I said to my father as we loaded up the trailer.

Yes, he was impressed and, being the consummate Southern gentleman, wanted to thank her himself. The shit-eating grin he sported when he returned to the car confirmed that he, too, had seen her abundant cleavage. The three of us were in for an interesting drive to Richmond, I thought.

During the trip, however, my parents told me that Aunt Lizzie had died from a stroke while gardening in her backyard a week before I arrived in Cambridge. My eyes welled with tears. I wasn't prepared to say good-bye to her, not until I could share my woolly adventure in Iceland. But I was comforted to learn that she went quickly. My great aunt had lived a good life, a life on her own terms.

And, for better or worse, she had just passed me the Hotchkiss reins.

After a brief stay in Richmond, I followed Tom Holden's advice and drove my cargo to the epicenter of Trust Fund Nation—the "Five Colleges" of western Massachusetts. In the town of Amherst, I found a vacant business storefront in a mini-mall on North Pleasant Street, one of the two main drags through the town.

I passed the sniff test with the landlord and, in a matter of days, did a cheaper-than-dirt build-out and hung a sign bearing the name The Nature of Iceland. I placed a column inch ad in the University of Massachusetts student newspaper to attract customers to what I called a "Sneak Preview Sale" on the last Saturday in September. Campus life was back in full swing, and local businesses were stuffing Benjamins into their cash registers again.

The sale was not just a success, it was a sellout. I mean a *complete* sellout. Not one item was left after I closed the doors that Saturday afternoon. So I remained closed for a month while I worked out a reorder with Hilda and found a customs broker to bring new merchandise in legally. I reopened the store in plenty of time for Christmas and kept it open until the end of ski season in late April. By that point, I had had enough. I was twenty-one years old, bored to tears with retail, and ready to resurface in academia.

Having established residency in Massachusetts, I enrolled that fall as an in-state student at UMass on a full-time basis. To pay my way, I continued to import woolen goods from Hilda and consigned them to a half-dozen shops in the area. I also got a part-time job waiting tables in the evening at the Elmwood Inn, a pleasant middle-class restaurant in nearby Hadley. My life was New Orleans redux, only better.

Iceland captured my spirit and changed my life. Although a near crisis and heartache went into the bargain, I found a way to manage. I was sure I would never face challenges like this again. How adolescent! This was just the tip of the iceberg.

CHAPTER 5

Marriage 101

AS A SEVEN-YEAR-OLD boy, I was caught mailing my twenty-five-cent weekly allowance to a camp counselor twice may age. She had doted on me that summer, and that made her my sweetheart. Pretty twisted, huh?

Now a student at UMass and long over Hurricane Lise, I was ready to play the proverbial field like a typical college student. But I was in Yankeeland—where them fast and loose girls roam—and first had to learn the ground rules.

There were established boundaries between the five colleges in the consortium. It was particularly evident when female students at Smith and Mount Holyoke ran out of available men from Amherst and Hampshire and wouldn't stoop to shopping down the road at the UMass megastore. They preferred to board studs from Ivies like Dartmouth and Yale onto green school buses—"fuck trucks," we called them—and import them into the valley to warm them over the long, cold weekends.

At first, I didn't go courting trouble off the UMass campus due to a certain Paula Hallberg, a fellow student from the eastern part of the state. Paula's biological father was a Swede, and as we now know, anyone of Scandinavian descent had the potential to lead me astray. She also lived off campus in a group townhouse in Amherst, conveniently located across the street from my apartment. After two months of sharing my bed every night, we decided to eliminate one rent payment and cohabit in my place. Living a carefree and idyllic life as college students, we went to class, worked part-time jobs, and screwed like rabbits.

Paula was neither a Richmond deb nor the type of girl I'd take home to Mom. She'd been raised in a small, blue-collar town in eastern Massachusetts, and her stepfather was a working class man. She would never be one to grow old and play mah-jongg with the ladies. Therefore, carrying on with her like this wasn't the *proper* thing to do. But I was in Yankeeland now, and I felt free to be a naughty boy without recrimination.

My parents asked a lot of questions about Paula and her family, but I didn't volunteer the little I knew. So they came to Amherst during the early stages of this courtship, ostensibly to visit me but mostly to check her out. I knew they wouldn't approve of her, but I was pleasantly surprised that they kept whatever comments they were probably dying to share to themselves.

Soon after leaving Amherst, they remembered that they'd left something behind at my apartment. They retraced the relatively short distance they'd traveled to retrieve it. They rang my doorbell and knocked loudly on the door several times, but no one answered.

After three days of celibacy, Paula and I could hardly wait to jump each other's bones. The moaning and groaning in my bedroom drowned out any possibility of my parents being heard. But they certainly heard us. Bless them for deciding to have me mail the item home and not making an issue about this carnal indiscretion.

Paula and I didn't last long as a couple. In fact, she dumped me because she felt I was getting too serious. She moved out without saying a word and took every piece of furniture in the apartment with her. When I went home with a buddy after school, we actually thought we were in the wrong apartment because it was so empty. I didn't know whether to laugh or cry. My only blessing was the certainty of Paula not being pregnant.

There had been no lead-up to the split—no battle royal, not even a simple misunderstanding that could've been blown out of proportion. I searched for answers. What had I done wrong? Had I really been too clingy? Had I been wrong to expect monogamy between us? I hadn't the first clue, but fortunately I was able to close the book on the matter without heartache.

I decided to break with tradition and expand my boundaries. A cousin from Richmond had just enrolled at Smith. The young ladies in attendance at this "Seven Sisters" college could easily hold out for appropriate suitors. Ordinarily, I would have been shunned as a UMass student, but my cousin kindly gave me proper entrée into her social network.

I was a bit clumsy on my first date—or second or third—with these refined young women. I stepped up my game and invited a young lady who hailed from Woodstock, Vermont, to dinner at my apartment. I didn't know how to cook, but I thought I could at least open two separate tins of Chun King Chinese food and blend the ingredients together. All I managed to do was cut my finger on one of the container lids so badly that I ended up in the hospital emergency room. That ruined my chances with that particular Smith prospect, but I got right back on my horse.

Once I became a bit of a mainstay on the Smith campus, I bumped into a good-looking package coming out of the dorm shower room into the hallway—wrapped only in a towel. She was pretty, in a natural sort of way, and preppy—but not overly so.

I was drawn to the curves beneath her towel and the unforced smile on her face. I introduced myself, and she didn't run away.

I quite fancied her name, Patrecia, and its unusual spelling. A graduate of the prestigious Hearst Preparatory School in Burlingame, California, Patty had, like me, a strained relationship with her parents and a tight bond with her grandparents. And like virtually every other college student in the '70s, this beauty smoked a little pot, snorted a little coke, and drank a lot of booze. She had a little devil in her, too. I was stunned by her confession that she and one of her best friends at Smith were sneaking out of their dorm at night to fool around with married policemen from the town of Northampton. Stunned, but not the least bit turned off. Love was in the air.

Patty came from wealth but didn't flaunt it. She was studying anthropology in earnest, not just going through the paces to collect her "MRS" degree. We began to gel, and our relationship had a good feel to it. As our feelings deepened, we boldly moved forward and shared our affection for each other with our families.

I first met Patty's maternal grandparents, who lived in an apartment in Fair Lawn, New Jersey. I found the two of them to be wonderfully warm and down-to-earth. They served as their granddaughter's safe port in a storm. Her grandfather—a retired physician—was a rather soft-spoken man. As he talked about his days growing up outside Ottawa and playing ice hockey, he opened up to me. This didn't go unnoticed by Patty and her grandmother, who made the sort of eye contact that suggested yours truly might be a keeper.

Next, we traveled to Raleigh, North Carolina, for me to meet Patty's parents, Stanley and Mae Beekman. They didn't hail from the South. Rather, they were transplants from Teaneck, New Jersey, a bedroom community outside New York City. They were "new money" and exuded all the signs of upwardly mobile wealth. I may have been the southerner in the room, but—make no mistake about it—*I* was the real misfit.

While Patty's father had climbed the corporate banking ladder, her mother had had the unenviable task of setting up one new house after another. She was also expected to host elaborate soirées for the seven-figure gang. Neither job came naturally. The way she hit the bottle suggested that she'd fallen back on booze as a mandatory stand-in for a husband on the move.

There was something terribly wrong with this picture, but never having experienced *their kind*—the demonstrably wealthy—before, I became a wee bit smitten with affluenza myself.

Patty's father was very large man, both in height and weight, whose physical presence dominated any room he was in. He spoke in a professorial manner but often without finishing a thought or keeping them in sequence. I tried really hard to engage him in conversation, but there was only so much I knew about Wall Street and he about Main Street. He never made much eye contact with me, either. I knew he'd be a tough nut to crack.

At the end of the 1977 academic year, Patty graduated from Smith with her bachelor's degree. She had applied and been accepted to the graduate school of anthropology at Berkeley. Since there was no hint of a future husband, Patty's family had no choice but to embrace that decision, and they urged her to matriculate immediately. But Patty deferred her decision for a year and chose to stay in the Amherst area to let me catch up to her. This upset her parents to no end. Although I neither encouraged nor discouraged this idea, they blamed me for Patty's perceived lapse in judgment. The relationship between her parents and us became quite fragile.

That year went by in a hurry. We did not live in sin, but we certainly didn't suffer from loneliness, either. I waited right up until graduation to accept a job offer in Washington, DC, at Stephen Winchell & Associates (SW&A), a new political fundraising agency established just two years earlier. Steve Winchell, a grassroots Republican mover and shaker, had just been awarded a large national account, and business was booming.

I hoped Patty would go with me to Washington. After proving her commitment to the relationship during my senior year in college, she made her position on the future of our relationship abundantly clear: a move south on her part would require an engagement ring on my part. This was certainly not an unreasonable demand. Uncharacteristically, though, I cooled my jets. I put my impetuosity on hold and stood my ground. Scared of commitment, I moved to the nation's capital alone.

Patty remained in Amherst, but only long enough to reconnect with Berkeley and move forward with her master's degree, perhaps as early as the fall. We were at a relationship crossroads. My male comrades certainly didn't help matters when they told me to let go of her—DC was "fat city" for a guy like me. Single women outnumbered single men by a seven-to-one ratio, so I wouldn't starve for affection.

From the moment I arrived in Washington, I had no downtime for dating. I lived in a Woodley Park home owned by a recent widow. We bartered free rent in exchange for yard work. No stranger to these duties from my years of experience at Halsnoch, I did a yeoman's job on her lawn and garden. I worked in the evenings after work and on weekends, too. She certainly got her pound of flesh out of me.

But the widow became high maintenance and too big of a pill for me to swallow. She ragged on me so often about working harder, I had no choice but to get the hell out of there and find myself a better arrangement. Luckily, a friend of Steve's was vacationing that summer on one of the islands off New England and allowed me to stay in his fancy Embassy Row home off Massachusetts Avenue, with no strings attached. Nice digs. Great location. Problem solved.

I liked my job at SW&A, but it was challenging to work for two owners with such different personalities. Steve was the majority owner, and we clicked right away. He was an "Aw, shucks" regular guy and a genius at his trade. Mr. Water. We shared the same sense of humor and didn't mind making fools of ourselves.

The minority owner was an attractive, yet manly woman—used "Jr" as a suffix—whom everyone called "Emmie." Ms. Oil. Although account managers like me officially reported to both Steve and Emmie, she carried the operational reins. She ran a tight, IBM-like ship—men were expected to wear only white or blue shirts with button-down collars, and facial hair was frowned upon.

Emmie had been a Young Republican in the Goldwater days and could spot a half-hearted Republican—like me—a mile away. She correctly sussed me out from day one. When I supported independent candidate John Anderson over Republican standard-bearer Ronald Reagan in 1980, she pleaded with Steve to give me the boot. He had my back, so Emmie tried to drive me away herself.

The two of us developed a strange ritual. I had my own office and liked for my desk to look *out* in order to properly greet people coming in. Emmie preferred it the other way around. On most Monday mornings when I went into the office, I discovered that Emmie had gone in over the weekend and turned my desk around to *her* way. This childish cat-and-mouse game continued for the entire time that I worked at SW&A. Neither of us felt any obligation to ever broach the subject or compromise with each other.

I raised my game to a higher level. Emmie had a special tree outside her office—a real eye-catcher that dwarfed the other greenery scattered around the company reception area and hallways. She was as fond of her tree as I had been of my old "Moonlight Over the Mountain" novelty. All of the vegetation in the office, especially Emmie's tree, received daily service from a plant doctor.

One Friday evening, a commercial printing vendor invited me, and a few other guys from the office, to a Baltimore Orioles baseball game. Sports tickets, golf outings, and dinner invitations were all perks of the job. We packed a cooler full of beer for the drive to Memorial Stadium to minimize the number we'd have to buy at the stadium. After the game was over, we arrived back in DC and made a pit stop at the office before heading our separate ways. We found the bathroom door locked, but none of us had a key. So we adapted by taking a long "group piss" into the pot of Emmie's beloved tree. Were we trying to kill the tree? Of course not. Were we dying to see if we could get a rise out of Emmie on Monday morning? You betcha.

Emmie noticed right away that her tree looked sickly, but there was no evidence of sabotage. It looked more like the specialist had given it too much food or water. Emmie didn't just pick up the phone and call the plant doctor; she first walked around the entire office to tell everyone that she was making the call and taking no prisoners. My coconspirators and I naturally wanted to eavesdrop on her conversation, but there was no way we could all do so together. We would've laughed too hard and let the cat out of the bag. To say Emmie ripped the plant doctor a new one would be a gross understatement. Fortunately, the tree lived, the specialist and I kept our jobs, and Emmie returned to being, well, Emmie.

Fun and games aside, I went to Washington looking to grow personally and professionally, not to behave like a frat boy. A good woman would cure that. Despite an abundance of beautiful and available DC women, I only had eyes—and time—for Patty.

Over the long Fourth of July weekend, I drove north to visit her. During the car ride, I had a lot of time to dwell on the physical and emotional distance between us. I decided that it was time to fish or cut bait. The fact that Patty was a rebel like me was too big of an asset to ignore. The instant I saw her, I dropped to one knee and proposed. My hasty decision meant I didn't have an engagement ring, but the promise of shopping for one the next day helped win her approval.

My parents were over the moon, constantly reminding me how wonderful it was for me to be dating a young woman whose parents had considerable money—new money, mind you—and how lucky I'd be to marry into a family like hers one day. My parents hardly knew Patty, and they'd never met her parents. But on the basis of my fiancée having a Smith degree, her dad having both a Princeton and Columbia education and a prominent job at a bank, and her grandfather having been a doctor, they thought she would make the ideal wife.

As for Patty's parents, they simply had to resign themselves to the fact that their daughter was never going to marry someone like her father. I made a huge mistake by waiting until after my proposal to ask for her father's consent. It was a clumsy way to start a formal relationship with my in-laws. They forgave me for only one reason: they saw the pseudosocial standing of my family, combined with their money, as the blueprint for good breeding.

The engagement forced me to find us a home. I signed a lease on a comfortable apartment in the Landmark section of Alexandria, Virginia. My new commute required the use of Metro buses and trains—in place of my feet. I wasn't thrilled about the change but, by big-city standards, I thought it would be manageable.

When Steve gave me my first promotion, it included a raise and a free parking space in the garage below the office. I tried driving to work, but in less than a month, and after a bad case of road rage—kicking another driver in the shins after he cut in front of me in slow-moving downtown traffic—I surrendered the parking pass and reverted to public transportation.

My whining to Patty fell on deaf ears. Her father had commuted for years by bus from the North Jersey suburbs to Manhattan and never lost his cool. In addition, she and her mother were busy planning the entire wedding. "Get on with it," she advised.

She was right. I was getting off pretty easy. I had one measly task: to show up on time in Raleigh. My father sponsored the rehearsal dinner at the downtown athletic club. I have no idea how he managed to pay that tab or to buy the new suit he wore that weekend, but he was proud to be able to step up to the financial plate for a change. I would do nothing to spoil his fun. In a rare gesture of goodwill toward my father, I'd chosen him to be my best man.

My other two groomsmen drove down from the Hartford, Connecticut, area to pick me up in Washington and deliver me to Raleigh. To celebrate the occasion, they shared lots of cocaine—the drug du jour—and bought me five minutes of fame with a DC hooker. Yes, I was guilty of being a cad, a pig, and a dog before the wedding, but I just thought of it as the symbolic last fling guys indulged in before tying the eternal knot. I had a clear conscience about the hooker but a raw nose from snorting too much coke. I had such a bad case of postnasal drip that speaking my lines at the rehearsal was a challenge. I excused myself for letting my emotions get the best of me. Luckily, no one caught on. Fiction won.

The wedding service and the reception that followed at her parents' house went off without a hitch. Our families played nice together, our friends were beautifully fed and wonderfully entertained, and Patty's shaggy little Chevy Chevette was packed full of wedding gifts for our drive back to DC. Because the national midterm elections were a month away, SW&A's fundraising machine was busy, and we had to delay our honeymoon trip until January.

From the start of our engagement to the final brunch party on Sunday afternoon, Patty had remained wonderfully cool as a cucumber. Weddings can be stressful events, but my wife maintained a resilient beauty of spirit throughout. I saw the same person I'd first met wrapped in a towel, and I had every reason to believe that marriage wouldn't change that. Perhaps I was confusing desire with love, but I came to appreciate all the nagging and prodding from my parents to snatch this special woman before it was too late.

Less than a year after our wedding, Patty and I opted to put down roots in Springfield, Virginia, a bedroom community about twenty miles southwest of Washington. We purchased a starter townhouse in a development near a man-made lake that afforded us some natural ambiance and reasonable shelter from a burgeoning population and never-ending real estate development.

This lifestyle suited my wife just fine. Our neighbors were nice, everyday folks who liked to party. She had grown up in suburbia and was comfortable in this environment. I thought I could easily adapt. The only things missing in our Norman Rockwell painting were the kid and the dog. But at age twenty-four, Patty didn't have a maternal bone in her body and made it clear that she didn't even want to think about having a baby until she turned thirty.

With very few distractions and stressors, I could focus on building a career. I quickly rose to the level of accounts supervisor at SW&A. I earned three promotions by becoming a good direct marketer. But as a registered independent, I'd hit a wall working on the agency's core business of raising money for conservative and Republican causes. I refused to drink the Kool-Aid, but having played a role in getting Ronald Reagan elected president, I was curious to find some way to capitalize on the "Revolution."

Knowing Steve was open to making a fresh buck or two, I created a business plan recommending the agency expand into the political merchandise arena and establish a new division to do so. I had a real passion for catalogs and enough knowledge to be dangerous. Raising my hand to become the head of the division played right into Steve's sweet spot.

Not surprisingly, my plan was approved, and we got our largest client to test the concept right away. Twenty products were manufactured and featured in the inaugural edition of *The Capitol Collection*, a catalog mailed to both individual donors and prime catalog prospects. It was a truly pioneering moment in the history of political fundraising. My hopes were high.

I also found some tasteful ready-made products that didn't make the *Collection* but were, in my humble opinion, certain to generate demand from supporters of President Reagan. My favorite was The Original Jelly Bean Tie, a woven silk-blend accessory designed on a navy background with a repeat of multicolored jellybeans jars. During Reagan's first term, this confectionery was found in every White House office and, as a result, flew off the shelves of candy and specialty stores across the country.

I was so bullish on the tie that I wanted to try to sell it myself. Steve and our client both gave me approval. I registered the business name The Oval Office as a sole proprietorship. I created space ads and placed them in conservative publications like *Human Events* and *National Review.* Media buys were based on performance of the ads, so I couldn't lose money. I received free publicity in publications like the *Washington Star,* the *New York Times,* and the *Wall Street Journal* and on television shows like *CBS Morning News.* In a year's time, I sold over five thousand ties in forty-eight states and eight countries.

Unfortunately, *The Capitol Collection* wasn't so successful. It was an idea ahead of its time. We learned after three catalog mailings that Republicans gave money for emotive reasons, not to receive a political souvenir in return. I had to make the recommendation to shut down the division—putting myself out of a job in the process.

Steve allowed me to stay at the agency until I found another job. I felt there would be no better time than now for me to transition into the catalog industry. Much as I'd dreamed as a kid about going to Iceland, I'd also dreamed about working at my favorite mail order company, L.L. Bean. I started networking and pursued every possible lead into the company. My timing was faultless; Bean was trying to hire a new space advertising manager. Even though legend had it that Bean never hired outside the company at this level, I threw my Casco Bay hat into the ring.

Patty was, let's say, 60 percent in favor of a move to Maine. She definitely preferred that I work for a mainstream, consumer brand like L.L. Bean rather than a small niche business like SW&A. But she didn't warm to the idea of being farther away from her parents. Was she growing closer to them? I wondered. If so, that was not a trend I'd welcome.

So there we were, both managing our respective expectations. But I *really* wanted this job. It was not only the right career path for me; it was also a fail-safe way to get Patty to uproot herself. For me, life in southern

Maine would be a big upgrade to the life we'd ever have in Northern Virginia.

My first interview at Bean was with the hiring manager and took place at a bar inside LaGuardia Airport in New York City. It went well, at least well enough to get presented to Bill Henry, the company's VP of marketing, at the company's headquarters. I should have heeded the precondition that getting to Freeport would be on my dime. After all, I was courting them, and they had plenty of internal candidates.

Even though it was February and bitter cold throughout the Northeast, I would just have to brave the elements to get to this interview. I drove to Boston the first day and got up early the next morning to continue to Freeport. A blizzard was on its way south from Canada, but it looked like I could beat it with an early start. The trip from Boston to Freeport was only 125 miles, and my interview was scheduled for 11:00 a.m., but I wasn't going to give Bean an easy out by not showing up—and on time. I left Boston crazy early at four o'clock in the morning.

I fully expected to arrive on the Bean campus with time to spare and to use it to explore their famous retail store from boot to canoe. Comments about their current product line would make a good conversation starter with Bill Henry. But it was snowing at such an alarming rate that when I finally crossed the border into Maine, my timely arrival in Freeport was in jeopardy.

My determination remained absolute, and by some simple twist of fate, I pulled into the Bean administrative offices at 11:00 a.m. sharp. The receptionist rang through to Mr. Henry's office but didn't get an answer—turns out Bill's assistant had left for the day, as had most of the other Bean employees. We were now in the middle of what weathermen were calling the worst storm of the season, and the Maine Turnpike was due to close down at any moment.

Bill Henry happened to be heading home himself. As he passed through the reception area with briefcase in hand, he spotted me. "You're not Stuart Hotchkiss, are you?" he asked.

When I replied that I was, he was incredulous. "What the hell are you doing here?" he asked.

Of course he was kind enough to keep our appointment, but he warned that we'd have to keep it short because the turnpike *was* going to close. I went through the usual battery of interview questions and offered reasons for Bean to hire me. Intermittently, Bill interrupted with statements of disbelief regarding my getting to the interview. He truly was impressed by my determination.

Our meeting ended with no commitment from Bill—just the usual "We've met with some pretty darned good candidates already" stall. I thanked him and made a beeline for my car and the turnpike. I'd made a friendly wager with Bill that I'd get out of Maine before the turnpike closed. I was winning until I got to the Kennebunk town limits and the "Turnpike Closed" barrier forced me to exit.

Right there on Main Street was the historic Kennebunk Inn, built as a private residence back in 1799. Not surprisingly on a day like this, there was no room at the inn. New England hospitality prevailed, however, and the staff graciously improvised so that the other stranded motorists and I could stay the night. After serving us hot bowls of homemade New England clam chowder, the proprietor cleared space for everyone on the dining room floor. She handed out thick Hudson's Bay blankets and kept the fireplace stoked all night. I was made to feel like a guest at the Four Seasons.

Despite the record snowfall, the state hustled to reopen the turnpike the next morning. The drive home was uneventful, and I made it all the way back to Springfield in one day. I'd written and rewritten in my head several dozen times the closing argument I'd make in a follow-up letter to Bill Henry. I didn't want someone else to get this job. How could they *not* hire me? Was any other candidate as committed as Stuart Hotchkiss?

Well, it was all for naught, and the legend—that I was merely a token outsider to make the job search look like an open competition—wasn't true. The man who got the job was none other than Chris McCormick, a recruit from niche direct marketer Garden Way, and now the president and CEO of Bean—and the first non-family member to assume the role. In the end, justice was served.

I chose to accept a backup offer with a small newsletter publisher in Bethesda, Maryland. It was a good bridge job and freed me from becoming pigeonholed as a political fundraiser. Fortuitously, I had stayed in touch with Bill Henry. Six months after our meeting, Bill was recruited to Time-Life Books (TLB) in Alexandria, Virginia, to become its new senior VP of marketing. He had kept me on his radar and recruited me to join his new team at TLB. My trek to Maine had paid its first dividend.

I was hired as the new house mail manager in the marketing department. It was an obscure job, and I'd be replacing a twenty-year incumbent who had never hired or trained an assistant. I admitted to Bill that I wasn't qualified for the position. He told me not to worry—none of the other candidates were, either. I worried anyway.

But I worked hard to validate his decision. Within a year, I could explain to anyone in the company how regression analysis was used to select the best prospects from TLB's customer file for direct mail promotions. Because this sounded so much harder than it really was, my colleagues thought I was a genius. My success made Bill look like a wise man. He kept telling me that much bigger opportunities lay ahead.

I was prepared for a long and fruitful career at TLB. I liked the job and the company so much that I ordered TLBOOK vanity plates for my car. I had a mentor who was going places and taking me with him. Work became my focus. I was not making my marriage a priority.

However, Patty was. By now, we had a dog. Parenting that little firecracker was so contagious that, in less than two years, my wife's maternal feelings, and eggs, were fertilized. That's right, to *everyone's* surprise, she was pregnant at the age of twenty-nine.

She remained a caring spouse, too. Despite the nausea and vomiting of pregnancy, Patty, along with two very dear friends, managed to plan a surprise party in honor of my thirtieth birthday. Kathy Uhrich and Patty had first met when they worked together at a local day-care center. They quickly became best friends.

Being a Smith grad and having access to family money to pay for additional education, Patty could have chosen most any career and written her own prepregnancy job ticket. But day care, followed by public school teaching, became her "wifely want." Her pay in both jobs was supplemented by an allowance from her parents, a generous—yet controlling—gesture. Very controlling. It pissed me off. And what a waste of tuition!

I truly wanted to honor my wife financially, but I didn't stand a chance.

Still, her work gained her new friends, and Kathy, a Seattle native, was the bee's knees. So was Bob, her husband, and we quickly became good friends, too. He and I evolved into fiercely competitive squash players, squaring off at least one night a week at a nearby Fairfax County recreation center.

On the Saturday before my birthday, Bob organized an impromptu late-afternoon match. It turned out to be a five-set doozy, with both of us ending the game covered with sweat. Our body odor was ripe enough to make a skunk wear a clothespin on its nose. We left the facility en route to Bob's house to shower and change clothes before meeting the wives for what had been billed as my birthday dinner. Out of the blue, Bob said we first had to make a detour to my house. I can't remember his ruse, but it was clever enough that I unsuspectingly bought into it.

When we got to the bright red door of my townhouse, I opened it and wasn't the least bit surprised to find a dark and empty interior. Patty and Kathy were supposed to be waiting for us at the restaurant. Within moments, someone dressed in a black robe appeared out of nowhere holding only a lit candle. Once he or she made a gesture for me to step forward, the lights came on, and there I was, frozen stiff in front of fifty or more guests. I was blushing from the surprise and preoccupied with my hygiene. Once I got to the bar and started catching up drink for drink with my guests, I began to relax and enjoy one of the best parties ever.

Clever Patty. She had invited guests to our home for an old-fashioned wake, a technique borrowed from my mother when she had planned my father's fortieth birthday party in 1957. The inside of the house was decorated like a funeral parlor, and my birthday cake had the shape and wording of a tombstone. Everyone cheerfully mourned the demise of my twenties and the unleashing of my thirties. I was grateful to my wife on so many levels. First of all, she had spent a lot of time planning and preparing such a wonderful and surprising party for me. But it was especially gratifying to see her take a page from a happy time in my parents' past and update it to the present just for me.

Patty's pregnancy and my job stability made it certain we'd be staying in the area for a while. But the time had come for us to move and buy a larger home, and one with a yard, for our expanding family. I now had a respectable salary, and Patty had built *herself* quite a nest egg from annual gifts of cash and stocks her grandparents made as part of their estate planning. In fact, her primary holding, Ma Bell, had just been broken up into seven separate companies. She had a good payday and, I thought, *we* deserved to spend some of it to buy a new home.

We could have easily managed to move up in the world. But she wanted no part of it. Her family may have been "new money," but they lived by that most sacred tenet of old money: Live off interest, never off principal. There was nothing I could do to change her mind. I became more and more resentful of her attitude that this windfall was *hers* and not *ours*. I was suffocating in this starter townhouse in Springfield, and the issue of money began to drive a wedge between us.

Both sets of parents were naturally surprised over Patty's pregnancy. Her parents still had a teenage son at home, so the thought of becoming grandparents at this stage in their lives wasn't even on the radar. All I heard on the other end of the phone when she called them with the news were two babbling idiots. I couldn't tell if they were happy or critical. But after deciphering their comments, I discovered this was indeed a joyous moment for them.

For my parents, the thrill of a new birth in the family fourteen years after Nicky's death had arrived not a day too soon. They immediately expressed their hope for a grandson to carry on the family name. I was the last Hotchkiss male from the bloodline that ran through Richmond and, until now, everyone had assumed our branch of the family tree was going to wither.

Our baby was due in September, but midway through Patty's pregnancy, we received an unexpected scare. She began experiencing vaginal bleeding which, at first, didn't appear to alarm her doctor. One exam later, we were told there was a distinct possibility of an early delivery. By early, I had no idea that I'd get a call one day at work in June telling me to rush to the hospital for the birth of my child. As a matter of fact, I didn't even get the call myself. I was away from my office and couldn't be found, so the person calling from the hospital asked to speak with my boss instead. He came looking for me to give me the news. When we bumped into each other in a hallway, he first congratulated me, then handed me my jacket and keys, spun me around toward the parking garage, and kept repeating that everything was going to be fine. How could everything be fine if my child was being born three months early?

I knew he meant well, but I didn't buy his pep talk. As I sped from one end of Alexandria to the other to get to the hospital, I tried to hold back an avalanche of tears. My anxiety levels were spiking, and my heart was pounding. I had no idea what to expect when I arrived, but I prayed to God that I'd find my wife and our child alive.

Our little boy, whom we named Jed after a Hotchkiss forefather, had already been delivered by the time I got to the hospital and was whisked away to the Neonatal Intensive Care Unit (NICU). Patty was in surprisingly good spirits when I arrived. Our son's prognosis was murky, but a team of doctors and nurses were working around the clock to save his life. Modern medicine could bring premature babies into this world with a high rate of success; keeping them alive presented the greater challenge. Every hour, Jed's condition changed, and his mother and I vacillated between elation and despair.

Our church rector came to the hospital and baptized Jed once his survival seemed in doubt. The hospital staff then rushed to remove all the wires attached to his tiny, two-pound frame and let father take over. I pulled him gently into my upper body to feel his heartbeat and experience his humanness. Patty had briefly held the living Jed after his delivery, but never again. Our son died peacefully in my arms.

We made arrangements to have Jed's remains driven to Richmond for burial in a new family plot at Hollywood Cemetery purchased to accommodate the newer Hotchkiss generations. Although my father kindly took care of matters with the funeral home, no one prepared me for what I would see at the gravesite. I had expected Jed to be buried in a normal casket. What I saw instead was something resembling a large white Igloo cooler, and it made me feel like we had stolen our son's dignity. He was so small and so innocent. This was way too cruel.

Jed's death created a vacuum in our lives that needed to be filled—by *something*—as soon as possible. We went through the usual "it either makes you or breaks you" heartbreak, but in the end, we decided the best way to honor Jed was to forge ahead and have another child.

Truth is, the excitement of the first pregnancy had masked the declining health of our marriage. I was operating in survival mode, not thriving mode. I should have cut the crap and engaged Patty in a real conversation about the salvageability of our marriage. Without mincing words, my passion for her was long gone, and my love was sliding like an avalanche down from the Matterhorn.

Despite these realities and the disbelief that having another baby might turn the marriage around, I reprised my role as lead actor in *Getting Pregnant*. Perhaps I was selfish. Perhaps I was fearless. Perhaps I was just a born risk taker. Whatever the label, once I made my decision, I let the universe conspire to make it happen and never looked back.

Patty remained my real concern. She'd become "Dolly, the Beekman sheep," a clone of her parents. Although they were quite generous in providing me with gifts, I still saw them as pagans. Never in my life had I never been treated or made to feel like such an outsider, which I resented with more and more venom as time went on. I could sit in their living room an entire day and not be asked a single question. Perhaps Patty deserved to hog the game of verbal ping-pong, but I viewed her style of play as both insincere and patronizing. The resolute, "money doesn't mean anything to me" young bride had transformed herself into a trust-funded, money-hoarding baroness.

Patty's father had invested a fortune in order for his daughter to officially major in anthropology and also snag a "MRS" degree at Smith. It would have been easy for her to find a husband with a lucrative future, like a doctor, lawyer, or investment banker. But rebel that she was, she landed me—a direct marketer. To Stanley Beekman, that was no better than a plumber's apprentice or a sweater smuggler. No wonder we could never strike up a meaningful conversation.

I was prepared to meet Patty halfway. Ironically, Bill Henry was the one to actually force my hand. Now president of TLB, Bill had been making overtures recently about my going to graduate school. He had laid it on the line: I'd only go so far in a corporation like Time Inc. (TLB's parent) without an advanced degree. He talked about the situations he faced every day as president, and I marveled at how much he knew about running a business. To become a wise leader like Bill, and richer in the process, just might earn me enough respect from Patty and her family to keep our marriage going.

Patty was pleased to hear this news, perhaps because it would please her parents, but certainly to stop my nagging about our needing to move. However, neither of us factored in the true hidden cost. There were no executive MBA programs in the DC area at that time, so my pursuit of excellence would require a lot of travel and time away from home. It would bring on stress in my life, and that just might kill the marriage.

CHAPTER 6

Executive Education

BILL HENRY WAS the gift that kept on giving. He had hired me into TLB and become my mentor. Since he had also lost a child, my grieving over Jed struck a chord with Bill and brought us together as soul mates as well as colleagues. For weeks, he consoled me with handwritten letters and daily visits to my office. He never once talked shop; it was all about taking care of personal business.

This big ol' Wilford Brimley look-alike morphed into the new Papa, the only one who could help me get out of my funk. In fact, he even suggested—practically demanded—that Patty and I bust out of town for a few weeks to his old stomping ground. Far from local Washington getaways like Rehoboth, Delaware, and Ocean City, Maryland, the southern coast of Maine offered copious amounts of lobster in many guises—rolls, salads, chowders, Newburgs, and scampis—at rock-bottom prices. It was binge eating at its finest.

Bill would be in Boothbay Harbor for a good portion of the summer of 1985, and he shared his itinerary with me so we could attempt to get together while Patty and I were in the area. Within days of our arrival, he invited me out for an afternoon of leisurely walking down Ocean Point Road. We would head all the way to his house on the other side of Linekin Bay. He started a little pep talk, and I listened carefully.

"You know, Stuart, the only barrier between you and the corner office is an advanced business degree." After Bill spoke these words, he forced a smirk as if to suggest that he had a surprise for me.

"What do you have in mind?" I asked in earnest.

I could detect a glimmer of excitement in my normally phlegmatic mentor.

He made me unmistakably aware that Time Inc. had long been a sponsor of Columbia University and the school's Master's Degree Program for Executives (MDPE). It was a Time-honored tradition that was about to end due to corporate cost cutting. Many of the company's best and brightest leaders had attended the program on the way to senior management.

To sponsor me for the program, Bill would have to climb a few corporate mountains, and I would have to sacrifice my personal life to get through the program. It would mean juggling school, work, and family all at once, and that would leave no time for Patty and me to work on us.

It was an all-or-nothing decision. Bill, the strong-and-silent type, was decisive and ready to act. He made it clear that I'd be a fool to pass up an opportunity like this, and I didn't hesitate to say, "Yes." Patty's father had always made work his priority, so I knew she would get it, no matter what challenges we faced.

The program was four semesters long. I'd be working at the same time. I could start as early as January, but I'd have to rush to apply. I'd be trying to make a new baby before I left for school. I had a fragile marriage. What the hell was I thinking?

Greed. I fell for it hook, line, and sinker. I was accepted into the program, and I took the plunge. Patty was two months pregnant by the time I matriculated.

Each semester began with a week of intensive study at Columbia's Arden House country campus, the former E. H. Harriman estate, in Orange County, New York. My MDPE cohort consisted of twenty-nine students in different stages of their careers. Officially, we were the class of 1987-II, but better known as "The Kamikazes." At the orientation meeting, we were asked to briefly introduce ourselves. I was so intimidated by the first dozen or so elevator pitches that I actually left the room to vomit before my turn came. Then the dean called upon me as Henry, my first name. I was completely flummoxed and never thought I'd measure up to the others.

After Arden House week, classes shifted to Uris Hall on Columbia's main campus in Manhattan and ran thirteen consecutive Fridays. I became a regular on the Eastern Shuttle between DC's National and New York's LaGuardia airports. I left work on Thursday afternoons to get to New York by the end of the workday and meet with my study group to discuss, dissect, and complete whatever assignments were due the next day.

On Thursday nights, I stayed in one of the many Time Inc. corporate suites at Hotel Dorset. The mid-rise building on West 54th Street was rather shabby and outdated inside, resembling an old English hotel that had seen better days. Smells of the past emanated from the flooring, curtains, and ventilation system, and fixtures were placed in awkward positions. Even a contortionist couldn't reach the toilet paper while seated on the throne.

Nonetheless, I found the place charming. The bar off the lobby was quite small, but celebrity regulars like sports journalist Howard Cosell helped make it a destination watering hole for New Yorkers. Best of all, the large dining room served cooked kippers and the juiciest fourteen-dollar half grapefruit money could buy.

We started classes early and finished late on Fridays, but that never kept a number of classmates and me from happy hour at The West End. This legendary student hangout served overcooked burgers and poured beer through dirty taps. And it rarely had an empty table. It was easy to lose track of time there. I always seemed to be frantically hailing a taxi on Broadway and enticing the driver to speed across town and over the Triborough Bridge so I'd arrive five minutes before the last shuttle departed for Washington.

Before enrolling in MDPE, I had thought of Manhattan only as a place to visit. I would have turned down a corporate relocation there in a New York minute. It was *too* everything—congested, noisy, and expensive. Nearly everyone moaned about their commutes to and from the Connecticut and New Jersey suburbs and the endless workdays.

But a month or two into my routine, I started to see the city in a different light. Getting around by taxi and on foot was a godsend compared with driving on the Capital Beltway. People in New York liked to discuss live theater and trendy new restaurants, not the federal government or the military. It put my mundane existence in a suburb of what I came to see as an overrated city like Washington into new perspective. I felt alive and spontaneous again and started looking for reasons to miss that last shuttle home on Friday nights.

I formed a special bond with a classmate and study group member who was the only other commuter, from Boston. He was responsible for his own lodging on Thursday nights. Since rooms at the Dorset always came with two beds, I was courteous and offered the spare one to him.

Although I doubted anyone at Time Inc. would care, I didn't broadcast the fact, either. People got hired and fired for silly reasons.

My roommate had been diagnosed with Type 1 diabetes as a teenager. He gave himself an insulin injection every morning and disposed of his spent needles just like he would at home—in the wastebasket. Between the doormen seeing the same two guys leave the hotel together every Friday morning and the chambermaids finding the needles, there must have been some juicy gossip about us.

After receiving my first-semester midterm grades and being pleased with the results, I made major "adjustments" to my Thursday-night routine. The rest of my study group felt the same way, so we began stepping out on the town. I was rubbing elbows with Hotel Dorset habitués and New York eccentrics. This was no longer a hardship; it was a party. And yes, I shared everything with Patty, even my vomiting into the boxwood outside the Dorset one evening after too much bar hopping.

Despite her pregnancy, Patty never made me feel guilty about leaving home. She told me she could manage just fine in the event of an emergency. Never once did I ask her if she'd like for me to stay home on a Thursday night and fly to school the next morning. I certainly didn't *have* to make that study group meeting anymore. By this time, the amount of work we did would fit in a thimble.

This balloon of nothing to worry about burst five months into Patty's pregnancy, in March, when she started to experience vaginal bleeding. Thank God it was the middle of the week, and I was at work.

We raced to her OB/GYN's office without even making the customary call to the doctor. Our second child wasn't due until late July, but the doctor didn't want to take any chances with another premature delivery. She performed an immediate cervical cerclage. After the procedure, total bed rest was ordered, and Patty took a medical leave from her job as a schoolteacher.

We survived the scare and remained stoical optimists.

Despite my grousing, we managed to muddle through, by the day and by the week. Patty's doctor had warned us that our baby could come a bit early, but by the time she reached the eight-month mark, any fears we might have had were alleviated. We had been cleared for landing.

So, on a Saturday night in late June, Patty and I went out to our local Chinese restaurant. It was meant to be a quick and easy date night. I was cramming for second-semester midterms and working long hours on Time-Life's annual budget. Patty was feeling tired from the pregnancy and couldn't stay up late if she tried.

Patty could finally relax and enjoy a meal—anything she desired. She ordered her favorite sweet-and-spicy, deep-fried chicken dish. After taking just a few bites, she started to feel funny and looked a bit frightened.

Her water had just broken.

"Check, waiter!" I yelled out, throwing double sawbucks on the table as I helped Patty get up and leave the restaurant. We were gone before the parting gifts of fresh orange slices and fortune cookies came with the bill.

Just past midnight on June 22, 1986, in the same hospital where his brother had been born, Samuel Hotchkiss was delivered one month early, weighing in at a strapping six pounds, five ounces. The original Samuel was the Hotchkiss patriarch who emigrated from England to America in 1638 via Massachusetts Bay. Twelve generations later, our son Sam was the only one in my family's bloodline to bear our forefather's Christian name. There were no complications, and Patty was doing well. We were blessed with a healthy and strong newborn child.

We started calling him Sam right away. Sam "the Man." At the same time, we started calling my parents—now grandparents—by the nicknames they had been given as youngsters. "Peg" was an obvious and cute nickname for Margaret, but "Bunks" bore no logic to Nelson. It was just one of those quirky family names that seemed to fit.

The simultaneous joy and stress of having Sam in my life added to an already hectic June. We took him home from the hospital on a Tuesday; two days later I was on a plane to New York. I hadn't gotten any sleep as a new father, a student, and one who budgets. I had consumed lots of coffee and was on a slippery slope.

As soon as the plane took off for LaGuardia, I felt like I was having a heart attack.

My ticker was racing, my arms and chest were in pain, and I had difficulty breathing. Panic was setting in. I wasn't having any new-daddy fantasies about Sam's first baseball game or piano recital. I was totally consumed with the possibility of never seeing him again.

When the plane landed, a gate agent at LaGuardia called EMS, and two paramedics arrived right away. They suspected that I had suffered a heart attack. I was placed on a stretcher and snaked through an insane number of got-to-get-to-my-destination-faster-than-fast passengers in the airport. It was unsettling to see strangers give me that pitying "he's a goner" look. The closest hospital was St. John's in the Elmhurst section of Queens. The five-mile trip usually took about ten minutes from LaGuardia, but it was six o'clock in the evening and the roads were chockablock with rush-hour traffic. It took over an hour to get to the emergency room of the hospital.

If I'd had a heart attack, I probably would have died in the ambulance.

Fortunately, the diagnosis was just anxiety and hyperventilation syndrome. I was released to the "custody" of my study group, who graciously came to the hospital and accompanied me back to the Dorset. I took some chill pills, had a good night's sleep, and took my exams the next day.

Patty was concerned about me and my health. We took a time-out from the usual bickering about living in Springfield, putting *her* money to use, and my nonexistent relationship with her parents. The conversations we had were tender and focused on Sam. This was a Hallmark moment and a viable turnaround point in our marriage.

But I didn't give love a chance.

I was mentally and physically exhausted. I continued to hyperventilate frequently. I developed debilitating symptoms of Obsessive Compulsive Disorder and became anxious about trivial matters at home and work. Something was wrong with me "above the neck," and I should have sought treatment.

But being a Hotchkiss, I didn't. I was drinking the same families-like-ours-don't-have-these-kinds-of-problems Kool-Aid as my parents, burying any inkling of mental illness under the rug. I blamed all of my problems on the rest of the world and masked my pain through the comic relief of MDPE.

For me, Columbia was no longer a sacrifice; it was a godsend. I could completely avoid the hardness of life for most of Thursday and all of Friday, then hide behind my weekend schoolwork and weekday career the other five. I was a complete coward.

By the third semester, my classmates and I turned our week at Arden House into a makeshift Bohemian Grove. No, we didn't stand naked against any California redwoods, but we certainly did things out of the ordinary that *stayed at Arden House.* We hosted cocktail parties and produced talent shows. Our drinking skills were well honed, but our stage skills were embarrassingly amateur.

Nonetheless, the show went on. A classmate raided his grandmother's closets in affluent Greenwich, Connecticut, and fit the ladies with Oscar-worthy wardrobes. And he laid out some pretty cool plaid bell-bottoms for the guys. We roasted our professors and ourselves. Most of the men with head hair colored it with removable spray paint. After our last performance, we celebrated by taking a late-night swim in the estate pool. The paint polluted the pool water and got into the expensive white towels we had taken from the dorm rooms to dry ourselves off. To make matters worse, someone tripped the fire alarm, and the Orange County Fire Department arrived on the scene at three o'clock in the morning to investigate.

The following Friday back at Uris Hall, each of us found, on our desks, a letter of reprimand, typed on University letterhead and signed by the dean of the graduate school of business. He chastised us for unprofessional behavior and put us all on academic probation. You could have heard a pin drop in the classroom.

"We're fucked," I exclaimed.

"I'm going to lose my job," sobbed the eldest member of our class, a late-forty-something female who worked in the treasury department at Philip Morris.

Grown men and women from elite Fortune 500 companies were shitting in their Calvin Klein underwear, trying to figure out how to get out of this jam. This was a real-time case study.

A few minutes went by before the classmate who penned the letter as a practical joke broke into irrepressible laughter. One by one, the rest of us looked at each another for reassurance and then let out a collective sigh of relief.

Even though her stunt seemed like harmless hijinks, it triggered a number of subsequent exploits to one-up her. After all, we were a competitive bunch.

And, yes, I became the unwitting centerpiece of a masterful encore.

After a strenuous workout on the basketball court, I took a long, hot shower to ready myself for dinner. All of a sudden, the stall door opened. A male classmate had a camera pointed in my direction and, until I covered Lord Vader with my hands, he only readied the camera. At the appropriate time, he started to click away, one "Burt Reynolds posing for *Playgirl*" frame after another. I rather enjoyed the photo shoot.

A week or two went by without hearing any talk of the incident, and I quickly forgot it ever happened.

What I didn't remember was that the camera used for this caper belonged to *me*! The unfinished roll of 35-mm film remained in the camera and got stashed away at home. Of course, Patty had access to the Kodak, and my classmate contacted her and asked to have the film developed. What she saw in the developed photos must have amused her, because she volunteered to order reprints and mail them to him on the sly.

What the two of them had really been doing in the way of photo reproduction came into focus sometime later on a routine Friday school day in the city.

The classmate interrupted one of our professors midlecture. Rather rude, I thought. Looking back on the matter, I realize the professor had to have been tipped off before the start of his class.

"The gentlemen of the class of 1987-II have a gift that they'd like to share with the ladies," announced the classmate.

What gift? I wondered. No one had mentioned anything to me or asked me to chip in for a present.

"In fairness to the ladies, I've put everyone's name in a hat and the person drawn will receive the prize," said the merry prankster.

He produced the hat full of names and asked one of the women in the front row to come up and draw one. A buzz about tasteful gifts started to gain momentum.

Then came the Oscar-like revelation, "And the winner is…Linda Garner."

Being a good sport, fair and proper Linda came forward to accept a cardboard mailing tube. She carefully removed a poster and unrolled it for the entire class to see. There, in full living color, was that candid of me in my birthday suit with a come-on-baby look and barely covered genitals. Needless to say, I went beet red at that particular moment in the classroom. My professor, a stern, bow-tie-wearing Brahmin—straight from the cast of *The Paper Chase*—let out the loudest laugh of all. After making sure every woman had the image committed to memory, Linda kindly returned the poster to me for destruction.

My fame as a model may have come and gone like an ephemeral dream, but Patty was now hip to my ways and kept a closer eye on my behavior. Maybe it *was* more than a bit of fraternal adolescence. Our marriage was fragile, and a real transgression would have snapped it in two.

I lusted for the bright lights of New Broadway, not other women, certainly not some woman to eff on the side. I kept telling myself this lie to the point that I believed it. I tried to make every trip back and forth to the city an adventure without ramifications. Keep things light and out of sight. Coming home in a foul mood meant that conversations would heat up quickly and boil over.

I spotted various and sundry VIPs flying the shuttle and made every effort to chat them up. Ed Koch, then mayor of New York City, held court across the aisle from me in a bulkhead seat and placed both of his size-16 wingtips on the partition in front of him; Gene Siskel and Roger Ebert debated movies as passionately on the plane as they did on their show; and economist Marty Feldstein read more policy manuals in an hour than I read textbooks in a semester.

My favorite elbow rub was with TV and radio personality Dick Clark, who was very gracious to me despite my droning on about Sam and fatherhood.

I learned that Mr. Clark had lost his only sibling, older brother Bradley, in World War II. That revelation won me over instantly. Despite his youthful appearance, his hands and head shook from an illness, maybe Parkinson's. I couldn't believe Dick Clark had a *flaw*. He looked so *perfect* on air. How maddeningly simple of me.

At the end of the flight, he graciously agreed to autograph a page in my notebook for Sam. "Is there anything in particular you'd like for me to say to Sam?" he asked.

Be creative, I thought. *Try and invent a quip that will associate Dick Clark with the show* American Bandstand. I had to be fast. The wheels had just touched the tarmac. "May I say it out loud?" I asked.

Before he had a chance to answer my question, I did so anyway. He gave me a "that's corny" look. But keeping his promise, he wrote it down word for word: "Dear Sam, Don't resist the TEMPTATION to be SUPREME."

After months of learning how to mingle with famous people and celebs, I endeavored to impress a colleague at Time-Life who was booked on the same flight home one Friday night. I was a marketer, he a financial type. It was time to dazzle.

"Success isn't about *what* you know but *who* you know," I goaded.

We spotted DC retail magnate Herb Haft waiting in our boarding area at LaGuardia. It was impossible to miss Herb with his coiffed white hair— a style borrowed from both Don King and Donald Trump. I mentioned to my colleague that Herb was a good friend of the family. I was challenged to prove it and happy to oblige. I had a nice buzz from a pitcher of West End beer before the flight.

I walked up to Herb, hand extended, and he actually cut short a conversation with someone else to greet me.

"Haven't seen you, Herb, since Robert and I were classmates at Harvard," I lied. Robert was the son who had graduated from Harvard Business School in the late seventies and was installed as head of several of his father's businesses. I'd never laid eyes on Robert before.

This got Herb's attention, so I continued. "You look fantastic," I said. He was flattered and flashed a smile only a dentist could love.

I then asked about his wife Gloria—to whom he was still married at the time—and we started to laugh and glad-hand each other. My colleague was stunned. He bowed to the master the entire way home.

I eventually admitted to my colleague that I was no more a friend of Herb than of Dick Clark, but the magic of my act still left him in awe.

"How'd you do that with a straight face?" he inquired.

"Marketing," I replied.

And the beat went on and on until May 1987. I would end up passing every course and completing my first and only on-schedule academic program. For sixteen months, I'd do a week's worth of work in three and a half days and, absent my little episode at LaGuardia, I never burned out.

Therefore, when graduation day came, it was a bittersweet occasion. My life would return to normal now that I was finished with graduate school, but I dreaded the thought of resuming my cookie-cutter life in Springfield. *Get through the ceremony*, I thought, *enjoy myself, and make my family proud.* I would deal with the demon of a dying marriage some other day.

Peg and Bunks drove up from Richmond, and Patty and Sam followed in a separate car from Springfield. I practically begged Patty's parents to fly up from Florida, visit their old stomping grounds in nearby Teaneck, and attend my graduation. They declined without even hemming or haw-ing. This was clearly not their idea of a family affair.

The night before graduation, all the graduating MDPE students and their guests got together for a meal at a restaurant near the Arden House campus. One of the members of my study group was by herself, so I in-vited her to sit with my family and me. She was a touchy-feely person, and she behaved exactly at dinner the way she would have any other day of the week. We were seated next to each other, and often throughout the meal, I'd get a "Having fun, Hank?" checkup and a harmless rub on the shoul-der. Her touching caught Patty's attention.

Hank is a nickname I've used rather selectively. It started at sleep-away camp back in the mid 1960s, when I would jokingly send postcards home signed that way. The name didn't stick then, and it wasn't until my days at Columbia that it had another audition. My study group started calling me Hank, and soon more of the class followed.

It may well have been the first time Patty had heard her husband called Hank, certainly by another woman. I'm guessing that caught her attention in equal measure.

After dinner, our guests were ushered back to Arden House. We of-fered them a sneak peek of the complex before retiring for the evening. Impromptu parties were hosted, and we jammed as many people as pos-sible into random student rooms.

My parents always had a gift for finding a good party, and we joined a spirited one in progress. Patty, however, did not follow us. When I realized something might be wrong, I left the party to go look for her. I soon found her in my room, packing suitcases.

"What are you doing?" I asked.

"What do you think I'm doing?" she shot back as she shoved Sam's diapers and extra clothing into a bag. "We're leaving!"

"What do you mean you're leaving? What's wrong?"

"Why don't you go ask your girlfriend what's wrong?"

"My what?"

"You heard me, your girlfriend. Don't take me for an idiot—she had her hands all over you." She was now shouting and bawling at the same time.

I couldn't believe it. Here Patty was, the night before my graduation, accusing me of having an affair with a dear friend whom I'd merely asked to join us for dinner. In return for my being a Good Samaritan, Patty was packing up our marriage, both figuratively and literally. She had just drawn first blood. Frankly, her timing stunk.

I left to rejoin my parents. When I walked into the room, the life of the party evaporated and the tension was palpable. Where was Patty, and why had *both* of us been gone for so long? Had something happened to Sam? The other guests were left stuck between a rock and a hard place. Most were ready to call it a night shortly after I left the room, but they were too polite to leave my parents stranded. The look on my parents' faces told me that they wanted to crawl under the proverbial Stearns & Foster and hide.

My parents, Patty, and Sam left for an off-campus motel, and I elected to stay, as planned, at Arden House. I wouldn't see them again until the start of the next day's graduation ceremony. My wife's attendance was now far from a certainty. On the way back to the motel, Patty lit into my father with abandon. I'm surprised *he* didn't pack up and leave.

"Did you see what your son did at dinner?" she shouted at my father. "How could you just sit there and not say something?"

Confrontation had never been my father's strong suit. "Patty, let's not have an argument now. We're all here to enjoy Stuart's graduation."

Patty thought she could get my goat by belittling my poor father. Smart tactic, but this was dirty pool. I had always kept my mouth shut around her parents, even when they stunk from egomania. My dad deserved way better. Since their first meeting, he'd been a complete gentleman to Patty, and attentive, too. Just because she had money—and he was docile—gave her no right to use him as her pawn.

"If I had just behaved the way Stuart did, my father would disown me," she neighed.

The more strident she got, the more silent he became. Neither one gave ground.

Peg knew how to calm a horse, so when my classmates and I paraded into the ballroom for graduation, all four members of my family were sitting, apparently contented, in the audience. There was a big surprise in store for them, and I didn't want anyone to miss it. The class valedictorian had declined to give the traditional graduation speech, and my classmates had kindly nominated me to replace him. It was one of the proudest moments of my life.

In preparing my speech, I had taken stock of how far I'd traveled from Richmond to Worcester to Reykjavík to Amherst and finally New York on my educational journey. But like any good manager would do, I put the focus on my classmates and introduced them like a Who's Who of American business leaders. I had become the carefree wanderer, and they were the chosen people.

My parents were beaming when I came down into the audience. As parents of the guy with the understated personality, they were held in high esteem. Patty was fidgety and wore one of her distant, überprivileged looks—a look I had come to know all too well. After all, her father had gone to both Columbia *and* Princeton. But she perked up when guests started to coo over Sam. This happy day would have to last me a long time. I knew there'd be plenty of ugly days ahead.

I wanted to do something nice for my father. He had just taken shit from his daughter-in-law and had my back. After a lifetime of criticizing a man who was a staunch defender of all things Hotchkiss, it was time to cut him a break. If he was a little set in his ways, not always the most deeply analytical of souls, well, he pretty much was trying to do the best he could. Which is all any of us can do.

Bunks and I were teamed in my car and headed for the Pennsville Diner in South Jersey, where we'd meet up with the others for a family meal before the final push to Washington. Between Arden House and Manhattan—a seventy-five-minute drive—I asked my father to take a walk down memory lane and wax nostalgic about the trips he had made to the city, both as a young married man and as a buyer for the gift shop. For the first time in my life, I listened carefully to what he had to say.

He wasn't big into details, but I got the general idea that the trips he made to New York were still very special to him. He had told me several times about his spur-of-the-moment jaunt in 1938 to watch the Joe Louis–Max Schmeling heavyweight boxing title rematch at a sold-out Yankee Stadium. His seats were in the nosebleed section, and by the time he had walked to the very last row of the upper deck, the fight was over. Lewis had knocked Schmeling out in just over two minutes in the first round.

I put the idea in his head that we had time to make a pit stop in Manhattan and still stay on schedule for the family rendezvous in Pennsville. I especially wanted to show him Hotel Dorset and some eye candy in Midtown. We drove into Manhattan across the George Washington Bridge and headed south all the way down Broadway, through Columbus Circle, then east on 54th Street to the Dorset. We stopped to have the doorman take a picture of us in front of the hotel, then continued on half a block to Fifth Avenue. As we were stopped at a traffic light in front of St. Patrick's Cathedral, Bunks jumped out of the car to have his picture taken again. It was a true Kodak moment!

After sixteen years, and almost by accident, I finally began to mend fences with the man who did his level best to raise me. I let go of my grudges—Halsnoch, Nicky's suicide, and my father's lack of motivation—and forgave him for being so wonderfully imperfect.

I had done all I could to make my parents happy. But their biggest fantasy—that I would marry into a wealthy family and live happily ever after—was just that. A fantasy.

CHAPTER 7

London Splendour

TWO MONTHS BEFORE finishing the Columbia program, management at Time-Life Books started to take notice of me again. Yes, I had lost some career momentum by making myself scarce around headquarters, but it was only a temporary setback. That impressive new sheepskin was certain to catapult me into a bigger job.

Bill Henry had left the company in late 1986, consigning my fate to his successor, John Fahey. A handsome and affable man, John had risen to the top through finance, not marketing. I knew I'd have to work hard to earn my way into his inner circle.

I was in no rush. I expected that the company would address my career needs when I resumed a full-time work schedule, but certainly not *before*.

Being in the office only three and a half days a week, I hadn't had time to brownnose the new president. John managed by walking around, and he popped into my office a few times, but we only made small talk.

One day in March 1987, I looked up from my desk and saw John standing in my doorway. He made an off-handed remark that made me realize I wasn't *that* invisible: "It's going to be a lot more expensive for us to keep you after you've graduated."

Truth be told, I had no desire to leave the company. But it was undeniable that my market worth was on the rise, thanks to Columbia. And I was not bound to the company.

A day or two after John's remark, his assistant phoned me to schedule a meeting. "Mr. Fahey wants to run something by you," she said. She volunteered nothing more.

No executive, except Bill Henry, had ever run something by a middle manager like me. It hardly ever happens in the corporate world. Something had to be up.

When I walked into John's office, he was charming as usual. After a little small talk, he got down to business. He was helping the head of TLB's European operations, a "Jack Mormon" named Howard Bingham, fill a vacant position in London with an executive from the home office. John had already struck out with several other candidates and was a bit exasperated. As John went through his ritual sales pitch, I interrupted him.

"Do you know I used to live in Iceland?" I asked.

That was a showstopper. He'd finally found someone willing to step outside of his comfort zone.

John offered to fly me immediately to London, and I happily accepted. We talked briefly about living abroad before John prompted me to ask a few questions. I had only one, and I asked it as truthfully as possible. The topic was canine separation anxiety: "What will I do with my dog Annie?"

He was dumbstruck. An expat job—in *London* of all places—was about to land in my lap, and I was worried about my dog? John must have thought I was batty, but being so desperate to check this search off his list, he gave me a mannerly response. "They put them in quarantine," he said. "It's some sort of rabies thing."

I didn't prolong the conversation. He confirmed that the company would cover Annie's transportation and kenneling costs. That was my cue that the meeting was over.

I wasn't going to let a wobbly marriage or the love of animals keep me from going to London to kick the tires. I booked a flight out of Dulles Airport for the next day.

The company had reserved a room for me at Brown's Hotel in the heart of Mayfair. Howard Bingham wined and dined me during my visit. He was eager to be a good host, but not in an unctuous way. Good chap,

I thought. No wonder Fahey liked the guy. The actual interview questions were puffball; we simply went through the motions. The only issue we haggled over was the job title—Howard wanted to downgrade it from VP of Marketing Services to a director-level position. Once I prevailed on that point, I had more or less committed myself to the job.

When I returned home, I asked Patty if she was up for an adventure. She didn't seem fazed in the least. She'd already learned the hard way from her mom that this was just part of being married to a guy on the corporate fast-track. The only issue for Patty was timing. Her mother had just been diagnosed with cirrhosis of the liver and needed a transplant. Living across the pond during a time like this was less than ideal.

We sat for hours talking about the pros and cons of the move—probably the longest we'd spoken together since our nights in the sack at Smith. The career upside for me was obvious. The financial considerations were significant as well. Besides a generous salary and bonus, there was a supplement for housing that was downright sinful. It all came down to our stomach for what could be another assault on our marriage.

We'd lost a baby. I'd gone off to New York for sixteen months to "study." Could an overseas move be the third and final straw to break the marriage? Yes, more than likely. Patty would be stuck at home in a foreign country with a one-year-old. She didn't make new friends that easily, and the American expat community was quite small for a city of London's size.

My folks were visiting at the time, and we invited their input into the decision. They weren't happy about the prospect of not seeing their only grandchild on a regular basis, but their moods improved when I started to peel the proverbial financial onion.

I went down a list of all the job perks, highlighting such things as housing, company car, country club membership, and home leave. I also predicted that the move would have a positive impact on my career down the road.

The idea of their son living like a pretend millionaire in London swayed them. Certainly I'd be able to afford to fly them over to London. Heck, we could even make a pilgrimage to the ancestral Hotchkiss birthplace in Doddington,

Shropshire, a rural village in the West Midlands region of England. We'd heard about that "dot on a map" from Papa many times. Until now, actually *going there* was a whole other story.

In the final analysis, we all agreed there was more to gain than to lose. In private, Patty and I talked about the worst-case scenario. We'd get an all-expenses-paid boondoggle in London, shake hands, and go our own separate ways. So we threw caution to the wind.

I called Howard to formally accept his offer, and the deal was done. We put our townhouse on the market; we got three competitive bids from moving companies; we started to look for kennels in England that would board Annie; and we went on a long and glorious farewell dinner circuit. We'd never stepped out so often or worn our husband-and-wife label so well. The hype that came with it—"the lucky couple"—was hard to deny. We were both great actors.

Things moved quickly. By the end of May 1987, three weeks after graduating from Columbia (yes, the same three weeks after Patty nearly walked out of our marriage at Arden House), I was on a plane bound for London with two suitcases and a footlocker full of dreams. I was excited over the new adventure I was embarking on but was on an emotional roller coaster due to the fragile state of my marriage.

Annie actually arrived in England ahead of me. She was flown over with the help of kennels on both sides of the pond. I waited anxiously to hear from the facility in Berkshire—sixty miles west of London—if she had survived the flight and made a smooth transition to quarantine. Although the personnel there assured me she was just fine and "full of beans," I craved visual proof. But keeping my promise to Patty, I cooled my jets until we could visit Annie together.

The company had leased a furnished flat for me at Shepherd Market, a small square in central London, until my family arrived and we could shop for a larger and more permanent home. It was both convenient and a short walk to the office, but I was constantly hassled by high-class prostitutes who did brisk trade there. They stuck to me—as I went to and returned from work—like flies on shit for the month I lived on my own. Considering the tenuous state of my marriage, I was concerned about how this would look to Patty when she arrived.

The day before Sam's first birthday, we became a threesome again. It was Sunday morning, and I'd thrown a bunch of dirty laundry in the compact washer/dryer combo unit before heading to meet my family. Although these machines had long been popular in Europe, I'd never operated such an appliance before. I hit the first button to make the thing run and left for Heathrow.

Patty, Sam, and I came back into the city by taxi. The driver pulled up to the entrance to my flat and helped us with the luggage. As soon as the "pros" saw me pushing a pram, I became invisible to them. I simply didn't exist.

Inside the flat, we discovered "lakes" of water everywhere. The three bath towels—a maximum load—I stuffed into the unit must have kept it from spinning properly. We used the few remaining fresh towels stored in the closet to mop up most of the mess. So much for the nap Patty had been planning.

We got in my company car and drove to Annie's kennel—*Your Pets*—on Bath Road, in Midgham, Nr. Reading, in Berkshire. Gotta love Royal Mail's exact requirements and one character spared for an already short word like "near"! This would be the first of at least twenty Sundays we'd make the journey. We brought a picnic lunch and other provisions to last the whole day, but the visit was limited, we learned, to *one hour* per week! There were no cutting corners, no bribing the owners. Annie's compulsory isolation was as hard on her as it was on us.

With a now-dry flat as our base, we started looking for a permanent place to call home. I asked both Howard and Andy Kaplan, the company's CFO, for spending guidelines. As expats, they'd negotiated their own deals and set some sort of spending precedent. Being low man on the totem pole, I certainly wanted to live within the company budget.

Howard and Andy recited company policy. Every expat was expected to pay 20 percent of his or her base salary as a contribution to rent. The company would pay the rest.

"The idea," Andy explained, "is for you to replicate the lifestyle you had in the states."

Replicating Springfield, Virginia, was not a pleasant thought. Trading in our modest townhouse for a posh residence in London, however, got me really excited. I couldn't begin to imagine what something like that would cost to rent.

"So would it be all right to look for a townhouse?" I asked him.

"Sure," replied Andy. "Just get the best deal you can."

I had just been empowered with wiggle room. The best thing to do with it was to play copycat. I told Patty to start looking for places in the same Kensington neighborhood as the Binghams and the Kaplans. How could I get in trouble for being a team player?

The Royal Borough of Kensington and Chelsea was, and still is, an affluent district of West London and a much sought-after place to live. We were attracted to its High Street shops, the Royal Albert Hall, Kensington Palace, and its two large green spaces—Kensington Gardens and Holland Park. As a rule, London homes were designed with very small gardens, or backyards, so it would be great to have not only one but two nearby parks for Sam and Annie to visit.

Almost right away, we found a three-story townhome on Abbotsbury Road, a thoroughfare connecting Kensington Road and Holland Park Avenue. It was also the western boundary of Holland Park. We had only to step across the road to access it. Most of the homes appeared to be owned by non-Brits and rented to expats, so the neighborhood wouldn't lend itself to meeting ordinary English families. But we were just people passing through town. It was by no means a deal breaker.

It was a good omen when we learned that a retired British military officer owned the house we wanted. His taste in furniture left something to be desired, but given the rent he was asking, I figured we had some leverage to ask for upgrades.

With contract in hand, I sheepishly went to Howard and told him that the rent on the property would be 6,000 pounds ($9,600) a month, plus utilities. My contribution would be just under $1,000 a month. Do the math. The company would be paying me, indirectly, almost *twice* as much in rent as it paid me in salary! Neither Howard nor Andy flinched. Obviously, it was a lower amount than either of them was paying.

And the hits just kept on coming. A company car—not just any wheels, but an Audi 100. Free membership in the Royal Automobile Club—steeped in tradition as a social and automotive club with access to two clubhouses—one in the glamorous shadow of London's Pall Mall and the other in the green countryside of Epsom, Surrey. A cost-of-living adjustment each month to compensate for higher expenses and currency fluctuations. Free tax preparation services for Inland Revenue and IRS filings. The company even paid the yearly license fee so we could access four television channels.

This was a far cry from any standard of living I'd enjoyed in life. But, in many ways, it also resembled the faux lifestyle of a place like Halsnoch— faux in the sense that someone else was paying the bills. And it would be fleeting. Once I returned to the states in a couple of years, the company spigot would be turned off, and this life of luxury would disappear.

There were so many ways to milk this cow. I discovered that London had an abundance of culinary erogenous zones, from chic restaurants like Cecconi's, Bibendum, and Le Gavroche to the less conspicuous Brick Lane curry houses. I typically budgeted fifty pounds a head for lunch and a hundred for dinner. And for mere "soft money," I could host lunch at the company's private dining room on the sixth floor of the Time and Life Building where one received white-glove service and had access to copious amounts of alcohol. After a meal there, my guests and I would smoke cigars on the patio off the dining room and take in views of the Henry Moore sculptures around the building, the surrounding Ritz Hotel, Berkeley Square, and other parts of Mayfair that couldn't be seen or appreciated from ground level.

Howard believed that travel was integral to the success of the business and that face-to-face meetings with foreign managers were always more effective than phone conversations. We had three offices on the Continent: Paris, Munich, and Amsterdam. We also had a very important licensee, Arnoldo Mondadori Editore S.p.A., in Milan. I would end up on an airplane at least once every week and collect so many entry and exit stamps that I needed to add extra pages to my passport.

Twice a year, the senior management team from across Europe would gather at what we called the Area Managers Meeting. A dozen or more senior managers from across Europe would assemble at a well-heeled venue for a bit of work and a lot of collegiality. It was my job to select the location, build the agenda, find the best restaurants, and pick up the tabs. Doing good work meant wearing out the "plastic" and earning hundreds of thousands of frequent flyer miles.

Having been in London for less than a month, I was able to attend my first such conference in Deauville, France, without having to plan it. All I was really expected to do was meet and greet my new colleagues. Naturally, I was eager to please. So when the European Editor, Kit van Tulleken, called an impromptu meeting during our afternoon free time to discuss the issues of translation for a new book series, I offered to attend.

Kit was a multitasker. Not wanting to forego her time in the sauna, that's where the five of us were instructed to assemble. That would be four men and Kit, a striking woman with a slim frame in her early forties. Unfamiliar with local custom, I headed to the sauna wearing a bathing suit. As I entered the room, I discovered that the dress code was European casual. Rather than be the odd man out, I removed my bathing suit. Yes, siree! There I was, as they say, in commando mode. I was so preoccupied with not getting a career-ending erection from staring at Kit that the entire conversation went completely over my, uh, head.

I wasn't the only American acting like a newbie in Deauville. A couple of senior executives from Alexandria had flown over to "observe" us, (i.e., to glean marketing intelligence that they could export back to America and to live like kings for a week). During their first afternoon recess, our guests ventured down to the main beach in Deauville and discovered that it allowed topless sunbathing. What it didn't condone, in the interest of good taste, were random photos our brethren took of luscious, bare-breasted women.

Once I returned to London, I did some real business. My first priority was to hire a new marketing coordinator as my primary subordinate. The incumbent was finishing up a job rotation and returning to her old job in the French office. There was no job description for the position, so the recruiter and I had to wing it.

We chose to run a blind ad, one that did not identify Time-Life Books as the hiring company. We wanted job seekers to think it was The Reader's Digest Association Ltd. running the ad, not us. They were far better known in the UK market. It read:

GLOBAL PUBLISHING COMPANY LOOKING FOR HIGHLY MOTIVATED INDIVIDUAL TO HELP LAUNCH AND MARKET NEW PRODUCTS ACROSS EUROPE. As a key member of the marketing team, the ideal candidate will have strong organizational and communication skills as well as the ability to multitask. Some language fluency in French, German, or Dutch a plus.

We didn't know how many CVs we'd receive. People weren't as "hungry" for jobs in those days, but we certainly expected to turn this search into a competition.

After two weeks, we had only one person worth interviewing.

Although Nigel Homer had studied to become a lawyer, he possessed no work experience relevant to the marketing coordinator job. What this English bloke did have was a passion for, and a vast knowledge of, the world's greatest drink—beer. That sealed the deal for me. I knew he'd end up teaching me as much about British real ale as I'd teach him about direct marketing.

I was right. We ate many pub lunches together, I encouraging Nigel to linger as long as he wanted. The quality of his work increased exponentially in the afternoons.

I was off to a good start and loved every second of my job. Having both Nigel and a personal assistant in place made it a lot easier to travel. I'd never spent so much money on travel and entertainment in my career, and I enjoyed the best that money could buy. My mistake was sharing too many details with Patty: the age and elegance of the hotel architecture, the expanse of the rooms, the quality of the food and wine. I never knew what "old" meant until visiting Europe.

Patty stopped listening after a while. The walls of our relatively new home on Abbotsbury Road were short and never changed color. Her contact with the outside world was limited at best. A meal out might be a midday snack at the Holland Park Café, if that. Regrettably, Patty wasn't a lady who lunched.

I shared this inequality with Howard one day. His immediate suggestion was for me to take Patty out for dinner on the company.

"Helps to keep them happy over here," he said.

I saw this gesture as both good and bad news. The good news, of course, was having the company foot monster bills at my favorite restaurants. The bad news was that wives of American expats became lonely—and sometimes, resentful—while in London. The Band-Aids provided by the free dinners eventually fell off.

As time went on, Patty was left more and more on her own. I didn't approach our weekends together with the same gusto as I approached my job or fully appreciate how desperate she was to break out of the mommy role now and then. Patty loved going to Holland Park and strolling with Sam and Annie past the Orangery, the cricket pitch, the tennis courts, and the fragmentary ruins of a Jacobean mansion called Holland House. Sam perked up when he passed the children's playground and the big sandpit. Annie, once she came back into the family fold, tugged on her leash when she sensed the abundant wildlife, especially the peacocks. It was a lovely habitat, for sure, but not one I could fully appreciate on a crowded day. And certainly not one I wanted to visit every weekend. My mind was elsewhere, perhaps Paris or Amsterdam. I was turning into a boringly selfish husband.

Unsuspectingly, I was also pushing Patty out of my life and into the background. Eventually, her "baby-whacked" life became so one-dimensional that it made sense to hire an au pair. This would afford her something of a life outside the home. Andy Kaplan and his wife had also discussed taking this step, so it seemed perfectly logical for us to share an au pair and split the cost. Since we had an extra bedroom in our home, we could hire a live-in caregiver, making the proposition even more reasonable. We did our own advertising and found an able young woman from East London—Cockney accent and all—who impressed both families. She moved her scant belongings to Abbotsbury Road and kept a respectful distance when she was off duty.

Once I knew Patty had another adult in the home with whom to interact, I didn't rush home if there was a chance to go out with a few mates for a beer after work. Not that I'd exactly bolted home before, mind you, but at least now I didn't feel so guilty.

Word got out that this "Yank" was normal, and my crowd of drinking mates began to expand. I became known as the affable expat, not just "over here" to bully the locals.

The feeling was mutual. I envied their work-life balance. Even a guy like Paul, our parking-garage attendant, scraping by on a tad more than minimum wage, made three-week holidays to Portugal a priority. I asked him, politely, how that was at all possible.

"Use your crust, mate," he said in Cockney slang. He was referring to my head, which rhymed with crust of bread.

One Friday evening in November, a young editorial production manager—one of Kit's direct reports—joined our group for a session. It was the first time I'd ever seen her out of the office. She had the kind of beauty one acquires from spending time outdoors, along with an infectious laugh. She loved everything about America and confessed her desire to emigrate there. She pumped me for information about the job market in New York. I'd seen this young woman present at meetings and knew she had talent. I would have gladly tried to help her, but the few contacts I had in New York at the time weren't particularly relevant.

Born in London to Irish parents, Doreen Murphy, then twenty-four years old, had come a long way for someone with a high school education. She'd even bought a flat in East London with her "man," the brother of a

117

previous lover. She sure charmed the pants off me. Sure, we flirted a bit, but I was in no position to make a play for her. It wasn't my style, and why contemplate adultery in the eleventh hour of a bad marriage?

I left the pub that night with a primed pump, but by the time I got home to Abbotsbury Road, I had nothing more than "brewer's droop." The house was as quiet as the night before Christmas. Sam was asleep, and Patty was reading a book. She was sitting in the living room and looked up for a second as I walked in. She seemed far more interested in the novel than she was in me. I felt like Patty was acknowledging me as a roommate, not as a husband.

"You missed another fun evening," I boasted.

This comment didn't stir Patty from her book, so I tried a different tack.

"I wish you'd come out with us once in a while," I asserted.

Patty wasn't much of a beer drinker, and she hated the secondhand smoke in pubs.

"I'm still waiting for Dee and Meryl to join me," she explained.

Dee Bingham and Meryl Kaplan wouldn't go to a smoky, boisterous London boozer if the host establishment were giving away luxury items from Asprey. It just wasn't their style.

I'd gotten cynical about the lack of life in our house. We never had neighbors drop by. We had no visitors lined up from the states. Patty's parents were unable to travel because of her mother's illness, and my parents always pleaded poverty. What a waste of prime London real estate!

"Let's use some frequent flyer miles and get Peg and Bunks over here in the summer," I suggested. As long as my parents could crawl, they'd accept a free trip to London.

We booked the trip and prolonged the ruse of our marriage. However, it did bring us good karma. Eventually others from America asked if they could come to stay with us, too.

Patty worked hard to roll out the welcome mat, whether they were her friends or mine. She enjoyed being around people with stories from back home and their kindred "I can't believe how expensive London is" remarks. I found most of their "Rah! Rah! America" conversations boring, but worth tolerating if it made Patty happy, albeit temporarily. The distraction of company alleviated some of the stress in our marriage. There was just one hard-and-fast rule: we could never air any of our dirty linen in the presence of our guests.

We spent an eye-opening weekend entertaining a couple from Pennsylvania. I had done some business with the husband, but I'd never met his wife. Perhaps we shouldn't have been so accommodating, but we were on a good roll. Hubby and I got along brilliantly on the golf course, but based on Patty's reports, Wifey was high maintenance. Our final night together, I saw it with my own eyes. She got completely smashed at a restaurant in the Connaught Hotel—a five-star establishment patronized by connoisseurs of luxury from around the world. She was the proverbial "loud American" and caused quite a scene. We thought her behavior might improve when we repaired to a discreet corner of the lobby bar for armagnac and port. What she really needed was a quaalude.

Keeping her on the premises was a huge mistake. The boring sophisticate actually had the chutzpah to scoop up two ashtrays etched with trademark Cs and stash them in her handbag as souvenirs.

This episode got Patty and me thinking. Maybe we should make ourselves *less* available and do some of our own traveling. We were in a great hub for European travel, and a wide assortment of countries and cultures lay mere hours away.

"If you ever have problems with your marriage, throw money at it," a wise man once told me.

I followed his advice. I took Patty to Paris for a long weekend. Maybe this would be the perfect tonic to turn things around for us. We stayed at one of the last remaining bastions of French tradition and grand service, Hotel le Bristol. *Les chambres et les restaurants* were stunning. Its small swimming pool—situated on the top floor of the property—was bordered by a teak walkway. We had a munificent view of the chic Saint-Germain-des-Prés neighborhood, Hermes storefront and all. Combining the iconic status of the hotel with the overall ambiance of Paris, you'd think Patty and I would have connected physically. It didn't happen.

There was no desire or lust between us. It was a clear sign that passion had fled the scene of our marriage. If we couldn't find romance in the City of Love and mess up the sheets at the Bristol, it meant our sex life had hit rock bottom. What was the point of continuing on? Why were we going through these false motions?

Understandably, Mae Beekman's poor health played a role in our inertia. Patty wouldn't consider a formal breakup while her mother was so ill, no matter how broken things were between us. But we both knew the jig was up.

For Christmas, we went to Florida to be with Patty's family. She flew over with Sam a week or so ahead of me. I had a weekend to myself in London before the journey home. By this time, Doreen and I had spent enough Friday evenings in each other's company at London pubs to embolden ourselves for a drive alone to the countryside. My mental distancing from my marriage was about to enter a new phase.

Doreen and I went on a day trip to the southern coastal town of Hastings, expecting that its history would lead us to some interesting places. In reality, Hastings was a pretty boring place, full of fish-and-chips shops frequented by tourists. We did find a nice coastal path to walk along and work up a thirst for a few beers. During the walk, Doreen brought out a joint she'd rolled before the trip started that was half-tobacco and half-hash. I soon found out why Europeans generally preferred such a mixture—the inclusion of tobacco seemed to get the active ingredients of the hash into the bloodstream a lot faster.

It seemed like an endless walk, not exactly a bad thing given the company and the buzz. Actually, I didn't want it to end. We fell down a few times from the influence of the hash, laughing uncontrollably. The drive, the walk together, the smoke, the laughter, the beers afterward, even the greasy fish and chips we succumbed to because we had the munchies, made me realize all the more how unhappy I was in my marriage.

If my arrival in Florida for Christmas showed *any* enthusiasm for being with Patty and her parents, then I was both feckless *and* a great actor. Only having Sam there kept me in the game. All the usual Beekman family crap I had put up with in the past was staring me in the face again. But for the first time, my voice was finally heard. They listened to me brag about my son.

After Christmas, the three of us made a pit stop in Richmond to visit my parents before heading back to London. I feigned illness while we were there in order to sleep alone and avoid being physically close to Patty. My heart ached for London and the new-and-improved lifestyle I had there. I couldn't get the fantastic time I'd had with Doreen in Hastings out of my mind, either.

Soon after Patty and I returned to London, we received news that her mother had undergone a liver transplant. The initial prognosis was favorable, but in short order, complications set in. She needed a second liver to survive. That she got, but it failed, too.

Patty and Sam flew immediately to Tampa once the family was told that Mae Beekman had only a few days left. Mother and daughter spent some quality time together and got some things off their chests. Moments away from dying, Mae released a report card of her daughter's life. I had made more of an impact on her mother than I ever imagined.

"Patty, you are so lucky to have found such a wonderful husband," Mae uttered, I admit, rather unsuspectingly.

This was the first of a one-two punch to Patty's emotional gut. By the time the words had time to sink in, her mother was dead.

I arrived in time for the funeral and got all holy and sanctimonious. During the time Patty and Sam were alone in Florida, I had finally answered love's call and broken my most sacred wedding vow, fidelity.

I would keep this to myself for now. We wanted to give her father a few months to grieve before breaking the news of our pending separation. Behind the scenes, we discussed the most amicable way of negotiating a property settlement agreement without throwing away a decade of friendship or contaminating a future of parenting.

My emotions were like dry kindling at the time, so I really didn't want to go the traditional lawyer route. I just knew where that would lead. We had heard of a new approach to divorce, where couples *shared* a lawyer. I was game to try.

Yes, I had graduated from Columbia Business School, but I was still very naïve and gullible.

CHAPTER 8

Divorce 101

FRIENDS OF THE Beekman family took me aside at Mae's funeral and encouraged me to be there for her husband, a new widower who had no experience in running a household.

"Call Stanley once a week and make sure he's got food in the refrigerator," urged one male friend and neighbor.

"Visit him when you can and get him out on the golf course," recommended another.

Yeah, right. Stanley Beekman, as aloof as he'd been all the years I'd known him, would suddenly accept me as his buddy? I didn't think so. But I felt his pain. He'd just lost the love of his life to a horrible illness, and it would be Christian of me to cut him a little slack. I prayed over the matter for a while and decided to be the better man.

Patty and I opted to ignore the horrible next steps in our relationship and play nice. We went ahead with earlier plans for a trip to the beautiful white beaches of Hammamet, Tunisia, traveling as "friends."

I'd never sunbathed in such intense UV light; in fact, it was the only time in my life that I experienced third-degree burns. We were also there in the middle of Ramadan, the Islamic holy month in which Muslims fast from dawn until sunset. Service wasn't just slow—it was nonexistent.

Unlike our experience in Paris the previous fall, our expectations about romantic feelings creeping out were nonexistent. We'd put intimacy away for good. It wasn't the right venue for that, anyway. Watching camels walk by on the beach had the same effect as heaping a tablespoon of saltpeter into my bowl of *lablabi*—it curbed my libido.

As soon as we came back from Tunisia, I headed out of the country again on a business trip. This company-wide extravaganza for all European employees was the promised payoff for hitting a profit goal. It was a much bigger crowd than the typical area managers' meeting, meaning the logistics were more complex as well.

Thus, I was merely one of several people on the planning committee. But it didn't stop me from heading out several days early to ensure a smooth-running affair.

Why wouldn't I want to extend my stay on the island of Crete? We'd be staying at the Elounda Mare hotel, a five-star Relais & Châteaux property that elevated privacy to a whole new level. While business travel had started to become a little monotonous for me, this trip would be anything but dull. It would also have far-reaching consequences.

There really were things that I needed to attend to, but the fact I kept on the down low was that Doreen was also leaving London early. We weren't on the same outbound flight together, but we would arrive the same day. There was no marriage to save, so I chose not to label it an affair. But I knew that in God's eyes, I would be committing adultery.

If anyone from the European operations saw Doreen and me together in public, I knew they wouldn't think twice about it. Our continental colleagues tended to mind their own business in such matters.

But there were Americans on site as well. And one of them, Jim Mercer, head of TLB International and Howard's boss, did mind. He caught Doreen and me in a PDA moment along a dirt road, well out of range of the hotel. We had rented a jeep for a day tour of the island and obviously weren't the only ones with that idea. Howard called my hotel room to pass along a message.

"Stuey," Howard said to me, "Jim saw you and Doreen kissing out in public today and thinks it would be a good idea for the two of you to lay low while we're in Crete."

Given that Howard, the messenger, thought of himself as God's gift to women and openly referred to young females in his employ as "birds," I couldn't help but hear hypocrisy oozing through the phone line. In fact, the warning didn't sound like it came from Jim at all. But I bit my tongue and thanked Howard for the heads up. Then I just carried on with my business and pretended the conversation never took place.

Doreen and I were friends with the woman who made the room assignments. I was to share a two-bedroom sea-view suite with my mate Ed Skyner, a book designer in the London editorial department. Doreen was to share a similar, adjoining suite with a female French editor who happened to be Ed's paramour. Then Doreen and Ed swapped rooms and, voilà, we were two very naughty couples.

We were more than five thousand miles away from headquarters and acted accordingly. The joy of rediscovering intimacy far outweighed any concern about my failed marriage. I threw caution to the wind and let it bluster.

I returned to London from Crete just before my parents' scheduled visit. There would never be a good time for me to come clean with Patty about Crete. Yet I feared her finding out about Doreen and me from another source. I had to man up and tell her myself. So I chose to spill my guts just before my parents arrived, fully expecting that Patty and I could keep this secret for another week or so.

I explained that my feelings for Doreen were real and that I planned to begin a new relationship with her once the separation commenced. I offered a slow, methodical wind down of our marriage to ensure as painless an outcome as possible for everyone, especially for Sam. As I was telling her everything, Patty was uncharacteristically calm. There was no screaming or shouting. Her tone of voice was neither bitter nor bitchy. She just kept asking questions about Doreen.

"How old is she?" Patty asked.

"Late twenties," I answered, with a slight exaggeration.

"Is she pretty?

"Patty, how am I supposed to respond to that?" I knew better than to answer that question honestly. It would serve no purpose to let Patty know that Doreen was a looker. Besides, it wasn't Doreen's considerable physical beauty that captured me; it was her vivaciousness and independence.

"Do you love her?"

"We're just getting to know each other."

She then switched gears and asked if this was my first "affair." I felt sleazy all of a sudden. Why hadn't I waited just a month or two longer before shagging Doreen? This was my first hands-free orgasm since Sam's conception, but it sure wasn't worth it.

Patty and I both started to cry.

Some of those tears must have been joyous ones for Patty. A husband lost is a dollar saved. After mother Mae's death, her grandmother, the family matriarch, had informed the family that she was changing her will. I was due to receive an equal cut of the grandchildren's inheritance. Ignorance was bliss; knowledge of this upcoming windfall may have been tempted me to lead a double life.

The next day, we met with our shared lawyer, an American working out of Pepper, Hamilton & Scheetz's London office. He informed us that he was obliged to be neutral and equated his role to that of a mediator. Patty and I were in complete agreement that Sam would continue to live with her back in the states. My visitations would be generous. Financial provisions for Sam would be ongoing and, of course, I'd be most generous with Patty in dividing our marital assets. The lawyer assured us that he would do everything possible to achieve an amicable settlement between us.

Patty and I were confident that our course of action would yield perfect harmony.

Then my parents arrived. Patty kept her lips sealed for a few days. We made that long-awaited pilgrimage to Shropshire to look for evidence of Samuel Hotchkiss and other family members from that era. We booked two rooms at a bed-and-breakfast in the town of Telford that was owned by a man with the last name of Hotchkiss. Perhaps Patty felt overwhelmed in such a potent familial setting. Equally, it must have struck her that Hotchkiss would soon become only a title. For whatever reason, Patty broke our code of silence and said to my parents, "Stuart wants to tell you about a horrible thing he's just done to us."

Mind you, she said this while I was driving nearly a hundred miles per hour on an English motorway. "What do I want to tell them?" I asked innocently.

"You want to tell them about Doreen."

My hands clenched the steering wheel with such pressure that the blood drained from my knuckles and turned them a pale shade of white. I looked over at Patty and snarled like a rabid dog. A long silence ensued.

"Let's just have a good time," my mother offered to break the awkward moment.

My father didn't say a word, but I'm sure he had his fingers crossed that there'd be no new confrontation. He couldn't have been looking forward to another tongue-lashing like the one he'd received from Patty at Arden House.

We arrived back at our house in London, and while Patty tended to Sam's needs, I asked my parents to sit down and hear me out. I was alone with them and comfortable in telling them my side of the story. I went through a chronology of events, from that infamous night at Arden House when Patty wanted out of the marriage to my doing the deed with Doreen in Crete a week earlier.

My father was uncharacteristically rattled. "Well, you sure picked a fine time to drop this bomb on us."

He was right. They'd schlepped three thousand miles to visit us. There was no such thing as a "free flight." Instead of having memories of a pleasant time spent in England, my father would remember having to be on pins and needles around his soon-to-be ex-daughter-in-law. He was tired of being Patty's whipping boy. Surely, if he took my side—which I didn't necessarily deserve—Patty would let him have it. The poor guy couldn't win for losing. His solution was to take lots of long walks to avoid both of us.

My mother, on the other hand, wanted to deny what she'd been told. She'd seen lots of her friends break up and get back together over the years. The penis had always wandered off to visit strangers but, somehow, managed to find its way home.

"You two will work this out," she advised.

If she actually believed, deep down, that a separation was inevitable, her worry would have been the reaction from friends in Richmond. Appearances *über alles*.

Patty gradually progressed into the role of victim. A Time-Life colleague from Alexandria and his wife were coming to visit the next week. I asked Patty if she would prefer for me to call and inform them in the most honest and straightforward way possible that it was a bad time for us. She said absolutely not; their airfares were nonrefundable, and they wouldn't have a chance to rebook anything on such short notice. She agreed once more to behave and keep quiet about the pending separation.

I should have known better.

Our guests enjoyed a peaceful two nights at the house before Patty had too much to drink the second evening and spilled the beans again. It was an awkward moment. In a matter of minutes, they were smack in the middle of our marital problems. Finding the situation too uncomfortable, they left to spend the next night at a hotel.

I felt we had been extremely rude to them and thrown their budget into chaos. I chose to move out of the house temporarily and into a room at the Royal Automobile Club (RAC) on Pall Mall and invited them back into our house. Our guests appreciated the gesture and accepted my offer to return to Abbotsbury Road.

This gave Patty a forum to present her—and only her—version of our breakup.

They kept her company until the wee hours of the night, drinking lots of wine and listening to my wife rant about my *affair*. As she told it, I, alone, had ruined our perfectly fine marriage—the outwardly perfect marriage they'd seen before we left Virginia. After several days of this brainwashing, they became Patty's faithful followers.

He was an unrepentant gossip and lost no time in exporting Patty's biased interpretation of events directly to the home office in Alexandria, Virginia. Lots of my friends and colleagues there became incensed over my trumped-up transgressions. By the time the story got retold for the hundredth time, I had slept with the entire female staff in England. And at least twice with each person.

Howard Bingham was in Alexandria during this time and heard enough to suggest to me that I completely avoid the Alexandria office until things calmed down. "Stuey, they'll cut your balls off if you go anywhere near there," I was warned.

Even with all this shit flying around, I still believed in the possibility of an amicable separation. But I started to feel a certain one-sidedness creeping in from the lawyer. Now that things were out in the open, Patty told her father what was going on. He heard about my temporary stay at the RAC and called me at the office with an offer: "If you remain out of the house until Patty comes back home, I'll pay all of your expenses at the RAC."

He was a wealthy man—excuse me, a man with sizeable material possessions—who could bully me with his wallet, and I let him do so. I tried to be as cooperative as possible with him. Now that Stanley Beekman was in charge, I knew the agreements Patty and I had made earlier were in the shredder and we'd have to start over. He advised his daughter to make sure the lawyer saw things *her* way or ditch him for one who did. Pity the latter didn't happen. I would have had at least a shot at justice with my own lawyer.

With her father's guidance, Patty was now out for a pound of flesh. She even hid the company car to gain negotiating leverage. She knew I couldn't involve Howard by telling him the Audi was missing, nor could I call the police to report it stolen because I didn't own it. Patty wouldn't reveal its location or give me the keys unless I agreed to give away the farm. The last thing I wanted was for anyone at Time-Life to get mixed up in my marital woes, so she prevailed.

I promised to give her all of our marital assets and touch none of her family money, including any future inheritances. That was music to her ears. I got the car back and Patty's promise to not play the adultery card. The other unresolved issues seemed like nickel-and-dime stuff at the time.

Patty's father flew over to make sure the nails were properly hammered into my coffin. The two Beekmans, and *our* supposedly neutral lawyer, sat across the table from me in the firm's conference room. The lawyer handed me a property settlement agreement that had been prepared with additional input from her father. Less than thirty days had passed from the initial consultation we had had with this lawyer to that day's meeting. And now, instead of mediating, the lawyer, or "MacArthur" as I came to think of him, was demanding the unconditional surrender of Japan—me—upon the USS *Missouri*.

Added to the agreement were stipulations for me to pay child support until Sam reached the age of twenty-six and to cover 100 percent of Sam's educational expenses, including college and graduate school, if applicable. Never mind that the Beekman Family Trust would cover that in full. I argued that point, softly, but was mowed down. There was a lot of other fine print, too, which I didn't fully comprehend but also didn't want to stress over at the time. I was young and successful, and I reasoned to myself that at least Patty wasn't asking for any of my future earnings.

"Stuart, this is a very fair agreement," Patty's father volunteered to break the ice. "It's a very standard agreement that I've reviewed and believe to be fair to both you and Patty."

The lawyer echoed Stanley Beekman's words, although he didn't say "Patty."

Realizing I was lawyerless, and screwed, I signed.

Patty's father wrote me a letter as soon as he returned to Florida. As always, he had to have the final word:

Your recent actions belie the person I've known all these years. But let me be clear—we will expend every dollar that we have to litigate against you should you not live up to your agreements.

Stanley Beekman's hand in architecting a win for his daughter was unambiguous and astonishingly apparent now. I realized how invaluable a strong father can be—especially one as money obsessed as he.

As Patty and Sam got ready to head back to America, I spent as much time with my son as possible. I showed up at Abbotsbury Road for his second birthday party and couldn't believe the number of people, mostly moms and their kids, in attendance. Had Patty had this large of a social network all along? Or had she hired them as extras to get my goat?

It was as much a farewell party as it was a birthday party. For me, this was no time to celebrate. I was losing both Sam and Annie.

Poor Annie had paid the ultimate price of relocation: six months in quarantine to enjoy just seven months of Holland Park. I was her king; she was my queen. I knew Patty and Sam would provide her with a good home, but it was painful to lose her, especially in a package deal.

I left the next day for a conference in southern England. My assistant forwarded details from Patty about their return to the states. The day of departure, that coming Friday, was also my last day of meetings. Howard had already cut me a lot of slack on account of the separation and wasn't happy about my need to leave early, but he acquiesced. Their flight was scheduled to leave at 9:30 a.m. out of Gatwick Airport. Barring any traffic jams, I could make it to the airport from my conference venue in two hours.

I left for the airport at 5:00 in the morning, made excellent time driving to Gatwick, and arrived at the South Terminal departure lounge five minutes shy of 7:00. I had prepared myself for some serious crying. Knowing that I might not see Sam again for months gave me a knot in the pit of stomach. I was also anxious about confronting Patty and her father. For all I knew, it could turn into a Jerry Springer moment.

At 7:15 a.m., they had yet to arrive.

They'd be coming by taxi and dropped off no more than twenty paces from where I was standing. As large a man as Stanley was, I couldn't possibly miss them.

Knowing that Stanley prided himself on military punctuality, I started to panic when the clock reached 7:30. Something was wrong. I asked airline and customs officials to please page Stanley Beekman, reasoning that if they were already at the airport, he would be more likely to respond to a page than Patty.

The page was made. I heard it clearly and succinctly over the PA system: "Will Mr. Stanley Beekman, B double-E K M A N, please contact any member of airport security for an urgent message?"

A second page was made minutes later. As I awaited an answer, I asked for help from every uniformed person in sight. My anxiety was spiking, and the vein around my right eye was bulging. I couldn't prevent my voice from cracking.

"Please, I must see my son," I wailed like a wild animal in heat. "Would you check to see if he has already passed through security?"

Each person I spoke to retained that famous "English calm." They didn't inconvenience themselves a bit. They merely told me that airport protocol would not allow anyone but a passenger to cross the security threshold. If my party had already gone beyond *that partition*, the one with all sorts of BAA warning signs, then I could speak with them only if they responded to my page. Simple as that.

I must have looked pathetic as I yelled out in the direction of the departure gates, "Sam-my! Sam-my!"

I prayed that somehow these words would connect with my son, the one I'd tried so hard to bring into this world.

Months later, Patty confessed that they had arrived extra early at the airport in order to avoid me. They couldn't stomach a final encounter, she said.

Who did she think she was kidding? This was all about brainwashing Sam into thinking I was such a loser that I hadn't even shown up at the airport to see him off. It was the tip of an iceberg so large it could sink two *Titanics*.

Patty had more control over my life now than ever before for the simple reason that she had my son.

I returned to my car and headed back to London a broken man. I was lost, dazed, and bewildered. As I merged onto the M25 motorway, I wiped away my tears and strained to look upward toward the heavens. "God help me!" I exclaimed. "This can't be happening!"

I was truly sorry for the way our marriage had ended. But I still couldn't believe that Patty would *really* use Sam to exact payback for the rest of my life.

CHAPTER 9

Twist and Shout

I HADN'T BEEN single in a long time, but there I was in London, some seven grams lighter around the ring finger. Doreen was more than a casual friend, and it was important to me to help her avoid the label of marriage wrecker. I knew I'd never be able to dissuade certain people from thinking that I'd left Patty for Doreen, and I wouldn't even begin to try, except for one person.

I didn't want my son, Sam, to grow up being brainwashed into believing such southern fried fiction.

By the same token, Doreen and I deserved the chance to evolve our relationship into something more serious now that I was legally separated. She was a part of the new "trinity," along with Sam and my career. In order to overcome the recent setbacks in my life, these three pieces had to fit nicely together. I did not have the opportunity to rotate one piece in and out like I'd had when I was as a student at Columbia.

Andy Kaplan asked me, very politely, to "adjust" my living situation. I completely agreed; it was unreasonable for a single guy to continue to receive such a lavish housing allowance. It was the least I could do for the company that had graciously paid all of Patty, Sam, and even Annie's relocation expenses back to Northern Virginia.

Change was everywhere. I was even losing my brew buddy Nigel Homer, who'd also become a personal friend. He'd fallen in love with an American exchange student in London, gone off on holiday with her to Minnesota, and come back a married man. When his new bride completed her studies in December, they'd be leaving England to begin a new life in Washington, DC. I handled this news pretty well, given that I'd be without someone like Nigel, who was forever teaching me how to laugh at myself.

But even bigger news was a letter Patty had written to John Fahey's boss—the CEO of Time Inc.'s book division—accusing me of using corporate funds to "screw Doreen across all of Europe." I was completely blown away. My initial instinct was to hire an assassin. But a prison sentence was the last thing I needed. I wisely decided not to give her the satisfaction of knowing that she was making my life hell.

I couldn't help but wonder what drove Patty to this madness. Didn't she consider that wrecking my career would jeopardize my ability to provide for our son? She could certainly afford to "bite off her nose to spite her face," but I couldn't pay child support without a job. I didn't mind her being vengeful—even if she was acting way over the top—but this kind of nonsense was unconscionable.

I decided to be proactive and ask Andy, who had been charged with looking into the matter, for a sit-down. I first apologized for having my marital woes visited upon the company again. I then went methodically through every out-of-town trip that I took over that past year and demonstrated as best I could—through travel vouchers and receipts—the impossibility of Patty's accusation. Andy heard me out, evaluated the evidence, and declared me innocent of all charges.

But ill fortune wasn't done with me just yet. Shortly after this disturbing episode, Howard Bingham introduced me to a suave, yet two-stone-overweight Englishman by the name of Kip Kirby. Together, they made an unannounced visit to my office. After a short introduction, Howard left. I didn't invite Kip to stay, but he did anyway. He started to ask a lot of questions about my job.

"Excuse me, sir, but what is the nature of your business?" I interrupted.

He shot me back a strange look, like I was the peddler and he was the client.

Was this even a sales call, I began to wonder? He gave no clues, but he spoke so intelligently about my area of responsibility that I figured Howard must have briefed him earlier.

"Have you been hired to do a project?" I continued to inquire.

Kip continued talking as if I had never asked any questions. He gave a "state of the business" speech, telling me how undermarketed our products were in the UK; how we needed to tighten reins on the European managers; and, last but not least, how much work there was to be done in *my* department.

Kip and I stood up to shake hands at the end of our meeting. There were no promises made, like, "I'll be back in touch," or "Let's make time for lunch." I became paranoid about possible scenarios. Was it possible that he was being hired by Howard to monitor my performance? Had Patty filed another complaint, and was Kip about to take my job? What the hell was going on? My one and only performance review was glowing; in fact, my year-end bonus had exceeded the target amount. So who was this *Kip Kirby* fellow, and why was he here?

I dropped by Howard's office later in the day and asked for some sort of clarification. He proceeded to gush about Kip and tell me how delighted he—and everyone else—was about the local stud joining TLB.

"Kip will be reporting to me," Howard said, "and I'm counting on the two of you to work well together."

Nothing more was volunteered, so I assumed I had just met my new peer. Then I thought for a minute. Despite being secure about my own job, something still felt amiss.

"Howard, is there something you're not telling me?"

"Stuey, what's your worry?" he answered back in a patronizing tone.

"My worry, Howard, is that you haven't told me I'm reporting to someone else."

"You and Kip will make a great team," he claimed.

Howard refused to spell it out. I was now going to report to Kip Kirby. Gentleness, equanimity, and benevolence were not native to Howard Bingham.

It got worse. Howard and I flew together the following week to Amsterdam for a monthly European Steering Committee meeting. During the flight, we sat and chatted with each other about business in general as well as topics on the meeting agenda. We shared a taxi from Schiphol Airport to the TLB office in town. We had an hour or so to kill before the meeting started, so I caught up on issues of the day with some colleagues. At the appointed hour, I proceeded into the conference room and took a seat. Suddenly, he tapped me on the shoulder and said, "Uh, Stuey, can you step outside for a minute? I need to speak with you."

I thought he'd forgotten to take something to the meeting and wanted me to contact London to fax it over. I should've been so lucky. What he told me was that I was no longer on the Steering Committee. The new guy was taking my place. I was history.

How red can a face get? The combination of anger and embarrassment can produce a pretty fierce hue. Experts say never to burn a bridge with someone professionally. I didn't just burn my bridge with Howard; I torched it.

"You've got to be fucking kidding me!" I yelled.

"Hold on there, Stuey."

"Hold on, my ass! And stop calling me, 'Stuey'! You bring me all the way here to Amsterdam and for what? To humiliate me in front of everyone?"

Why *had* he brought me here? Why hadn't he just told me in London that I was off the committee? And why did he always ignore my pleas to stop calling me "Stuey"?

I wasn't finished with "Howie." If you're going to get ejected from a "game," make a public spectacle out of yourself like baseball manager Earl Weaver.

"We spent an entire plane ride together to get here," I continued, "and I didn't hear one word from you about this, you fucking coward! First you don't even have the decency to tell me I have a new boss, and now this! What is your goddamn problem?"

He left me standing there fuming and returned to the meeting. What could I say to those who had just witnessed my meltdown? I told them the truth. I went office to office and cube to cube and gave everyone in the Dutch office an instant replay. Then I hopped in a taxi back to Schiphol and sucked down nearly a dozen small-glass Amstels before flying home to London.

I was now faced with a professional dilemma. Should I quit in protest or simply coast along until my work visa expired? The only person I could trust to give me sound advice was Andy Kaplan. Next to Bill Henry, Andy was the straightest shooter I'd ever known.

Andy and I chatted about career paths in general and the possibilities of my next company assignment in particular. The bottom line, according to Andy, was that I had to get back to America before I could jump ship. The odds of getting a job with a different company back home—not to mention the potential relocation costs I'd have to absorb—would be far better if I sat tight and waited for TLB to determine my next move.

Thanks in large part to Andy's counsel, I chose to try and turn a negative into a positive and make nice with Kip Kirby.

I invited my new boss to sit down and listen to me. I characterized our future together as a mutual codependence. I would stay in London till the bitter end. I would prove myself to be invaluable to Kip. I'd start by telling him where all the proverbial bodies were buried. And I was prepared, if necessary, to throw Howard Bingham under the bus.

I pointed out Howard's strengths and weaknesses to Kip. To his credit, Bingham was masterful with numbers. He had been a terrific chief financial officer before his promotion to president. On the other hand, he meddled too much in marketing. He would beat up the area managers if they came in a fraction over budget on planned advertising expenses. Then, to be a spiteful bugger, he'd invest in extravagant Pan-European direct mail package tests just to try and prove that "London" could beat the "locals" at their own game. I also told Kip that if Howard tried to export his management style to America, he'd be sued for sexual harassment.

As soon as the dust settled, Jim Mercer reached out and threw me a bone. He was moving his office from Alexandria to London, and he and his wife were making the move at some point in the near future. They came to London and found the perfect home to rent on the first try. But it was too early to commit. Rather than risk losing it, they asked me to take immediate possession and house-sit for them, rent free. I was over the moon. I'd eventually have to downsize, but for the next three months, I lived in Jim's palatial digs and entertained my friends royally.

The timing was perfect. Doreen had given "notice" to her man, and they'd decided to sell their flat in East London. With Jim's blessing, she became a frequent overnight guest at the palace. By the time the Mercers eventually got to London, Doreen had sold her property and I'd found my own corporate flat off the Fulham Road in South Kensington. We decided to play house together.

To celebrate our new living arrangement, Doreen used some of the money from her real estate deal to take me to Venice. It was November 1988, and we experienced unseasonably cold weather. The wet air made strolling the canals unpleasant, so we opted to stay under the duvet in our room. The payback, unfortunately, was hell. I started to experience horrific pain in my left testicle. Perhaps if we'd come up for air once in a while, this wouldn't have happened. I'd had blue balls in the past, but this was an entirely different level and duration of pain. When we returned to London, I went straight to Harley Street, noted since the nineteenth century for its large number of private specialists in medicine and surgery, to see a urologist.

The prolonged twisting and wrenching of my lower anatomy during our sexual marathon had cut off the blood supply to my left testicle and killed it. I remembered what Howard had told me earlier—that folks back in Alexandria wanted to cut off both my balls. Well, they'd soon have to settle for one. The left testicle had to be surgically removed.

It felt like I was being stripped of my manhood at every turn. At least the surgery, performed at the private Harley Street Clinic, was a doddle. This medical center—more hotel than hospital—was patronized by the world's megarich. I was assigned a large private suite, where nurses served me proper afternoon tea on Royal Worcester china. And being covered by BUPA health insurance, it was entirely free.

With the procedure behind me, I was left in a narcissistic coma. The bum testicle had been replaced with a prosthesis during the surgery. I struggled for days to look at myself in the mirror. My testicles were no longer close to being the same size, and I obsessed about being able to "perform" again. I was extraordinarily anxious over something I couldn't control. Another bout of déjà vu.

With Doreen's support, we bridged the gap between abstinence and abundance just fine. In less than three months, we were at it again. Yeah, baby.

But the really big orgasm occurred when it was announced, out of nowhere, that Howard Bingham was returning to Alexandria! Doreen and I both screamed when we heard the news. The man who had wined and dined me to come to London, then unceremoniously dumped me, was a goner! And, Jim Mercer, my new ally, was going to serve as his replacement, at least for the time being.

This news boosted my interest in prolonging the London tour. Despite getting off to a rocky start, Kip Kirby and I had become bona fide comrades, and he offered to help me find a way to stay. We discussed the few scenarios that might pique management's interest. There wasn't much opportunity for growth, even laterally. Only one thing was certain—I could not prolong the status quo.

The most plausible move was managing director of the English market. But the incumbent didn't appear to be on the ropes or leaving anytime soon, so I proposed a job swap, in which she would gain more exposure to American management and the new product development pipeline that started in Alexandria. I felt more than ready for the managing director job, and Kip promised to approach Howard, whose vote still counted, and Jim with the idea.

Howard was distracted at the time with personal business. At the top of the list was a private farewell party that he and his wife were planning. Engraved invitations requesting the pleasure of one's company at the ultraposh private club, The White Elephant on Curzon Street in Mayfair, had just been mailed. The couple was also heading to Utah for a couple of weeks. *Mormon stuff*, I reckoned. Kip didn't get to Howard before he left town.

When Howard returned to London, he was like a skeleton of his former self. He had lost too much weight, making his bespoke Savile Row suits look poorly tailored. There was also a big gap in his mouth from a lost tooth. He looked more like a homeless man than an executive. Something was very wrong with this picture.

Word got out that the farewell party had been canceled. All kinds of rumors circulated, but soon the truth was revealed: Howard and Dee were headed for a divorce. All the animus I had felt toward Howard was suddenly gone. He looked awful, and I'm sure he felt awful. After what I had been through with Patty, I didn't wish divorce on anyone.

For the first time in our relationship, I visited with Howard and did most of the talking. I was speaking from the heart. I offered my help. Howard was extraordinarily humble.

Nothing changed Howard's opinion of my professional talents, however. When Kip finally had the opportunity to pitch me for the new job, Howard was not swayed. Instead of suggesting that the idea was crazy because of too many moving parts, he simply told Kip I wasn't creative enough to do the job.

Howard probably didn't mean to batter my professional ego again, but I was offended. I knew at some point in the future I'd prove him wrong. But for now, he had control. His remarks guaranteed I'd be heading back to the states and, in all likelihood, Alexandria. Although I'd be closer to Sam, it would be a terrible career move. The visceral reaction of my former colleagues to my split from Patty was a curse. There had to be another plan.

TLB management must have arrived at the same conclusion. I was encouraged to get on a plane to New York to interview for a new position at Book-of-the-Month Club (BOMC), another Time Inc. subsidiary. Although Jim Mercer told me to go into the interview with an open mind but to feel comfortable saying no, the realist in me knew better. My options were practically nil.

Chris Linen, now both CEO of the Time Inc. book division and president of BOMC, was embarking upon a plan to merge TLB with its sister division BOMC under his leadership. While TLB was a direct marketing company that happened to be in the publishing business, BOMC was a publishing company that used direct marketing as its primary form of advertising. The corporate cultures were entirely different, and the geographical inequality didn't help matters. Still, Chris sensed there was enough synergy between the two companies to pull this off. He went looking for "change agents" to join his army.

Once I heard that change would come through evolution, not revolution, I was sold. That's how I liked to manage. I also embraced the idea of getting in on the ground floor of something new and daring. The role of planning, buying, and analyzing all the print and direct mail advertising for the seven book clubs under the BOMC corporate umbrella was being shifted to a new media department. I was offered the job of director and told to hire my own employees. For someone as independent as me, this wasn't a bad gig.

I told Chris that I would throw myself into this job for a year or two as long as we both knew that I expected my next job to be that of a club general manager. He didn't promise me anything, but what he did say was reassuring: "Stuart, you help me now, and I'll certainly take care of you down the road."

I believed Chris, but I didn't commit to the job that instant. Instead, I brought up the topic of Doreen. She was dying to get to New York, so I suggested a package deal. Getting her into the country would be so much easier if she had a job, too.

Chris had no obligation to accommodate Doreen, but word had already spread to him that she was cute and smart. That combination always got a man's attention at TLB. All she needed at the time was a "bare bones" J-1 Visa, the type issued to au pairs, nannies, exchange students, and business interns. It could be obtained at the click of a finger from someone in the human resources department at Time Inc.

Both Chris and Jim worked their New York connections, and Doreen landed a job right away at a new *People Magazine* spinoff scheduled to launch in early 1990. Many thought the new *Entertainment Weekly* would be short-lived. The failed launch of information-packed *TV Cable Week* back in 1983 still spooked a lot of rank-and-file executives. But the negative gossip didn't dissuade Doreen. Her attitude was that all she needed was to get her foot in the door at Time Inc., and the future would take care of itself. She was spot on.

I flew over in August 1989, and Doreen followed in a few weeks. I was starting a new job with a clean slate. The baton dictating my corporate future had finally been passed from Howard Bingham to Chris Linen, the son of an ex-publisher and president at Time Inc. As luck would have it, Chris was a graduate of a small, well-known New England prep school founded in 1891 with money from the estate of Benjamin Berkeley Hotchkiss, a very distant relative.

Uncovering such a potentially powerful connection was purely accidental. Chris and I were simply making small talk one day at a urinal in the BOMC office.

"Great school, all the Linen men went there," he remarked.

After we had both zipped up our pants, I thanked him for helping Doreen get the job and gave him one of those sons-of-privilege pats on the back. I then leaned in close to his ear and muttered the Hotchkiss School nickname, "Son of a Gun."

CHAPTER 10

Green Card

I SEEMED ALWAYS to be rushing into things. Moving to New York with Doreen, after the ink on my separation papers from Patty had barely dried, was no exception.

Perhaps I wanted the world to see this higher level of commitment to Doreen as a precursor to a second marriage. It was all a bit fuzzy back in 1989, except for one thing. I needed someone to love.

Unlike Patty years before, Doreen didn't need a marriage proposal in order to make the move to New York City. She'd longed for this opportunity for eight years since completing her O-levels education, the equivalent of American high school. She danced at the mere mention of a holiday to the Big Apple. When I asked her to move there, she practically turned into a ballerina.

The company put me up at the historic Algonquin Hotel in Midtown Manhattan, a convenient walking distance from Book-of-the-Month Club's offices on Lexington Avenue. The hotel was a company favorite on many fronts. Its best-known tradition was hosting the members of the Algonquin Round Table, a celebrated group of writers, critics, actors, and wits. Some of the members of the round table also served as members of BOMC's board of judges, the ones who declared the club's monthly selection.

I liked traditions, even more so after living in a venerable city like London. The hotel was such an institution that even its house cat was famous. I liked being able to come "home" after work and make myself comfortable in the Blue Bar. But my account balance at the Algonquin kept soaring, and BOMC let me know about it. It was time for me to find my own place, although I wasn't looking forward to shelling out a small fortune on New York real estate.

I began looking in earnest for a rental apartment, something comfortable enough for two. There were so many unique neighborhoods in the city. At times, I felt like it would be easier to just throw a dart at a map of the city than to try to reasonably choose.

After seeing a lot of property that was simply out of my price range, I started to focus on the Upper West Side of Manhattan. Being adjacent to my old Columbia University neighborhood of Morningside Heights, the area felt familiar. Still, being a first-time apartment hunter in New York was a dizzying experience. It required a blend of determination, luck, and payola. Building superintendents, to a large extent, are the gatekeepers to affordable apartments in livable buildings.

To expedite the search, BOMC hired a company that specialized in finding apartments. After all, time was money. I told the agent assigned to me that I wasn't going to grease anyone's palm, so she directed me to a new, mid-rise apartment building that had a set-fee structure and standard rental agreements. The Boulevard offered several impressive amenities: twenty-four-hour concierge service, a common area for kids, and a seventy-five-foot indoor swimming pool. Admittedly, it felt more like a hotel than a residence, but signing a short-term lease allowed me to get my mind off real estate and onto work.

Back in London, Doreen was winding down her affairs and waiting for her work visa. She also spent some quality time with friends and family. If any tears were shed, they were happy ones.

Her parents were her biggest supporters. They didn't lay any guilt trip on Doreen for moving so far away *and* shacking up with a new beau. Peter and Dora Murphy practically pushed their daughter out of England. As emigrants themselves, they knew that opportunity had just knocked so hard, it had ripped the door off its hinges. Doreen, a mere high school graduate, had just landed a professional-level job with a Fortune 100 company at the epicenter of the business and financial world.

My own parents strived to remain neutral. While protecting their own interests as grandparents, their continued contact with Patty served me no harm. They knew little about Doreen or her background, and I preferred to keep it that way. My mother had to know, and even empathize with, the uphill battle a woman faced in life with only a high school education. She just didn't know how to articulate her feelings. And my father had long ago stopped meddling in my affairs. He was too afraid of losing his only living son.

So I simply touted Doreen as a business phenom, which wasn't far from the truth. Her new job at *Entertainment Weekly* started a few months ahead of the magazine's launch. She was hired as a financial assistant, a surprising choice given that she had only editorial production experience. There certainly was no shortage of candidates with MBA degrees vying for an entry-level position such as this at Time Inc.

Just as everyone who vouched for her predicted, Doreen immediately excelled in her new job. Her good looks and English accent were the proverbial icing on the cake.

I worked long days at BOMC staffing my new department. I felt a sense of reward training young men and women who were passionate about their jobs and their careers. The new media department quickly earned its stripes, and my peers recognized me as a good manager. Knowing myself as the type who bores easily, I hoped my newfound state of contentment would last.

Five months after finalizing my property settlement agreement with Patty, I was issued a higher order by the Virginia court: a final decree of divorce. I was now free to remarry. This change in status manifested itself into an inescapable conclusion—engagement—so badly camouflaged we might as well have eloped to Vegas.

Always one to do things "back-asswards," I suggested to Doreen that before we made our engagement official, we first explore the real estate market. I had enough money for a down payment, and our combined income would qualify us for a mortgage. We liked the Upper West Side and, in particular, Riverside Drive, a winding and scenic north-south

thoroughfare on the extreme west side of Manhattan. Anything farther
west was a waterfront park and then the Hudson River. When one found
a suitable apartment for sale on "the Drive," it didn't pay to procrastinate.

We didn't. In a matter of days, a real gem at the corner of Riverside
Drive and 82nd Street came on the market. It was a cozy two-bedroom
apartment—the owner advertised it as a "doll's house"—tastefully refurbished with granite floors in the dining room and hallways. It offered no
views of the Hudson, but looking north from the seventh-floor living
room, one could channel Jimmy Stewart in the movie *Rear Window*.

We took the plunge and moved into our new apartment just as
Entertainment Weekly launched its first issue and partied all night long to the
beat of the Pointer Sisters and their "Wang Dang Doodle." We fit in like
the perfect couple.

Impetuous as ever, I went to the Diamond District on West 47th Street
in Midtown Manhattan to do some window shopping. Heck, it didn't cost
anything to look, and I thought I could fend off high-pressure salespeople.
Besides, after buying the apartment, the money I had left couldn't possibly
buy an engagement ring of modest size and clarity, something fitting for a
bride-to-be like Doreen who, unlike a lot of New York transplants, had yet
to develop extravagant tastes. Foolish me. Even the discounted stuff caused
sticker shock. After an hour of haggling and a visit to an appraiser, I convinced
myself that I'd gotten one hell of a deal and I parted with my money. All of it.

"Gor, yeah!" she exclaimed in sealing the deal. That's all I can
remember.

We spent the next several months looking for a minister who would
marry us in a reasonable time frame. As a divorced man, I was not allowed
to marry a practicing Catholic like Doreen in her church—unless I had my
first marriage annulled. No way was I going to have Sam reclassified as a
"bastard." Even my own Episcopal church required a second timer like me
to ask for and be granted permission. I didn't have any local church connections, but a good friend did. As the senior warden of her parish, she ran
interference with her priest and the New York bishop, and we were quickly
approved. Preparations were soon under way for our wedding.

Doreen Murphy and I were married on Saturday, September 1, 1990, at Church of the Good Shepherd in the Kips Bay neighborhood of Manhattan. It was the loveliest day possible for a wedding. New York was enjoying unusually mild and dry weather, and it was Labor Day weekend to boot—thousands of city dwellers would head to the Hamptons and other nearby beaches for the final weekend of summer. It seemed like the hundred or so people gathered for this occasion were the only ones in town.

I gave the selection of my male attendants great thought. Meaning no disrespect to my homies from the first time around, I settled on three stable and drug-free friends from different parts of my past: my Columbia classmate and Hotel Dorset roommate, who served as best man; my TLB colleague and "next-door neighbor" in Crete; and one of my old safecracker friends from Richmond and St. Christopher's.

Everyone we invited came to the wedding and the reception except for my son, Sam. His mother forbade it. She said he was too young to attend. I didn't understand why this was Patty's decision alone to make. But all too aware of her potential for wrath and recognizing as well the truth of Sam's tender age—four—I decided to back off. My father hadn't allowed me to attend Papa's wedding to Elise, when I was eight, for the very same reason.

We held the wedding reception aboard a rented yacht that sailed leisurely around the island of Manhattan. Many of Doreen's relatives had come to America for the first time to share in the event. As the Statue of Liberty came into view, the scene of our foreign guests—their heads bowed and tears in their eyes in remembrance of family members from long ago—was heartrending. Our boat came to a complete stop no more than twenty yards from the shores of Liberty Island and that iconic symbol of the American Dream. After a few moments of contemplation, prayers, and photographs, we resumed sailing, grateful for the spirit of camaraderie on board.

Our honeymoon took us to Margarita Island off the northern coast of Venezuela. We turned a stopover on the mainland into an overnight stay at Hotel Avila, the aged grande dame of Caracas hotels. Billed as a quiet oasis above the city, it was anything but. All the locals who came and went from the hotel were "packing heat" due to the high rate of crime. We couldn't wait to move on to our final destination, Isla Margarita.

Once we arrived on this Venezuelan island, we bolted by jeep for the remote north side. We had a thing for islands and jeeps, ya know. It was an extremely quiet and simple way of life, about as diametrically opposed to life in New York as one could get. We kicked back and enjoyed a romantic and restful stay. *La vida es magnífica!*

Once home, time passed more quickly again. Before we knew it, it was Christmas and the start of our first holiday party season as husband and wife. Like most couples in our situation, Doreen and I agreed to attend only our respective company parties. I felt my staff would feel less inhibited if attendance was "employees only." I was hoping people would let their hair down at the party, and I intended to partake as an equal.

The BOMC party turned into a raucous evening that lasted for hours. We started out in formal surroundings at the Rainbow Room at Rockefeller Center. Then a good number of people headed down to Bowlmor, a trendy bowling alley then located in Greenwich Village, for a few pitchers and frames. We ended the evening at the Gramercy Park watering hole Pete's Tavern, where celebrated regular O. Henry wrote *The Gift of the Magi.* Pete's wasn't meant to be our last venue. Despite being a very forgiving place, Pete's was where the liquor caught up with us. We managed to get ourselves kicked out for inappropriately loud and otherwise sloppy behavior.

On the way out of the tavern, and for no reason other than my extreme intoxication, I picked up a patron's briefcase and took it with me without breaking stride. I took the damned thing home, stared at it the next morning, and tried to put two and two together but couldn't seem to come up with four. Despite my uncertainty, I took the briefcase to work with me that morning in the hope that someone in the office who had been with me the night before could explain my seemingly obscure motives. A colleague explained that I had simply taken the briefcase as if it belonged to me. Embarrassed does not begin to describe how I felt about what I'd done. Obviously, the idiot staff member who let down his hair and couldn't handle his liquor was me!

I looked inside the briefcase and found a name and phone number. I called the owner and lied, identifying myself as a Good Samaritan who had found his briefcase outside of Pete's Tavern the night before. The gentleman was so relieved to hear this news. I offered—no, I begged—to take the briefcase to him, but he insisted on coming to me himself.

"Mr. Hotchkiss," he said to me over the phone, "this is the kindest thing that's ever happened to me in New York, and I have to thank you in some way."

Feeling even guiltier, I simply came back with, "Can you get to the old Playboy Building on Third Avenue in an hour?" BOMC had added so much staff, in addition to my department, that I was no longer working in the main building on Lexington Avenue.

When the owner showed up at my office, I noticed a number of partial heads poking out of office doorways as I presented him with the briefcase. I couldn't really blame them. The *last* thing they expected to see was me—the kleptomaniac—being hugged and adulated by his victim. In the New Year, I resolved, I would go to church more and to bars less.

January reform set in as planned. It was a good month to take in some new movies. Doreen and I attended the opening of *Green Card*, a romantic comedy about an American woman (Andie MacDowell) who enters into a marriage of convenience with a Frenchman (Gérard Depardieu) so he can obtain a green card and remain in the United States. Doreen and I laughed at the absurdity of the questions asked at an Immigration Service (INS) interview in the movie. We agreed that life could never imitate such art.

The movie served as a warm-up of sorts for our own interview with INS. We were about to take the first step for Doreen to become a permanent resident alien. After being processed, she would receive an initial "green card," valid for two years. Aside from the many documents we were asked to produce and fill out, there was a live interview with a female agent. The questioning lasted over fifteen minutes, but we kept our cool.

"Please tell me the color of your wife's toothbrush," the INS agent asked me—almost to the word the way we'd seen it asked in the movie *Green Card*.

"Blue," I replied, "with soft bristles and a rubber tip at the end for her gums."

"Do you and your wife sleep in the same bed?"

"Yes!" I answered with a wide smile on my face that I held long enough to make sure the agent saw it.

"Does your husband ever snore?" she asked Doreen.

"Yes," she replied, but I wished she could've lied to spare me the embarrassment.

Our answers affirmed that our marriage was entered into for legitimate reasons. Doreen earned her first green card. The agent then went to her computer to mark us down for a renewal appointment two years out. She found the first available date and instructed us to mark our calendars for Monday, April 5, 1993.

Somehow I sensed I had a conflict that day. I asked the agent for a new date.

"You'll get pushed out several months if you can't keep this date," she advised.

I wasn't going to challenge the Feds, so we kept the appointment. As soon as we got home, I checked my calendar. I had been right. My beloved Yankees were to open the 1993 baseball season against the Cleveland Indians that day. But the game was in Cleveland, so I wouldn't have been able to go anyway.

In fact, I thought life was grand. Doreen and I were nailing our jobs, enjoying our apartment on Riverside Drive, and making lots of new friends. I'd proven myself worthy beyond a doubt to BOMC and Chris Linen. In fact, I was going to make my case for a promotion over lunch with him the following week.

Unfortunately, the lunch wasn't just postponed, it was canceled.

Chris made a surprise announcement that week. He was leaving not only BOMC, but also Time Inc., to head up Warner Music Enterprises.

This meant his grand plan to merge TLB and BOMC under one management umbrella was finished. Those of us who had joined Chris's move to BOMC with promises of better jobs had just lost our Moses.

Jim Mercer was called in to serve as president of Book-of-the-Month Club. Ever the gentleman, Jim took me to lunch to discuss the fallout from Linen's departure. He let me know that there was considerable tension between the veteran BOMC senior managers and the old TLB interlopers like me. I didn't see that from my office on Third Avenue, but I knew Jim wouldn't bullshit me at a time like this. Presently, Jim had to cater to a whole bunch of newly vitalized BOMC "lifers" who were back in power.

As a result, my chance of a promotion in the foreseeable future just wasn't in the cards. I thanked Jim for his candor and asked for one favor: to please find a way to cash me out of the company as soon as possible. I wanted out of this dead-end situation. I was prepared to chart a new career path for myself as a marketing consultant, provided I had a little nest egg.

Consulting was not merely a pretend job to tide me over until I found a real one.

I had two goals in mind. First, I wanted to pursue clients in industries outside of publishing to expand my horizons. Perhaps, I thought, I could take another shot at L.L. Bean or another big player in the mail order industry. Second, I knew from my media experience that direct mail list brokers—the ones who facilitate the rental of names and addresses of prospective customers to countless direct marketing companies—made a lot of money when they landed a couple of big, as in Book-of-the-Month-Club big, clients. I wasn't a natural-born salesman, but I thought of auditioning for the part while I was still relatively young—and connected to media buyers at BOMC.

I assured Doreen my "gamble" would pay off, promising her that no matter what, I'd continue to contribute the same amount of money each month toward the household expenses. She thought I was nuts, but she couldn't offer any sound reasons for me to not go for it, particularly since her lifestyle would not suffer. Besides, I'd always listened more to my own inner voice than to those of others. I wasn't looking for her permission.

Everything came together nicely. In less than two months, Jim Mercer called to let me know that my ship had come in. He'd gotten the company to agree to eliminate my job. It was very clever, and generous, on Jim's part. My severance package would include six months of salary and cash for unused vacation. I couldn't have been happier.

I made my first pitch for business to direct mail veteran Bob Castle, part owner of a list brokerage and management company called Uni-Mail. A New Yorker to the core, Bob had grown up in the Bronx. He was Mensa smart, and his passions were many. Two of them—baseball and statistics—intersected with mine. It was obvious that Bob was an old industry hand worth getting to know, so I asked him out on a date.

After sizing me up, Bob offered to hire me as both a retained consultant and commissioned list broker. On the brokerage side, he wanted me to focus only on landing BOMC as a new client, no others. I argued that we should aim higher.

"Stuart, my boy," Bob asked, "do you have chutzpah?"

"What's chutzpah?" I asked. Waspy guys weren't supposed to know.

Bob laughed his ass off. His point was both made and taken. I would have been chewed up and spit out by the competition as a rank-and-file list broker in New York.

However, the role of consultant was tailor-made for me. Bob was stuck trying to develop a proprietary software application to attract new business. Another consultant, David Hoffman, who'd worked with Bob for years, had the technical knowledge. Bob had never worked client side, so he struggled with the design of the user interface. Hiring me to partner with David hit Bob like a ton of bricks. I was paid to devote two days a week to this project and nothing else.

For six months or so, Bob and I saw eye to eye. But at some later point, a power struggle ensued. Always cost conscious and mass-audience driven, Bob wanted a shrink-wrapped, one-size-fits-all application that every direct mailer in the country could use right out of the box.

"Impossible," I argued, but he bristled at my pushback.

If Bob wanted to establish credibility with the top industry players, it was in his best interest to heed his consultant. I wasn't trying to one-up Bob; rather, I was trying to make him look smart. Every company had a unique way of doing things, especially the data they stored and analyzed and the terminology they used. How could Bob possibly argue with a guy trying to protect his company's image?

I'd find out soon enough at an extremely important demonstration for catalog retailer Fingerhut at their headquarters outside of Minneapolis, Minnesota. Then a giant in the mail order industry, Fingerhut sold modest, everyday merchandise to millions of middle-class Americans. But their direct marketing acumen was off the charts. For us to have a chance of installing our software at Fingerhut, we'd have to pull out all the stops.

David and I met Bob for breakfast in our Minneapolis hotel the morning of the presentation. We had already tweaked the demo version with some proprietary Fingerhut terms that I had gleaned from a company executive in advance. Regrettably, Bob still couldn't think beyond the one-size-fits-all approach. He went ballistic when I told him what we'd done and told us to "strip it out" before the meeting.

Right there in the restaurant, Bob and I went at it. I had plenty of chutzpah that morning. I wouldn't give an inch.

"Bob, I'm not going to jeopardize your integrity or mine by going in with some watered-down presentation for a company as sophisticated as Fingerhut," I shouted. "Right, David?" I looked at my codeveloper for moral support.

David wisely kept eating his bagel. He couldn't afford to lose Bob as a client. I rested my own case and swore to Bob that after this demo, I was done.

To please the boss, we stripped out the meat of the demo in the hour or so before show time and gave the presentation Bob's way. Fingerhut gave us, as I expected, a very ho-hum reaction. After we finished, Bob and I agreed to discuss matters back in New York where cooler heads might prevail. David and I killed the afternoon at the Mall of America in nearby

Bloomington, riding the indoor roller coaster and getting legless in the upper-level sports bar before heading home.

Waiting a few days before sitting down with Bob didn't change either my opinion or my hotheadedness. I told this man—the client who was singlehandedly keeping my consulting business alive—that I couldn't work with him anymore.

Ever the professional, he said to me, "That's fine, Stuart. No hard feelings, and I want you to know that I'm still willing to pay you brokerage commissions should we land the BOMC account."

Defiant—and idiotic—I told him he could keep his money. *After all*, I thought, *he'll never land the account without me.* I nearly guaranteed his failure by calling some of my contacts at BOMC and ratting out Bob. Sharing details of our estrangement was grossly unprofessional and only made me look like the fool.

I'd probably just pissed away a sizeable chunk of income when Doreen decided she wanted to spend some money on new decorations. She raved about some funky cowboy artwork by a new artist she'd discovered at a local restaurant. She wanted to buy all three paintings on display and make them the centerpiece of our living room. It was hard to say no to something she was so passionate about, so I agreed to spend money I didn't have on something I didn't like—which set up a bad precedent, as it turned out.

Once Doreen realized how much she liked the new artwork in the living room, she was motivated to redecorate the entire apartment. Most of the furniture in our home had a distinctly colonial, Hotchkiss look—recycled in large part from my first marriage. Updating the apartment with a nod to Doreen made infinite sense, but the timing stunk. We had nothing left in the way of savings. Foolish me, I gave in and became a pretended convert to man-made materials.

Last, but certainly not least, Doreen constantly pushed for a new puppy. Since I had Sam, she wanted us to have our own living thing, but not a baby. Not for some time, anyway—a feeling I heartily seconded. Outside of Manhattan, I would have been delighted to get a dog. Losing Annie had left a hole in my life. But raising a puppy in a New York apartment required a big commitment from both parties. The initial year or so of housebreaking and the requisite three or four walks each day required one of us to be close to home at all times.

I was looking for work and needed flexibility. Some of the more lucrative consulting gigs would require overnight travel. I also found myself on a train to Washington, DC, once a month to visit with Sam. Doreen's job, although devoid of travel, could easily require twelve hours a day. It was a delicate subject, to say the least. Most couples likely struggled less over the decision to have children.

I was able to put off the decision—for now—but it was going to keep coming up.

One thing I couldn't skimp on or ignore was the celebration of Doreen's thirtieth birthday on April 6, 1993. I was certain a clever and "large" celebration would make my deserving wife feel quite special. Doreen downplayed the event—how English—and gave me no clues about how she might want her big day planned. All I got was the usual "I'd prefer that we not do anything" line. Given the number of times she responded that way, I should have seen the writing on the wall.

Don't listen to her, I thought. Having been surprised at that age myself, I chose to ignore the soon-to-be tricenarian's wishes and forge ahead.

I struggled to come up with a shocker. There was no point in doing something this big half-ass. Doreen's mother and sister over in England were lacking in ideas. Her colleagues and friends in New York came back to me empty-handed as well. I was prepared to ditch the whole surprise thing and take Doreen over to England for her birthday, but the business of producing *TIME Magazine,* her new and bigger job, got in the way.

Her mother and sister, along with her sister's two children, did come to New York for a short, prebirthday visit that March. As it turned out, the focus wasn't on Doreen. Her sister was going through some major marital problems, and the three women had a lot of catching up to do. Our apartment became a place full of sad conversations.

From the little I heard, I felt like a star compared to the philandering hubby.

I was left to my own devices as far as Doreen's birthday surprise. Media planners use a term called "reach" to set their objective for the total number of people exposed to a campaign. "Why shouldn't I find a way to let as many people as possible find out about her birthday?" I pondered.

The paper edition of the *New York Times* sold two or three lines of advertising space on the bottom of its front page. Most of the ads were personal, celebrating birthdays, anniversaries, Bar and Bat Mitzvahs, and similar occasions. A typical ad read, "Love to dear Katie on her 21st Birthday from Mom and Dad." Seldom, if ever, was a last name included and never was there any description of where the person lived or worked.

I called the newspaper's advertising department and explained that I was interested in using this space to help broadcast Doreen's birthday: "My wife is turning thirty years old, and she hasn't given me a clue what she wants," I explained. "I'd love for her friends and colleagues to call her on her birthday."

I happened to be preaching to the choir; the ad rep had just turned thirty herself and thought my idea was terrific. "In fact," she said, "make it sound like she's in a funk about her birthday."

I quickly cobbled the following ad copy and read it to the rep: "Doreen Murphy turns 30 today, and she is very sad. Please call 212-522-XXXX to offer her comfort."

The rep sent it in for review. Within hours, I received two separate calls from the *NYT* copy police asking if I had Time Inc.'s and my wife's permission to use her office phone number. They took the matter of privacy seriously, but not seriously enough. I told every color of lie and said that I *had* obtained permission, so my ad copy was published verbatim and with a real phone number. Eight million people or so could now dial straight into Doreen's voice mail.

By the time Doreen got to work that morning, her mailbox was already stuffed. By the time the day ended, she'd received hundreds of live calls and messages from around the country. Many more greetings would've gotten through if she'd had time to continually empty her mailbox. The majority of the calls were from strangers, and many went into great detail about how they got past their own "Big 3-0" moments. Trading was suspended on the floor of the Philadelphia Stock Exchange as a large chorus of money lords sang "Happy Birthday" to her over the phone. Even her boss at *Time* got into the spirit of things by attaching an enlarged copy of the ad to his tie.

To put it mildly, Doreen did not appreciate my humor, not even one iota. Anyone who knew her and saw or heard about the ad thought that it was wonderfully clever, but they didn't have to live with her. She was boiling mad when she got home that Tuesday evening and refused to even talk to me.

Just the day before, Doreen had been much happier. We'd gone down to the INS building for our green card renewal appointment, the one that had been scheduled two years earlier. We sat in front of the agent, holding hands the entire time. I was relieved to feel warmth in Doreen's hand despite the uncertainty of the questions we'd be asked or the agent's decision.

Unlike the previous agent, this new one cut to the chase. She wanted to hear the love in Doreen's voice. "Are you here today merely to have me renew your green card?" she asked bluntly.

"Not at all," Doreen answered. "I love my husband very much, and we're very happily married." She said it with such passion, it made both the agent and me blush.

The interview concluded with best wishes from the agent. Doreen's green card was now encased in platinum. There would not be another interview for ten years, by which time Doreen might well have applied for citizenship.

We didn't go out that evening or the night of her birthday, either. But we did have a dinner reservation for Wednesday night, and I had planned a double celebration of her expanded alien residence and thirtieth birthday. The ad in the paper almost knocked the whole evening on its head, but not quite.

Doreen never intended to miss this date. She had her own agenda, I realized later. I ordered what I expected to be the first of many rounds of drinks and, when it arrived, I was ready to deliver my toast.

Just as I was opening my mouth, Doreen blurted out, "Please don't take this personally, but I don't want to be married anymore."

As I heard these words, I was raising a mojito cocktail to my lips. It became hard for me to hold it at that moment because my fingers started to sweat more than the dewy, ice-filled glass. I continued on and took a long sip to stall for time and gather my thoughts. Normally this blend of rum, sugar, and lime was a pleasing experience.

"You what?" I exclaimed as the taste of my fancy-pants cocktail turned sour.

"You 'eard," she snapped back in cockney brogue.

She doesn't want to be *married*? Was I hearing her right? Don't take this *personally*? I was a faithful and committed husband—how could I take it any way *but* personally? Someone must have spiked my drink. I released my grip on the cocktail glass before it slipped out of my hand, and I asked her, "Is it another man?"

"No, it's not that," she answered.

"Is it another woman?" I asked next.

This question wasn't meant to be cruel, but I didn't know what was going on. In my dazed state, I was grasping at straws.

"Don't be a pillock," she hissed.

I asked her if the ad in the *Times* was the tipping point.

"It pissed me off, as you well know. But it's not that, either."

I could've continued on with a list of questions like these, but it seemed pointless. I was certain all of her answers would remain the same. I was trying to absorb the news, but nothing was making any sense.

I then leaped upon her family's recent visit in March. I had a hunch that her sister's problems in her marriage were being visited upon ours.

"Actually," Doreen answered, "my sister and my mother are two of your biggest supporters. They actually argued with me to stay in the marriage."

Whether there was some justifiable reason or not for Doreen's decision, this last answer clarified one thing: she'd been contemplating leaving me for at least a month or more. And *after* we purged most memories of

Patty from the apartment, which left me even more perplexed. Why was she being so capricious? And why with me? Why now? I wanted to bend light somehow and become invisible, but I couldn't.

Hey, I wasn't perfect, and I could rattle off a dozen things about me that I'm certain annoyed her. But were any of those things deal breakers? I didn't think so.

The most upsetting and humbling consequence of getting dumped was becoming a two-time loser in marriage. I took great pride *this time* in getting my shit together as Doreen's husband. I had eyes only for her. I balanced my life between Sam and her as best as I could. I was fond of and enjoyed being with her parents. Things were pretty wonderful for two years and change. Where had I gone wrong?

My heart and mind didn't want to go to the issue of the green card, but how could it not? Had she been in love with me on September 1, 1990? I'd certainly thought so, but now I couldn't be sure. Was our whole marriage a scam? Clearly, Doreen timed our visit to INS two days earlier perfectly. Thanks to me, she now had legal permission to remain in the United States for another ten years!

It seemed a bit churlish to contact INS and report her. But, yes, I did compose one, two, maybe three letters to the agency, all left on my hard drive for a day's reflection, all dragged into the trash and never printed and mailed. Mindful of Patty's earlier letter to Time Inc., I wouldn't—no, I couldn't—stoop to that vindictive level.

As timed passed, we had a few more fruitless discussions. She never veered from her position and became emotionally unavailable. I simply had to accept that Doreen wanted to move on. By the weekend, I was sound enough to say to her, "I can't force you to stay, so if you want out, just take what's yours and go."

As Shakespeare put it, "Ay, there's the rub." My definition of what was hers and Doreen's definition of what was hers were two diametrically opposite points of view. Frankly, I'd done most of the heavy financial lifting to buy and maintain our only true joint asset—the apartment. Equitable distribution in New York would leave Doreen with peanuts. And why wouldn't she be more of a giver than a taker anyway? She's the one who wanted out of the marriage. A two-year marriage, I hasten to add.

When all was said and done, what Doreen demanded—more than half the equity in our New York apartment—simply wasn't gonna happen. Not this divorce.

CHAPTER 11

Two-Timer

I COULD NOT figure why Doreen had chosen to dig her heels in and refuse to be reasonable. Yes, she knew I'd been far too generous in my first divorce and was a bit of a negotiation patsy. But by now she wanted 70 percent of the equity in the apartment!

Where did she come up with a figure like that? I wondered as I prepared myself for a cold war. I couldn't shrug the sense of foreboding away.

And she didn't let up. Doreen rushed to purchase a puppy she'd always wanted, a pure male Weimaraner, whom she named Wedgie. He was cute, I admit, but a handful. Doreen trotted off to work and left the high-strung animal in a crate all day. Soon into this ritual, when I was trying to work from home, I heard little Wedgie yelping inside his cage. When I checked to see what was wrong, I found him flailing around inside the crate with his mouth stuck on a wire of the door. I pried him loose, accepted some wet licks of gratitude, and all was well.

But I was so disturbed and angry about what happened that I called Doreen at work and had her pulled out of a meeting. I was now the one doing the barking. I told her that if I hadn't heard such a commotion, he could've hung himself to death. She dismissed this as sheer nonsense and said I was "mentally disturbed" for calling. The next call, I told her, would be to the ASPCA.

Not long after, Wedgie became seriously ill from an unknown weakness in his immune system. One day I found him lying, lifeless, in his crate. When I opened the door and picked him up, I was grateful and astonished to find him warm. I could feel him breathing and his heart softly beating through his nearly motionless chest. I kissed him and cuddled him and ran with him in my arms down to the street, into a cab, and off to the neighborhood vet.

They kept him overnight for tests and observation, and then delivered the news—he should be put down. Doreen never actually said as much, but I always felt she thought I willed this to happen. Nothing could have been further from the truth, and I thought that my actions in trying to save Wedgie deserved at least a thank you.

As we argued over the apartment, I realized that we needed to start living separate and apart before one of us killed the other. I was also looking for greater job stability, since my marriage was coming unhinged. I sent an SOS to my current roster of clients and anyone else willing to help, hoping to network my way into a real job.

One of those clients, Rodale Press, was a private, family-owned book and magazine publisher located in Emmaus, Pennsylvania. They had an impressive array of titles, like *Prevention* and *Men's Health*, and a well-respected direct marketing operation. They responded quickly to my inquiry. So quickly, in fact, that they were my first—and only—interview. Rodale's ranks were almost entirely homegrown. The company had a devil of a time persuading anyone from a big city like New York to consider moving to their corporate campus in the bucolic pastures of Lehigh Valley.

Rodale talked specifically about my joining them as a marketing director in their book division. With my international experience, executive education, and big-city background, I was viewed as the proverbial change agent they needed. Anthony Russo, president of the division, made it clear to me that should I join his team, the expectations of my performance would be quite high. I thrived on that sort of pressure. I was expected to bring new ideas and be a leader. It took only this one meeting for Russo to ask me for references. I took that as a sign of a looming job offer.

I suggested Russo contact Chris Linen and John Fahey. He knew them both personally.

"How about one more person?" Russo inquired. "Someone who directly managed you."

We both knew who that someone was. It was a small industry. *What the hell?* I thought. I gave him permission to contact my old nemesis, Howard Bingham.

Within a few days Russo called me and invited me back to Emmaus. That seemed a bit odd. While Chris and John had given me glowing references, it turned out that Howard Bingham had slammed me. Russo now wanted to hear my side of the story—face to face. I was honest with him and told him that Bingham and I had a checkered history. It concerned Russo enough that he held off on his offer. I suggested that he speak with Jim Mercer, who might shed some light on Bingham's remarks. Somehow, Jim cleared the air, and Rodale made me an offer. I accepted, but it worried me that Russo had so much respect for my former boss. The last thing I wanted was to work for a Howard Bingham disciple.

Even though it was paramount to try and settle matters with Doreen before leaving for Pennsylvania, we still couldn't come to terms. I hired a real shark of an attorney to try to dynamite her out of the apartment. He was no match for Doreen. After burning through my initial retainer and spending over a month trying to get me a decent offer, he surrendered and quit.

I was still co-owner of the apartment and its mortgage, but living in rented accommodation—a bed-and-breakfast called Fogelhaus—on the side of a small mountain near Rodale's headquarters. Doreen continued to live—quite happily—in our apartment by herself. Stubbornly, once I started paying rent for a place to live in Pennsylvania, I stopped paying my share of the New York mortgage. Upon learning this, Doreen stopped paying her share as well. While we both knew this could lead to foreclosure and credit suicide, neither of us blinked.

Although Anthony Russo had hired me, I actually reported directly to another supervisor. It was an arrangement that Russo wanted for the short term, and frankly, I liked the man—a great person in every regard—assigned to manage me. I had already learned quite a bit about how Rodale operated from him when I was a consultant. A month into the job, new boss man Aidan Flaherty took me out for a beer after work to tell me how well I was doing and to encourage me to keep bringing new ideas to the table.

The very next day, Russo asked me to his office. I honestly expected him to mimic Aidan's comments; instead, he used this opportunity to essentially reprimand me. He told me to start doing things the Rodale way. That was the way to become successful in my job. He made it very clear that I was being way too independent in my actions.

I was confused. I thought that I'd been courted, and paid a premium, to be that dynamic, cosmopolitan, out-of-the-box thinker that comes to Rodale only once in a lifetime. Yet I was being told, in no uncertain terms, that I had to learn to play by their rules and no others. Whose rules were they anyway? I wasn't vying for Russo's job. All I wanted to do was help make the company's bottom line grow and the people around me feel valued. I didn't respect Russo's "shepherd and flock" approach to managing either, so I ignored his admonition and continued my ways.

Before I barely had a chance to unpack my suitcases, I went from feeling adored to feeling trapped at Rodale. Job-hopping wasn't common, or wise, in those days. Besides, there were only a handful of companies in the mail order book business and very few personnel secrets.

One of these companies, however, was Time Inc. In 1992, they decided to relaunch a book business that had failed under Oxmoor House, a sister company located in Birmingham, Alabama. *They must be staffing up*, I thought. It certainly wouldn't cost anything to investigate them.

The head of the new venture, called Time Inc. Home Entertainment (TIHE), was a wunderkind and former *TIME Magazine* circulation director named Dan Gitman. I'd previously interviewed with Dan for a renewals manager job at *TIME* before leaving BOMC. Although he hadn't hired me then, I must have made a good impression on him. When I called Dan to let him know that I was at Rodale, he made time for me.

Furthermore, we agreed to sit down later in person and share "best practices." The content of the two companies didn't overlap, nor did our current or prospective customers. In other words, we weren't direct competitors, and we couldn't be accused of giving away company secrets. So Dan and I expected to meet sometime in December, once I returned from a two-week vacation to the Patagonia region in South America. I'd booked this trip before being hired, and Russo had agreed, although quite reluctantly, to the time off when I accepted his job offer.

I couldn't get away from Rodale fast enough. I expected to get two things out of this trip: breathtaking views of what many travelers considered the most striking scenery on the planet and a little self-indulgent nookie. I was suffering from a bad case of DSB—deadly sperm backup—and needed a cure.

My first stop was Buenos Aires, Argentina, for a bit of Parisian-like dining and people watching. I was impressed by the number of bookstores and by how many streets were named for writers. But I was awestruck by the vast affluence adjacent the even higher amount of poverty. While I thought poverty in the United States was disgraceful, it was far from what existed in Argentina. Inflation was out of control. The majority of the population was lower class. There were only two social classes, upper and lower; the middle one had vanished.

A common tourist like me could enjoy a five-star meal for less than ten dollars. I traveled outside of the city by *colectivo* (bus) to experience this for myself. I dined on Argentinean *asado* (barbecue) cooked on an outdoor *parrilla* (grill), paired with a "jammy" Malbec wine at one of the many outdoor restaurants in the surrounding suburbs. Each night, I was invited to join groups of complete strangers at their tables—no one eats alone in Buenos Aires.

My next stop was the Swiss-inspired ski resort city of Bariloche. It didn't bother me that I was visiting during the off-season. I felt quite refreshed and distanced from the fifteen million people and the sweltering late spring heat of the greater Buenos Aires conurbation. Bariloche was making headlines in the international press after it was reported that Nazi war criminals had been hiding out there since the war ended. I ignored all the hoopla because I was on vacation and trying to meet beautiful young women, not old Nazi geezers. No such luck.

From Bariloche, I rode on ferries and motor coaches across the majestic lake districts of Argentina and Chile. We crossed many different lakes, and it took a lot of effort getting up, down, and all around in one day. I wasn't complaining. The landscape was dotted with beautiful lakes, captivating glaciers, freshwater rivers, impressive waterfalls, lush forests, thermal hot springs, and dormant volcanoes. There was so much to behold I suffered a case of sensory overload. I crashed from sheer exhaustion that night in the Chilean port city of Puerto Montt.

I'd purchased what was called an open-jaw ticket and would be flying home from Santiago, rather than Buenos Aires. I had a couple of days left to get to the Chilean capital and several options from which to choose. The only mode of transportation I *hadn't* used up to this point on my trip was rail, so I went to the train station in Puerto Montt to inquire about schedules and prices. When I got to the ticket counter, I found three other travelers queued up for the trip to Santiago. They all spoke English and kindly invited me to join them, so I bought a ticket and climbed on board. The service was known as *El Rápido del Sud* ("Southern Express") but these seasoned travelers warned me that the trip—a distance of only 569 miles—would take a full day. Didn't bother me at all. What good is vacation if you have to rush?

I had no idea a train could move so slowly. I doubt it ever topped forty-five miles per hour. We stopped along the way to drop off and pick up everything from mail to milk to migrants. To pass the time, my new friends led me to the café car and introduced me to the local cerveza. Paying eighty cents a bottle, the four of us—two Bavarians, a Californian, and a New Yorker—cleaned out the barman.

We stepped off the train in Santiago completely blitzed. It was midday, and I needed both a nap and a place to stay for the evening. I stumbled upon a cheap and cheerful hotel just off Avenida Libertador General Bernardo O'Higgins, a large boulevard in downtown Santiago and arguably the longest street name in South America. O'Higgins was a Chilean independence leader of Irish and Basque descent. His name was plastered everywhere, and it reinforced the feeling one gets in Santiago of being surrounded more by Europeans than by traditional South Americans.

After checking into my room and taking a long siesta, I ventured out for drinks and a bite to eat. A quaint and informal self-service restaurant on O'Higgins caught my attention. It had a good-size crowd that skewed young and female. I chose a table next to two cute, young women who smiled back at me when they realized I was undressing them with my eyes. Yes, they were young—no more than college age, if that. They oozed sex appeal and carnality and made me forget how old I was. We used smiles and giggles as our lingua franca and somehow managed to keep one another entertained.

A few local studs found their way to our table. They knew my cuties and acted as if their presence had been expected. After we all drank a few Pisco Sours—a South American cocktail made with a liquor distilled from grapes—I was invited to join the group and head to a party at someone's apartment.

Once there, one of the women, Xaviera, paired up right away with the guy who must have been her boyfriend. The other woman, Catalina, floated for a while and eventually ended up in my corner, or I should say, on my lap? After a few more Pisco Sours and some serious smooching, Catalina and I were out of there and back to my hotel. I never knew a woman could be so sexy. She showed me sexual positions I hadn't known existed. By the time she was done with me the next morning, I *had* to go home. My one good testicle was in circulatory shock.

When I returned to the real world, I knew immediately that living in the woods just outside the depressed, blue-collar town of Allentown—yes, Billy Joel's Allentown—was not for me. Furthermore, the winter blues had just set upon us. I would never be able to call a place like this home. I craved big-city life.

I reconnected with Dan Gitman at TIHE. He was still eager to meet, and I *insisted* that I go to New York. Russo never liked for his key staff members to leave campus without a stated purpose, but I had a unique situation with my apartment and Doreen and, therefore, a dynamite alibi.

I asked Dan to keep our meeting confidential. Well aware—and fearful—by now of Russo's management style, I was damn sure that if he found out I was talking with Time Inc., there'd be hell to pay.

Dan invited his operations manager to our meeting. Monica had worked with Dan previously at *TIME Magazine* and was the glue of his current business. The three of us talked freely and shared a lot of useful information. So useful, in fact, that the two companies should have explored a mutually beneficial marketing partnership. But I was not going to be the one to suggest that to Russo or Flaherty.

Monica and I promised to pull together some additional information and become the respective point people for ongoing conversations. We all liked the idea of meeting again on a regular basis, perhaps once a quarter. In an effort to rotate venues, Dan and Monica volunteered to come to the Lehigh Valley in the first quarter of 1994 for our next meeting.

The winter of 1993–1994 came roaring into the Lehigh Valley. Constant snowfall created hazardous, barely navigable roadways. Added to this mix were unseasonably cold temperatures. Rodale workers who lived far away from Emmaus had to make an effort to commute to the office, even when it became dangerous to do so. If they didn't show up for work, they were charged personal days. No excuses.

The week before Christmas, a jolly good vendor invited several of my colleagues and me to dinner for the holidays. Since an invitation like that was rare, the forecasted blizzard that evening didn't stop us from attending. We all had a splendid time and drank way too much. When we left the restaurant around one o'clock in the morning, the roads were slick, and new snow was in the air. I didn't think I was that bombed and felt safe driving home.

I had purchased a new Honda Accord when I moved to the Lehigh Valley. I ambled along a main road at a safe speed and a good distance behind the car in front of me. It slowed as we approached an intersection with a traffic light at the bottom of a hill. I tried to as well, but my brakes wouldn't hold. I hit a patch of ice and slid into the oncoming traffic lane as I headed down the hill. There was no way to slow down or steer out of harm's way. I flashed my headlights at the oncoming driver as he passed through the intersection and began his ascent up the hill. We were doing about twenty-five miles per hour and crashed head on.

My airbag deployed, but without any air. I hit my head on the visor but, thank goodness, not on the windshield. After my car came to a stop, I sat dazed and looked down at the droopy airbag covering my frontal area. After I regained my focus, I immediately got out of my car to go check on the condition of the other driver. He was already out of his car and standing tall. I apologized profusely. I knew that insurance companies warned their policyholders to never admit guilt, but for Christ's sake, I hit the poor guy head on in his own lane of traffic!

It was snowing quite heavily by now. A cop arrived shortly and took statements from both parties. He didn't stay long as the moisture made it impossible for him to write a detailed report on paper. He told us to go back to our cars and sit tight. Tow trucks were on their way.

When my guy arrived, he asked me where I lived. As soon as I told him, he shook his head and started to laugh. "Buddy, that's clear on the other side of South Mountain. I can barely get you to the base of it in this weather."

The Rodale parking lot was very close to the base, so that's where the man took my car and me. The only way forward was to walk—three miles up and over the mountain, through two feet of accumulated snow, in street shoes, with a fuzzy mind. Maybe I should have slept on the floor of my office rather than walk to Fogelhaus, but I didn't want to draw any attention to myself at work the next morning. So I trudged home. Two hours later, I got out of my soaking-wet clothes and slept for a few hours.

I got up at my usual morning hour and repeated my steps back over the mountain to Rodale. I had on proper footwear, but I didn't feel well at all. I saw little white spots whenever I closed my eyes. I had a ringing noise in my left ear. There was a painful and swollen bump on my forehead. The fresh air didn't cure what ailed me. I arrived at the office dazed and disoriented, and I prayed that someone would show up soon to help me.

Lo and behold, one of my three assistants arrived at his office just a few minutes later. He took one look at me and knew immediately something was wrong. He escorted me to his car and buckled me into the passenger seat. We drove to the emergency department at St. Luke's Hospital in Allentown. There, the medical staff determined that I had suffered a concussion in the accident.

"Mr. Hotchkiss, did you sleep last night?" the doctor asked me.

I replied that I had slept, but only for a few hours. I thought my *lack* of sleep was his concern. He lectured me, saying that people with head injuries can fall into a coma if they fall asleep after severe head trauma. After hours of tests, I was released from the hospital. Bed rest, fluids, a mild pain reliever, and ice to the bump on my forehead were the only things prescribed, so I was relieved that the damage was minimal.

I was back at work the next morning. It took only a few days to get back to full speed. Russo never asked how I was doing, but he was sure keeping score. On the payday after my accident, I looked at my check and noticed that the gross and net amounts were lower than usual. I went to the payroll department for an explanation. They told me to check with Russo's executive assistant, who was responsible for submitting timesheets. She did some research and reported back to me that I had been docked a day's pay for missing work. What hypocrisy! The fact that the publisher of *Prevention*—and all that mantra about work-life balance—could toss aside a traumatic injury like this seemed so capricious to me. I marched right into Russo's office.

"Are you shitting me?" I asked. "I was in the emergency room being treated for a concussion, and you docked me a day's pay?"

President Russo was completely unmoved and didn't say a word.

"This is barbaric," I said full of frustration and anger. "I won't stand for it."

The gloves were off. I helped myself to a seat in his office and started to recite my own "ten commandments." Among other things, I told Russo that I needed the freedom to act as a change agent. I suggested that I report directly to him. I asked for a higher salary. And, for good measure, I told him I wanted to spend less time in the Lehigh Valley. I hated it there. Indeed, I was so rattled, I kept referring to it as "Happy Valley," a colloquialism for the Penn State College area.

Russo took all of this in but didn't show his hand. He promised to get back to me, and in less than two days, he did. He was standing his ground. He would make no changes. I let him know that I wanted out. I told him that I would not actively look for another job until I'd been at Rodale a full year, presuming he wanted me to stick around. He did. He'd paid a premium—in the form of a five-figure hiring bonus—to get me to Rodale, and he wanted his money's worth.

Soon after my meeting with Russo, my assistant—the one who drove me to the hospital—confided in me that I was being "investigated." He had just been grilled by Russo, Flaherty, and a member of human resources for details about the night of the Christmas dinner.

He shared some of their questions: "How much did he drink?" "What kind of shape was he in when he left the restaurant?" "Were drugs involved?" He hated being put in the middle, but he was a loyal dude, not a member of the flock.

Someone at Rodale was scared shitless. They were either out to cover their asses legally or smear my name. I was now stuck in two bad marriages at the same time.

A week or so after my conversation with Russo, I received a phone message from Dan Gitman asking me to get back to him. I presumed he was calling to lock in a date for our next meeting in Emmaus. It seemed a little strange that Monica—who was supposed to be my point person—hadn't called, but I didn't read too much into it.

I called Dan back and, after a minute or two of pleasantries, he got down to business. He wasn't calling about the next meeting at all. He was feeling me out to see if I was interested in going to work for him at Time Inc. He conceded that since I'd just started working at Rodale, it was unlikely that I'd want to uproot myself so soon.

Little did he know! I wisely kept things very close to the vest and played hard to get, but I listened to him with the renewed hope of a man thirsting in the desert who sees an oasis before him. I hoped that what I was hearing wasn't a mirage.

Dan couldn't have built the infrastructure he had in place at TIHE without a trusted operations lieutenant like Monica. Now he needed someone with her talents who could focus on marketing and new product development. Timing is everything. I couldn't convince Gitman before I left BOMC to hire me, even though I had over a decade of direct marketing experience. But right now, after a mere five months of almost identical experience at Rodale, I was a prized recruit.

I went to New York to interview with Gitman's boss. If she liked me, then I knew he'd make a formal job offer. My car accident had left me with neck spasms that flared up under stress. During the interview, I was nervous as hell and had trouble speaking. It was not the best way to try and impress a Time Inc. executive. I felt as though I'd come across as some sort of freak, and I certainly thought I'd failed the audition.

Thankfully, I was wrong. Gitman's boss had even persuaded him to offer me a more lucrative compensation package than the one he had ballparked earlier. To top it off, he threw in relocation expenses back to New York, despite the fact that I already co-owned an apartment there. Throwing that extra money at Doreen was the first thing that came to mind.

I feared that my resignation from Rodale would be sticky, so I asked Gitman for three or four weeks to make the transition back to Time Inc.

"Give them two weeks' notice," Dan pleaded. "I need you to start right away."

I offered to try, but I also wanted to preserve any last ounce of reputation I had with Rodale. It was a Friday, and I went immediately to Aidan to share the news. I made it clear to him that Time Inc. had come after me, not the other way around. I hadn't broken my earlier promise to Russo. We agreed that three weeks' notice would be a good compromise. Gitman could certainly wait an extra week, I figured. As always, Aidan was understanding and professional and offered to broach the subject with Russo over the weekend so my own conversation with him—hopefully, first thing Monday morning—wouldn't come as a shock.

I rehearsed my resignation speech several times before arriving at my office early on Monday morning. I planned to take some time to get settled before heading over to Russo's office. When I got my keys out to unlock the office door, I noticed that it was ajar. I couldn't see anything inside the office at this point, but I sensed something was much amiss. When I opened the door wide, I saw Russo sitting in my chair at my desk. I thought I was dreaming.

"Have a seat," the president said, pointing to the visitor's seat.

I followed orders—which he loved—and sat down. Russo obviously wanted control, and for once, I let him have it. That's how a lame duck acts.

"Aidan and I met over the weekend. Have you reconsidered your decision to resign?" he queried.

I told him I hadn't. I went off script a bit, but I essentially repeated everything I had told Aidan on Friday. While I didn't make my resignation personally, I can't say the same for Russo. He pointed to several empty boxes he'd brought with him and told me to start packing my shit.

"I'm going to sit here and watch until you are finished. And don't take any longer than thirty minutes."

He sat and patiently scanned each item as I removed it from my desk drawer or shelf and placed it into a box, hoping, of course, that he might witness me trying to steal company property. I very calmly continued my packing without saying a word. Knowing myself as I do, I was surprised that a cascading anger didn't well up inside of me. But I was getting what I wanted and heading back to New York, so why rub it in?

As I was packing, Russo proclaimed, "This is the first time I've ever had to do something like this."

I later learned from other Rodale employees that I was merely part of a long list of "tossed outs." Russo took great umbrage when anyone resigned on his watch.

As I was being unceremoniously shown the door, I let Russo know that I'd walked to work that morning and needed to retrieve my car and come back to collect my boxes. He was so eager to get me out of there, he actually helped load my boxes into his pickup truck and drove me back to Fogelhaus. Silence saturated the ride as we drove up and over

South Mountain. After unloading the truck, I couldn't resist one parting shot. I reminded Russo that since I'd formally resigned, he still owed me two weeks of pay whether he allowed me to work them or not. His eyes narrowed with anger. I was worried his pride would rupture. Through a cutting smile, he told me, "You won't receive another dime from this company."

Still holding one of my boxes, I calmly replied, "You'll lose that fight. It's company policy."

His smile disappeared. Far too many times, he'd thrown some manner of these very words at me when I negotiated with him. How dare I throw them back in his face? I didn't wait around for his reply. I turned and walked to my front door, leaving him fuming in his vehicle. When I got inside, I called human resources, and they agreed to pay out the standard two weeks' notice.

I was a little nervous calling Dan Gitman and telling him what had just transpired. But he simply brushed it off, happy to be getting me sooner. Two weeks later, in fact, I was back in New York City, working at Time Inc. and living on Riverside Drive.

But a lot had changed, and I had to get used to a very different living arrangement. Doreen had commandeered the master bedroom and dead bolted the door. Following suit, I did the same with the smaller bedroom. She'd replaced Wedgie with another Weimaraner puppy and was raising it without a cage. Each morning when I came out of my bedroom, puddles of piss greeted me. She had actually trained the dog to do his business there. And she refused to clean it up.

Any conversations between us, few as they were, always became elevated to shouting matches. I couldn't keep on living like that. I had to let go my feelings of surrender or whatever it was that had me stuck on a certain settlement amount. Reason started to prevail over insanity. Yes, I was ready to pay whatever price necessary to buy her out.

But it was a dicey move at the time, because we'd now missed six mortgage payments! We had to be at or near default, I knew. So before I made another offer to Doreen, I went through a pile of mortgage statements, found the most current one, and called customer service to explain my side of the story. I especially wanted to learn just how deep a hole we'd dug.

Our mortgage seemed to have magical powers. Since I hadn't opened any statements in a while, I hadn't read that the current owner of our mortgage had recently bought it from the original lender. My call was transferred to a loan officer who searched our account. She found no delinquencies. Almost four years of payment—and nonpayment—history had evaporated in the sale. She even did a quickie credit history to verify. No black marks anywhere. I was a model borrower. We were merely a month behind in our payments, and that had not yet been reported to any credit agency.

I confessed to the loan officer that I wanted to pay off the mortgage to avert any more missed payments. She crunched some numbers and gave me the bottom line. The number seemed far too low, so I asked her to repeat it. I heard right the first time. The payoff amount reflected a discount of 8 percent. She wanted to get rid of this potentially toxic loan as much as I did.

The bank's offer was time sensitive, and I needed to act fast. I approached Doreen with what I told her would be my final offer. It was much too generous, but I was using found money from the bank and Time Inc. to subsidize it. Doreen turned it down. Without any hesitation or premeditation, I went over to a very large and delicately crafted bowl she'd presumably acquired since our separation and picked it up.

"Do you like this bowl?" I asked.

"What are you doing?" she shot back.

I dropped it right in front of her, and we both watched it shatter all over the floor.

"Sorry, it slipped," I said.

"Are you crazy?" she exclaimed.

"No, I'm not crazy, I'm just clumsy. Tomorrow, I bet I'll have another accident and ruin something else." I wasn't bluffing in the slightest.

I couldn't have been more straightforward or honest. All of my possessions were out of the apartment and in storage. It finally dawned on me that I had power. If necessary, I'd even paint mustaches on the cowboys in her living room artwork.

I don't know if it was the seriousness of my demeanor or the madness of my desperation, but Doreen finally caved and agreed to accept my latest offer. I called a new lawyer to draft a property settlement agreement. Doreen signed it, and I gave her a nice, fat cashier's check. I then closed out the old mortgage and opened another, in my name only. I gave her ample time to move out of the apartment. I've bumped into her only once, in a New York subway car, since she left.

More good news was right around the corner. Bob Castle called to inform me that Uni-Mail had just landed the BOMC account. He thanked me for my participation and told me I'd start to collect my commission in a few months. I was touched by his forgiveness and generosity. It brought two true comrades back together again, and we maintained a marvelous friendship until his death in 2006.

After making some major repairs to the apartment, and ridding it of filth, I had a home again. I stepped out often with old friends and colleagues, sparing no expense at restaurants with great food and wine lists. I was a bachelor again and loving every minute.

But I needed physical love, and the kind I'd experienced with Catalina in Santiago would have been heaven. Those were orgasms for the history books, but history often repeats itself. Leave a special moment in time like that alone? Me? In a most characteristic manner, I didn't. I checked inside my wallet to see if her contact info was still there. It was!

I wrote to her and told her I'd be passing through her hometown of Punta Arenas on business. For some reason, I was afraid to be honest or sound too anxious. Nonetheless, I had a reply within two weeks.

"Dearest Stuart, my love, please come to visit me and my family," Catalina's letter started. "I hope I will make you happy here in Punta Arenas."

I was thrilled by her response. It was inviting and filled with innuendo—and it also left me curious as to why she mentioned her family. I'd be 6,500 miles from New York and wanted no part of a shotgun wedding. If she had just issued a warning, I ignored it. I booked my trip three months out, in November, and started doing Kegel exercises. I was ready, as they say, to get my freak on.

I worked around the clock to earn David's respect. One or two weekends a month, I entertained Sam in New York, as he was finally old enough to fly back and forth from Northern Virginia as an unaccompanied minor. I exercised by walking back and forth to work, nearly an hour each way. Without such distractions, those three months would have taken their sweet time in coming.

When the time came for my vacation, I was friskier than ever. It was a long, three-stop flight to Punta Arenas. Catalina met me at the airport. She was dressed for work and wearing some sort of tight-fitting uniform that made her look even hotter than I remembered. Despite how weak I felt from a lack of sleep and fresh air, I could have done her right there in the arrivals lounge.

Catalina couldn't dilly dally. She was under time constraints at work. We took a taxi from the airport into town, where she dropped me off at a hotel near her office. She'd already made a reservation there in my name. She told me to take a nap and regain my strength. She'd be back after work to pick me up in her car, and we'd head out to her parents' place for dinner.

She drove up to the main entrance of the hotel that evening in a cute little import that reminded me of a Yugo. We made a quick exit, and it wasn't long before we were navigating dirt roads. Deep into her parents' neighborhood, I came to realize that many residents had probably never seen a foreigner before. They started to follow the slow-moving car on foot. By the time we stopped and parked the car in what seemed to be the middle of nowhere, there were scores of children staring at me like I was some sort of NBA star. I was a foot taller than most adult males, and I wore trendy American clothes.

On foot, we followed a short and winding path that led us first to the backyard. We passed by a live pig that, it turned out, was soon to become our dinner. Catalina's father and grandmother came out first to greet me, then her mother. They were all extremely gracious and made me feel right at home.

But there was another young man standing nearby who didn't come over to introduce himself. He was a shy boy, not at all like Catalina. I presumed he was her brother, but they were different in appearance and personality. My doubts were confirmed when she realized the boy and I hadn't been introduced to each other. She grabbed his hand, led him to the populated side of the yard, and parked his teenage flesh and bones in front of me so I could get a good look.

"Stuart, please say hello to my boyfriend, Alvaro!" cooed my Lolita.

Huh? Her boyfriend? This was going to get interesting in a hurry.

The father and boyfriend killed the pig right there in the backyard then drove a skewer through it and cooked it rotisserie style. We dined al fresco. I'd never eaten pork that tasted so good. I watched Catalina and her boyfriend hold hands throughout and after dinner. I needed a lot of Pisco Sours to take this all in. I guessed I'd misread her letter. Or maybe I read much more into it than I should have. I had Catalina call me a taxi to take me back to my hotel. I couldn't begin to unravel the mystery of this Chilean Cleopatra.

The next morning, Catalina called, hoping to find me in my room. I had just woken up and taken a shower. She told me to stay put. She was coming to the hotel, and my room, at exactly 11:30 a.m. She arrived promptly and alone. She was full of apologies as she started to undress. "Sorry I didn't tell you about my boyfriend. We can still make love, can't we?"

Given that I'd traveled 6,500 miles to do exactly that, as often as humanly possible, we got right down to business. Turns out she was not her usual self, but I wasn't complaining.

Catalina tried to flatter me while we were lying next to each other in bed. "You know, Mama *really* likes you."

She said the word *really* so seductively that I started to feel a bit uncomfortable.

"And she's the same age as you," she added in for good measure.

Somehow, I managed to steer the conversation away from Mama and back to us. *We* were the ones about to head out of town for a dirty weekend and perhaps do some light hiking and nature watching in Torres del Paine National Park.

It was quite a smooth journey to the middle of nowhere. I was pleasantly distracted by ample guanaco and pumas and the three distinctive granite peaks soaring abruptly from the terrain as we neared our destination. When we got inside the park, I saw parts of the Southern Patagonian Ice Field that made my head torque like a wide-eyed tourist. Those deep blue lakes were so vivid in color from the very small rock flour suspended in their waters.

We hiked, got sweaty, soaked our shoes, and played hard in the wild. So, yes, it did end up being a dirty weekend, but not like any before.

Back in Punta Arenas after a few days, we spent dinner again with her family. We enjoyed another exceptional meal—and much stronger Pisco Sours, it seemed—under the stars. But this time, immediately after dinner, the boyfriend said goodnight and left. It wasn't more than two minutes before Catalina came over and sat in my lap, in full view of her family. Their admiring looks suggested that she had just snatched a sugar daddy.

I was getting quite comfortable when Mama came over and tapped me on the shoulder to try and cut in. "Won't you dance with me, my *Stooart*?" asked Mama.

The added alcohol had taken its hold on me, and I said yes. I warned her that I couldn't dance. She was buzzed herself, and there was no one within earshot to translate my exhortation. She held me tight and led me to a little room in the back of the house. This was not a tango or some other sort of sanctioned dance I'd learned at cotillion back in Richmond. Mama maneuvered me against a wall, unzipped my pants, and began slowly performing fellatio on me. My fear of Catalina and her father hearing us in the next room was mitigated by Mama's sensual and rhythmic movements. We finished our "dance" and rejoined the rest of the family in the front room.

No one asked where we'd been or why we were gone so long. Nothing was said at all. Everyone just sat around in a circle with big smiles on their faces. Did Mama have an open marriage? Was her husband waiting to sort this out in private back at my hotel? Was the whole freaking episode some sort of sexual shakedown? Ten minutes later, I was out the door, with no one to direct me back to town.

Panic began to set in. I was all for family activities, but what had just happened was way too bizarre, even for me. If I could've changed my flight and gotten the hell out of town that evening, I would have done just that. Instead, I moved to another hotel in downtown Punta Arenas, one frequented by moneyed British expats. There, I could dwell in their midst and avoid Catalina for the duration of my trip. Or so I thought.

When I arrived at the airport, three days after the last "tango," Catalina and her entire family were there to bid me adieu. I'd forgotten she had my outbound flight details. Grandma had food, Mama had a religious icon, and Catalina had her boyfriend. Her father told me he had cleaned his car especially for this ride to the airport. When they stopped at my original hotel, they were told I'd checked out. I felt somewhat guilty. Perhaps this entire experience had been a mere expression of local hospitality that was ever so foreign to me. All the same, I was one happy amigo when the plane departed Santiago.

Normally, I could use work to drown out all sorts of distractions, but not this recent escapade. It still had me wrapped up like a mummy. I was disappointed in myself. Yes, I was an out-there kind of guy, not easily embarrassed, but this sort of kinkiness wasn't my bag. All my life, I'd been searching far and wide for new and healthy experiences. I thanked my lucky stars for getting me back safely from the dark side of the planet.

Not only had I made it easy for Catalina to track me down at the Punta Arenas airport, I had enabled her, with the gift of my business card, to stay in touch. I'd hardly been at the office a week before she started burning up our fax line with love letters, all written in her native tongue and decorated with hearts and kisses. Sheepishly, I retrieved them from the communal inbox. Once, and only once, I asked a Spanish-speaking coworker to translate one of the letters for me. She read halfway through the prose before putting it down. She couldn't skim another portion. "Too much information," she said. "And too weird."

Let's take an inventory: I was a month shy of forty, and I'd already run away from home, lost a brother and a son, been held up driving a taxi, grown marijuana, smuggled sweaters, exploited a president, been twice married and divorced, lived like a millionaire, received a free Ivy League education, had a midlife crisis, and busted a nut. My career was the only thing left unscathed, despite numerous attempts to nuke it.

Cupid may be adorable, but don't let that baby face fool you. I should have hired a supermodel with really pointy stilettos to walk all over him!

As a self-imposed penance, I spent the next four months celibate. I put more effort into my work than I had in years. I made my apartment look and feel grown-up and came home to it every night. I kept reminding myself, "Three strikes and you're out." I was more than happy to sit on a few pitches.

One day, a Columbia classmate called to check in on me and my love life. I told her that I wasn't seeing anyone and, no, I wasn't available. She was working for a state financial agency in Virginia that was represented by the New York law firm of Brannon & Black. She wanted to set me up with a law associate there, someone she'd talked with over the phone many times but had never actually met in person. Her rationale was incontrovertible: "Hank, you're divorced; she's divorced. You have a nine-year-old son; she has a nine-year-old son. You live on the Upper West Side; she lives on the Upper West Side. It's a perfect match."

My friend and I haggled quite a long time, and I finally gave in to an introduction, simply because having a fellow single parent in the neighborhood, as a friend, might come in handy. Sam was still a regular visitor and, frankly, needed a dad with better parenting skills. She put in a call to her lawyer friend, Linda Murphy, and told her to expect a call from me, using my Columbia alias, Hank.

I didn't reach Linda the first time, and I left a message without thinking, calling myself Stuart, as was my usual custom with strangers. So when she returned my phone call, leaving a voice message for me in return of the one I left her, she seemed to stumble a little bit with her intro. She wasn't sure whether to call me Stuart or Hank, and I could hear it in her voice.

Linda and I had three or four marathon chats over the telephone. This seemed auspicious, since I rarely spoke to any female on the telephone for more than fifteen minutes. Never get them started. But Linda and I had racked up hours of talk time and spilled our guts about what was going on in our lives. Then came show time. We agreed to have our first "official" date. We planned on drinks after work at a venue convenient to the Theater District. Linda had tickets to a play that night at eight o'clock. I decided we should meet at the Atrium Bar in the Times Square Marriott Marquis, a large space that would in no way suggest intimacy—even though it was a hotel bar.

As was my custom in meeting new people for the first time, I would be holding a copy of *TIME Magazine*. We were supposed to meet just outside the main entrance to the bar. Definitely not wanting to screw up this momentous occasion, I scheduled my time to arrive a full ten minutes early. That plan would have worked like a charm if the National Academy of Television Arts & Sciences hadn't been holding their Daytime Emmy Award Ceremony at the hotel that evening. Cell phones weren't around yet back in 1995, so we couldn't alert each other to the mayhem. The place was crawling with so many teenyboppers that finding Linda would take nothing short of a miracle.

To top it off, our signals were mixed up. Linda had gone *into* the bar, found a free table, and ordered a drink while she waited for me. I kept circling *around* the bar thinking I'd find her somewhere on the perimeter. At first, I ruled out the possibility of her being in the bar since it was so crowded. So I continued to wait by the entrance. But time went marching on, and it got closer and closer to the time she would be shoving off for the theater. I thought, *What the heck? If I don't go in the bar now and check every table, then we leave everything to fate.* That could cripple a man's journey.

Remarkably, I did find her sitting at her table with a finished drink and a settled tab. How did I know it was her? She looked much like a young Lauren Bacall, but her aura was sultry yet cool. Only someone from the Midwest could be that patient and even tempered. She was surprisingly cordial for someone who had, for all intents and purposes, been stood up. I apologized and asked if I could explain my tardiness over a quick drink. Five minutes later, I was walking her out of the bar and to the Palace Theatre at 47th Street and Broadway. Her friend was there, waiting anxiously. She quickly introduced us, and in they went to see their show. I had every reason to believe that I'd never see Linda again.

The next morning, I strapped on my rollerblades and went to Riverside Park for some exercise. I wanted to burn off some of my frustration. Yes, I had picked the wrong venue for our first date, but it was an honest mistake. I had been as eager as she to show up on time. Just as I was letting my imagination go wild, I bumped into Linda; her nine-year-old son, Ben; and their dog, Ruffy. They were heading home after one of Ben's West Side Little League baseball games. Linda was dressed down and wearing no makeup—something that embarrassed her but that I found sexy. She thought for sure that my seeing all of her baggage in one place was going to chase me away. I genuinely caught her off guard when I called later that night to apologize again for my poor planning. Apology accepted. It didn't take much temerity to ask for and receive another chance.

Anyone who could rebound from a disastrous first date like ours had to have a great sense of humor. It made the chase even more enjoyable. The biggest obstacle for me, honestly, was her maiden name: M-u-r-p-h-y. Spelled exactly like Doreen M-u-r-p-h-y. I felt it would be impossible to keep from slipping and calling her Doreen. That's the sort of thing that can land a guy in "couples' jail" for a long time.

I studied up for the second date. I researched as much as possible about Des Moines, Iowa—Linda's hometown—and researched some of the more famous people from there, including actress Cloris Leachman, actor Bill Daily, writer Bill Bryson, and the designer known simply as Halston. I made notes next to each name and tucked the list inside my pocket just in case I needed to take a peek during a time-out.

Linda was duly impressed. We dined at the old Sfuzzi's on Broadway near Lincoln Center. The next morning, I had an early flight to Richmond, but that didn't deter me from staying up as late as possible. We enjoyed ourselves and more than made up for the botched first date. I found myself heading in the right romantic direction.

I called her as soon as I returned from Richmond to ask for another date: "How about coming over to my apartment tonight and watching the Michael Jackson and Lisa Marie Presley interview with me?"

To my delight, she said she would. Watching the made-for-television special was somewhat obligatory because of my simultaneous work on another Time Inc. property, *PEOPLE Magazine*. It was important to stay up to date on the latest pop-culture headlines, if for no other reason than to impress the magazine editors. They could be great allies at work. That being said, I realized that keeping up with America's "darlings" wasn't everyone's cup of tea. Although Linda was a great sport that night, I eventually discovered how much she reviled the whole *PEOPLE* franchise.

Technically, this was our third date. If I listened to my buddies, this meant it was time to hit the sheets or part ways. But I wasn't thinking about the so-called rules that night. I was merely enjoying the company of a woman whom I found to be titillating. All the same, Linda was thoroughly bored with the interview. As soon as I expressed my displeasure, too, she sat down on my lap and started to unbutton my shirt.

"What are you doing?" I asked, assuming it was just a little flirtatiousness during a Plymouth Neon commercial.

"Just relax," she replied. "You're going to enjoy this." And I did.

CHAPTER 12

Cherish

Cherish is the word I use to describe
All the feeling that I have hiding here for you inside.
You don't know how many times I've wished that I had told you.
You don't know how many times I've wished that I could hold you.
You don't know how many times I've wished that I could mold you
Into someone who could cherish me as much as I cherish you.
> —From the song "Cherish," The Association, 1966

WHILE MY LOVE for two other women—each for different reasons and in very different ways—had driven me to the altar, I found my expanding love for Linda to be a cherished one, a blend of rapture, felicity, and respect.

Linda's "move" the night we watched television left no question that she was a passionate woman. Her combination of Irish and Italian ancestry made a potent mix that helped me overcome my relationship fears and got me back in the saddle. I was mindful that her forwardness was in no way suggestive of her readiness to make a commitment. She'd been deeply wounded by her first marriage and divorce. The legal marathon with her ex-husband had been one for the books—by Linda's account, a landmark case still talked about in New Jersey. She was left with a financial mess to clean up. But most important, she had a son to think about. Ben was emotionally scarred from the divorce, having been caught between parents who were both lawyers and often still dueled with each other.

I'd only met her son once, and by accident. Linda didn't want to introduce me formally until we were an item. After two months of dating, she felt it was time, but she still wanted to be cautious. So she staged an outing to the multiplex cinema on Broadway and 84th Street. We met there under false pretense and, in neighborly fashion, agreed to see the same movie together. After the flick, Linda left Ben and me alone for a moment. I walked with him outside the complex, and we grabbed a spot on the street bench that Linda had designated beforehand.

"What is your favorite sport?" I asked.

"Uhm, baseball," he answered with that classic word that crosses "uh" and "um." Perhaps that extra second broke the tie with football.

"Who's your favorite team?" I asked next.

"The Yankees!" That one was shot out of a cannon.

He was two for two in my book. Now came the moment of truth. One can often judge the character of another, even a little boy, based upon the athlete he idolizes.

"Who's your favorite player?"

He took a bit more time to answer this question than the first two.

"Cal Ripken!" he answered thoughtfully.

He was a kindred spirit! I praised him for having such good taste and promised him a treat for playing my game of trivia. As Linda rejoined us, I took his hand, and we all crossed Broadway to head to the local Häagen-Dazs shop. By the time we finished our huge servings of Pralines & Cream, Ben and I were like old pals.

As ready as Linda was for me to meet her son, I was equally as ready to introduce her to close friends. I invited an easygoing, married couple to dine with Linda and me at my apartment on a Saturday evening. Per our usual custom, we were preparing to feast on some new fare I wanted to make, and they'd be bringing something rare and expensive from their wine cellar. I'd just migrated over to California Cabernets myself, and they wanted to expose me to some "pucker" bottles they'd purchased on a recent trip to Napa Valley. It didn't cross my mind how Linda might react to copious amounts of alcohol. My friends certainly wouldn't mind if she got a bit tipsy—in fact, they'd probably like her even more if she did.

Before the dinner party, Linda was nervous about meeting my friends and was consumed with her desire to impress them. That Saturday afternoon, while shopping at Bloomingdale's for a new outfit to wear, she had run into an old friend from Des Moines. They'd decided to go out for a drink so Linda could discuss dinner party strategy with her. Well, the old friends got carried away, and one drink turned into many.

My friends arrived on time, but Linda was late—by almost an hour! And when she did arrive, she was in the bag. She tried to hold a conversation but couldn't. We encouraged her to go lie down on my bed, where she proceeded to pass out. The dinner party continued, and my friends were great sports about the whole episode. Linda missed a fabulous meal and some great wine; I missed an important cue.

After tidying up a bit, I went into the bedroom to arouse her. It took some doing, but I had to get her home. She had a babysitter to cash out and a son to parent the next morning. I got her home in a cab, paid the babysitter, tucked her into her own bed, and said good night. Presumably, we would speak the next day.

The following day, I was sitting in my apartment and heard something being slipped under my door. I got up and found an envelope that bore Linda's handwriting. Curious to see what she had to say, I ripped the envelope sealing flap open to find:

Hank, I can't begin to tell you how embarrassed I am about last night. You have every right to say that our relationship is over if you feel that way. I'd love it if you would give me a second chance. I won't blow it again like I did last night.

Being the poster child of bad choices myself, I couldn't hold this one transgression against her and bolt. She appeared to have far more upside than downside. Yes, I admit, the warning signs were in my face. Linda had even admitted that her father battled alcohol for decades, forcing her to grow up in a fractured environment. In time, I also found out that her habits ran much, much deeper than booze.

It was time for some serious man talk.

How fortunate that three good friends and I were about to celebrate our recent fortieth birthdays in grand style by knocking a little white ball around the Ring of Kerry in southwest Ireland. We had reserved plush hotel rooms in Killarney—our base—and tee times at world-class links courses like Ballybunion Old, Waterville, and Tralee. We hadn't booked the trip ourselves, but we did our own driving in a modest, white, and narrow bread truck. How we managed to get that beast of a vehicle back to the rental agency without stripped gears or any dents was a minor miracle.

By sheer coincidence, we happened to be following the same itinerary as then University of Kentucky men's basketball head coach Rick Pitino and a good number of the school's boosters. Coach Pitino was being wooed by these wealthy Wildcats to remain at the southern college and not head to the NBA as head coach of the New Jersey Nets. It was fun watching the television reports broadcast out of the states with Pitino sitting at the next table, his only concern at that time being why he three-putted so many greens.

Not surprisingly, the topic of Linda was tabled until the end of the trip—and well after my own personal *Caddyshack* moment. If you haven't heard of this Harold Ramis–directed movie, then you must not be a golfer, or an American! While we were playing the Killeen Course at the Killarney Golf & Fishing Club, the heavens unexpectedly opened up on the tenth tee. We found ourselves playing in the same "heavy stuff" that Bishop Pickering encountered in the movie. My friend, Walter, can tell a better story, but like the bishop, I started to have one of those "I can't quit now" rounds when I reached the par-five eleventh hole in two shots. The rest of the foursome could barely even find the green and had long stopped keeping score. The heavy stuff came down all right!

It was as cherished a moment as that August day back in 1969 when, at the age of fourteen and playing in a twosome with Nicky, I shot a three-under-par 66 on the Westhampton Course at the Country Club of Virginia. It was the first and only time I recall that Nicky—instead of carrying the usual grudge of losing—tipped his cap to me, as if to say, "I'm really proud of you."

Golf can do wonders for a guy and make him think straight, too. My buddies agreed that I should give Linda a second chance. She was clearly a head turner based upon my descriptions, and hell, nobody's perfect. Why go back into the dating jungle when I had the perfect ten? All right, nine and a half. When our plane landed back home at Newark Airport, there she was to meet me. By limousine! The guys gave me lots of winks and raised eyebrows as we left the terminal.

There was so much more to this wonderful woman than the occasional lapse in judgment. Linda was a polished lawyer, well respected by her peers. She was masterful at bridging competing sides of any argument and was a calming influence when more hot-headed colleagues wanted to resort to open warfare. Against formidable odds, she excelled in an industry dominated by men. She was a self-made woman and never carried a chip on her shoulder about her humble beginnings.

She was compassionate, too. Linda stood by me during a long and unwinnable war I waged against Dan Gitman. This man had one of the smartest minds I've ever come across in business, but he was a classic bully boss who couldn't appreciate any talent unrelated to numbers. He constantly sniped at my output and made sarcastic remarks about my financial acumen. His browbeating management style made my prior nemeses, Howard Bingham and Anthony Russo, seem like a couple of small, annoying gnats. Dan was a big ol' north-woods black fly, in my face 24/7. At night, Linda would patiently listen to my daily dispatch. She wasn't impartial to me or judgmental toward Dan; rather, she'd offer constructive advice and send me back into combat the next morning.

To be fair, there was a good side to Dan. We played poker together with other Time Inc. colleagues at least once a month after work. The games were often held at my apartment. He was as fun and engaging as everyone else—not the greatest poker player, but never a sore loser and always magnanimous if he happened to come out on top. I couldn't figure out why he never showed his affable side in the office.

At the heart of our struggle, I was a creative person—and a relationship builder; Dan was a bean counter. I did my best to count and recount the beans over and over again and come up with the right answers. But even after several iterations, my numbers didn't match. It was frustrating because I thought of myself as a perfectionist.

"Stuart, this is a very important job," he'd tell me, "and if you're ever going to master it, then be more committed in the future."

Bean counters were the ones getting promoted, so I heeded his advice. I went to work earlier and left later, but no matter how long I worked, I'd still receive handwritten missives attached to my work. Sometimes they ran on for so long that as I took several minutes to read them, Dan—ever anxious for a rebuttal—would appear in my doorway and just stare. When I'd look up, he'd say to me, "Just bring it with you to my office! It'll be quicker if I just fix it myself."

It became a demoralizing issue for me and for the people who worked for me. I hired really good managers—talented, well-rounded professionals with great character and the ability to think strategically. But none of us were as good or as fast as Dan with numbers. He often went around me to bully my subordinates, as well. We became gerbils in a cage, running on a financial-reports wheel that never stopped spinning. I became the team shrink, fielding late-night calls from my staff. They went out to bars after work to try to forget their days. After several glasses of truth serum, they turned into mumbling, broken-down wrecks.

I knew my situation was kindergarten compared to what Linda faced every day in a New York law firm. So I continued to lean on her for advice. Her bosses yelled and swore and had temper tantrums every day. She could handle that sort of toxicity, but I couldn't. I started to lose sleep and suffer from anxiety. I went for a period of weeks without any sleep. I felt like I was coming out of my skin.

Linda told me one day that she wanted to treat me to something *special*—something that always did the trick for the associates in her firm.

This would be my first experience with precious white powder in nearly twenty years, since the bachelor party before my first marriage. When you do coke after such a long absence, a little bit goes a long way. It was a powerful high and led to great "junk food" sex. The habit lasted for about a month, with us romping just about every night on apartment floors, in the backseats of taxis, at a Johnnie Walker Scotch–tasting event, and at any other venue that would make the next high feel unique and ecstatic.

During these high times, I stayed up half the night. I couldn't get to sleep when I wanted or needed to. I got by at work for a week or two, but then I struggled to stay awake during the day and focus. I was lost and couldn't find my way back to normal. I eventually stopped using—cold turkey—as did Linda, but the upheaval lingered.

One reason I had stopped this lunacy was so we could entertain my parents on one of their rare visits to New York. It was a celebration of their fifty-fourth wedding anniversary, and this would also be Linda's first time meeting my mother. We took them out to dinner at the Rainbow Room and watched my parents dance cheek to cheek for hours. Their well-coordinated steps wowed everyone there, and I was one very proud son. All those years of practice and routine Saturday-night outings with other Richmond couples at Tantilla Garden and "The Club" certainly paid off.

After dinner, the four of us took a taxi to Linda's place, where we had a nightcap and enjoyed a game of cards. It was late, but that alone couldn't explain why Linda kept confusing clockwise with counterclockwise in terms of the flow of play. When she excused herself to go to the bathroom, both my parents were unusually frank.

"That girl's got a screw loose!" offered my governed-by-correctness parents.

Wow, talk about the pot calling the kettle black! I defended her odd behavior to the hilt, but I didn't man up and confess that I was equally guilty. Sure, I didn't want to ruin another trip for them like I'd done back in London, but, more importantly, I didn't want to burst their bubble. I wasn't just someone making his own way in the Big Apple; I was the "*so* successful" son stroking checks to keep them flush socially.

Truth be told, I was falling apart at work. I couldn't sleep. I couldn't focus. I had recurring tremors in meetings. I had no other option but to reach out to a resource I thought only *weak* people used—the company's employee assistance hotline. They moved quickly and got me in to see a psychiatrist in less than an hour. I was welcomed by Dr. Gerald Laufer at his office on Sutton Place—the extreme east side of Midtown Manhattan. No white jacket. He was a pleasant, easygoing man, someone who made me feel like I was being invited into his home rather than his medical practice. I led in with statements about my job dissatisfaction but withheld any information about the coke. I didn't mind being diagnosed—yet again—with anxiety and depression, but I did feel it necessary to revert to the Hotchkiss tradition of denial; I definitely didn't want to be labeled as a drug addict.

Dr. Laufer could only help me with what I told him. He probed my unhappiness and frustration at work. We talked about my relationship with Linda. He asked no questions about drugs and alcohol—perhaps I looked too clean-cut for that. I hemmed and hawed until he forced me to talk about something that he could actually fix, like the stress and anxiety caused by Dan's overbearance. In addition to ongoing psychotherapy, Dr. Laufer prescribed the drug Klonopin, an old standby for many docs that helps treat seizures and panic attacks. I took it and experienced some improvement, but it wasn't any "wonder pill." So I limped through therapy with Dr. Laufer for over a year to find a more permanent way to deal with my issues. Eventually, I got back into the work saddle, or at least the Time Inc. barn.

Linda had her own mounting pressures. As a single mother in the New York City legal industry, she had taken herself off the partner track. Although earning a decent income by virtually anyone's standards, she was burdened with the crosscurrents of New York City rent, private-school tuition, the cost of after-school care for her son, and a tsunami of post-divorce debts. Despite all her efforts to remain afloat, the buzzards who constantly circled and picked at her financial carcass made bankruptcy inevitable. This was a painful decision for this proud woman who had overcome childhood poverty, paid her own way through college and law school, and made it all the way from Iowa to the Big Apple by herself.

After she filed her bankruptcy petition, I invited Linda and Ben to live with me so she would be able to reduce her expenses and achieve a level of financial peace going forward. Despite having some reservations about its impact on Ben, she agreed. He moved into the small bedroom in my apartment—the old jail cell I'd called home in my final days with Doreen. Coming from an apartment with a much larger bedroom for sleeping plus a spare one for toy storage, it was a significant downsize for him. As working single moms often feel compelled to do, Linda tried to pacify him with credit cards. This is not a judgment on my part, because I'm all too aware that I was the same way with Sam. Despite being space challenged, Ben was a true champion.

Ben now had full-time use of what had essentially been Sam's room when he came to visit me. That meant that one of the boys, most often Sam, would have to camp out in the living room when the family was a foursome. Sam and I spoke about the situation everyone was facing, and he agreed to be a team player. So it was in this atmosphere of mutual acceptance that our new and blended family had its beginnings.

By the time Linda and I had lived together for a year, that darn marital bug crept into my head once more. This was new territory for both of us—two other people would make this a package deal. It would be wise to speak with both Sam and Ben first and find out if they were ready for this union. Surprisingly, there was nothing to discuss. They both said they were thrilled and begged to be part of the actual proposal. They were willingly sworn to secrecy as I shopped for a fitting engagement ring and choreographed a memorable knee-dropping moment.

Memorable, unfortunately, in two ways. After buying the ring, I raced home to call Chubb Insurance to purchase a valuable articles rider to my homeowners policy. It was denied. Denied? I was a good customer with no previous claims, or so I thought.

Turns out, after Doreen and I had either separated or divorced—I can't remember the exact timing—I had neglected to cancel the rider on *her* ring. Big mistake. She called Chubb to report it lost—it "slipped off her finger and went down a storm drain"—and they took her word. I was never consulted. I argued insurance fraud; Chubb told me to take my risky business elsewhere.

Despite that one final "fuck you" from Doreen, and two days after Christmas 1996, Linda, Ben, Sam, and I had the opportunity to exchange our gifts with one another. Being a blended family, we had to be flexible with dates during major holidays. I had packed Linda's insured-through-Allstate engagement ring in several layers of boxes. The outermost one was stamped with a clothing brand logo to throw her completely off the scent. The boys egged her on to open this gift first, but sensing it was something special, she saved it for last.

"Hurry, hurry. Open the box," screeched the boys.

It took a while to burst open three carefully wrapped gift boxes, but Linda finally got to the prize—the one covered in velvet. The look on her face suggested she knew there weren't earrings inside. This was something *monumental*, not just special.

"This is from the boys and me," I started my proposal. I had to pause to let her compose herself. "*We* would like to ask you to become my wife."

Linda merely whispered, "Yes," because she was all choked up, but we all knew what she was trying to say—"*Yes, yes, yes!*" for herself as well as the boys.

We spent the day making celebratory calls. What a beautiful couple and family we made! This was the marriage for which we had both paid the ultimate price—exceptionally bad judgment, three times combined. The only other "lottery win" that could have entered our orbit at this time was a job change for me. I wasn't going to let Dan's carping burst our bubble!

There was more magic to come. A senior colleague at work tipped me off about a new job opening up and the company's plan to slate me for an interview. I balked at the news because it wasn't a marketing job.

"You must have me confused with someone else," I said.

The position of executive creative director for all of Time Inc.'s New York–based magazine titles was normally filled by a homegrown writer or artist. My superiors, however, felt that I brought to the table a sorely missing and critically needed skill set.

"No, I'm certain they are leaning toward you because of your management skills," my colleague reaffirmed the now-declassified information.

While I readily acknowledge that I was no numbers genius, I had become recognized as the great compromiser—that soothing intermediary between two adversaries, like Time Inc. Home Entertainment and the Time Inc. Editorial Department. TIHE only used content from the magazines to create its book products, so while the editors derived nothing from Dan, he most definitely needed them. His abrupt manner and palpable sense of entitlement did not always go over well with the magazines' editors. I was always the one sent in to soothe bruised egos and get both sides working together again for the common good of the company.

Time Inc. management trusted that I could utilize these skills to heal the schism that had developed between the creative and circulation departments. The company needed someone to rebuild harmony between the "buyers" and "sellers" of various creative services so that the expense of maintaining an in-house "ad agency" could be justified. I felt honored to be recognized as a leader and to do something more fulfilling than spreadsheets. And I would be free from Dan.

My family was rooting for me all the way. When I got the job, I called Linda at work to share the good news. When I came home that evening, after announcing my departure to Dan, I found a trail of handmade signs in my apartment building, starting in the lobby and leading all the way to my front door.

"Free at Last!" read one sign.

"No More Dan!" read another.

I kept swatting through the somewhat cheesy "Good Luck" and "Congratulations" balloons to get to my front door. There, I saw the largest and best sign of all: "The War Is Over!"

I wondered what in the world my neighbors thought. There was a Holocaust survivor living on my floor, and I didn't want him to think we were referring to *that* war. He had called the police on me before, mistaking Thor's hammer signs on my Icelandic blanket for Nazi swastikas.

I embraced my new job and surroundings right away and with humor. I worked with one of my new staff artists to create a very unconventional memo announcing myself to the staff. It was titled "The Purpose," written in my own words, describing why I, the presumed enemy, had been chosen for the job. It was designed with the picture of me taken in 1973 with long hair and a Van Dyke beard—scanned right off my hack license. It was a total icebreaker.

That instant rapport between my new staff and me was a tonic. In less than three months, I ended my sessions with Dr. Laufer and wound down my meds. I still needed something to help me sleep. The scars from the coke binge would never heal.

As Linda and I moved forward with our wedding preparations, the ceremony presented difficulties or, more appropriately, the officiating of the ceremony presented us with a challenge. Linda, a Catholic, wanted a ceremony in her faith. I had no quarrel with this; however, the church did. After all, she was a divorced Catholic, and I was a twice-divorced Episcopalian. It was suggested to us that if we sought and received annulments of our marriages, the church would be able to perform the marriage. Once again, this was completely unacceptable to me—and Linda. If our former spouses were deceased, this issue would have been moot. Wishing they were dead right now didn't help. We needed another plan.

By default, we chose to get married by a minister from the Unitarian Church of All Souls in Manhattan. He was a jolly fellow and graduate of both Yale University and Union Theological Seminary; furthermore, he was a world traveler. We hit it off beautifully. Since we couldn't book a wedding in his church anytime soon—which we both wanted—this gourmand suggested that he perform the ceremony at a restaurant.

Linda and I loved to dine at Montrachet, an up-and-coming eatery located in the Tribeca neighborhood of New York City. The entrance was inviting, the service was relaxed and low-key, and the food was five-star. At the time, it was also one of the hardest reservations to get in Manhattan. While at Book-of-the-Month Club, I had conducted business with Montrachet's energetic owner, Drew Nieporent, who had moonlighted as a sales rep while building his restaurant business. Given our past relationship, I was certain Drew would accommodate us on short notice.

On May 9, 1997, we had the exclusive use of Montrachet's private room for our service and reception. Linda and I exchanged vows before our priest and forty-or-so friends. Both sets of parents were skeptical about the longevity of this union and boycotted the festivities, but Ben and Sam were there and stood up for us. Sam's presence at this wedding more than made up for anyone else who didn't attend.

During the luncheon that immediately followed the service, Linda asked me to take off my wedding band for a moment.

"I'll never take this off," I told her lovingly.

"I know, but please take it off just this once and look inside."

I took off the band and discovered that it had been engraved on the inside with a sentiment, "I will forever *cherish* you," and our wedding date, "5-9-97."

"Do you know the power of this statement?" I asked. I was overwhelmed by her choice of words.

"More than you will ever know," she added.

I felt a volcano of emotion and passion inside me. I held her tightly, trying to keep from erupting, but it was no use. I cried like a baby. No one had ever made that sort of statement or promise to me before. The woman to whom I'd given a second chance had carved it in "stone." Dollars to doughnuts, *this* marriage was going to work.

Complain as I might about my parents, our wedding day did feel incomplete without them. I took for granted that time would validate our decision. My parents had grown fond of Linda, and I expected that trend to continue as they aged. Equally, Linda's fondness of them taught me how better to love and appreciate my parents, no matter how late in life I'd be able to do so.

The timing of this renaissance was immaculate, because it coincided with my father's losing battle with prostate cancer. Bunks had not been to a doctor since his mandated army physicals during World War II. As a septuagenarian, he began to have nagging aches and pains that accelerated to excruciating back pain. Peg was finally able to convince him to see a physician. The diagnosis didn't shock or defeat him.

His first treatment decision for the disease was to have hormone therapy, but this proved ineffective. He then elected to have radioactive seeds placed in his prostate gland, but this, too, failed to provide the cure we all hoped for. Bunks had already decided against prostate removal surgery, and we respected his wishes.

Linda only knew Bunks for a short period of time, but as a living tribute to him—the consummate walker—she joined me in trekking the entire length and width of Manhattan Island on his last Father's Day. We felt his presence the entire journey, and we later shared with him the hundreds of pictures taken over our thirteen-hour pilgrimage. We got all of this done in the nick of time—Bunks passed away on our second-month wedding anniversary.

I had tried desperately to be with him until the end, but it wasn't meant to be. I'd visited him two weeks earlier, fully expecting him to die a quick death. His pain was overwhelming, and he refused to go to the hospital. His home was his castle, and that's where he was determined to remain, no matter what.

Transcendental meditation teachers frequently use the phrase "letting go," the beautifully simple yet abstract and often elusive act that certainly applies to both living and dying. Since I'd been practicing a bit of TM to help with my anxiety, I had taken my father into the spare bedroom of his home and shared a little of what I had learned.

"You know you're going to die, don't you?" I asked him softly.

"Yes, I know," he answered with no elaboration.

"Good," I said. "You won't die alone."

"I want that," he pleaded. "I can't take the pain anymore."

We held hands, talked openly about death, kissed each other on the cheeks, said our good-byes and love yous, and prayed to God to receive him right then and there.

That's right, we *both* prayed to God. My father had always labeled himself an atheist, but he was the nicest, most Christianlike person I knew. He was a civil, honest, and quiet man and never uttered a bad word about anyone. At that moment, he found God; I'm certain of it. He never said anything he didn't mean.

"Bunks, it's OK to let go. Just try. I'm right here with you."

"I'd give anything to go," he begged. "Please, God. I'm ready."

Seeing him in such pain brought back memories of Nicky lying on the athletic field with a bullet in his brain twenty-six years earlier, but that was my own little hang-up, not his. And not something to be shared.

My mother was in the kitchen with a good friend who'd been keeping her company for weeks. They had no idea where the men were. But having been away from them for some time, I was afraid they might come barging in and unbind this scene of intimate and spiritual connection.

Yes, he tried to surrender, and yes, he made his peace with God, but it was not his time to go, not yet. Yet again, his pain seized control. The only humane thing left for me to do was call an ambulance. The paramedics came and whisked him away to Stuart Circle Hospital. He was heavily medicated and made to feel a lot more comfortable. The next day, I asked his doctor for the truth. He told me, in this setting, my father could live for weeks.

"Mr. Hotchkiss, there's nothing you can do at this point. It would be better for you to just go home."

Between the morphine and his willingness to let go, he suffered only two days longer. I missed one of the most important events in life but took comfort in learning that, in the end, Bunks reverted back to his halcyon days as a proud and ambitious VMI Keydet. He saluted all the nurses and doctors, and he sang some insane doggerel about his year as a Brother Rat.

When Peg called me with the news, she was strong and proud. "Your father was the greatest gentleman I've ever known," she told me that day. "You were a very fortunate son."

Providentially, Linda and I had already planned our honeymoon to Eastern Europe in August to accommodate some of Ben's summer activities. I had been agonizing over the possibility of being out of the country when Bunks died, but he didn't let that happen. He passed on July 9. We went to Richmond for the funeral and remained there for several days to keep Peg company. We returned for another visit a few weeks later, just before the big trip. It helped us both fly away with clear consciences.

We arrived first at the splendid Hotel Gellert in Budapest, Hungary. Playing the "just married" card upon our arrival, we received an upgrade to a massive suite with a balcony overlooking the Danube River. Among its many splendors, the hotel offered its guests access to the famous Gellert Spa. I was a massage rookie, so when a rather large Hungarian man dressed as Hercules lathered me up with industrial-strength soap and twisted and tenderized my limbs and muscles into positions that defied the laws of physics, I winced. Linda and I subsequently spent a lot of time in our hotel room, not just as romantic honeymooners but also as bruised fruit.

Once we had a taste of international luxury at the Gellert, we decided to go native. We found quaint, family-owned restaurants with traditional cuisine on the western (Buda) side of the city. Walking in their doors, we were met with the smells of stews, paprika, and goulash. I thoroughly enjoyed the traditional fare and also accepted Linda's dare of ordering lard cakes made from deep-fried pig fat. I should have tried rubbing them on my bruises rather than eating them.

We left Budapest by train for a quick round-trip excursion to Prague, to see its many cultural attractions. No sooner had we walked the relatively short distance of the Charles Bridge and crossed the Vltava River than we stumbled into a beer house teeming with hospitable locals. On the night train back to Budapest, we were enlightened, all right. Scores of Romanian gypsies sang soulfully the whole way home, ignoring even what sounded like official orders from border patrolmen to shut down the party.

Then we traveled by rental car to three distinct geographical areas of Hungary: the Tokaj-Hegyalja wine region, the Puszta Plains, and finally, Lake Balaton. Sadly, my remembrances of the last leg—what many in this landlocked nation call the "Hungarian Sea"—centered upon the untimely death of Diana, Princess of Wales. We were glued to local-language television trying to grasp the details of this horrible tragedy. A still picture of Diana captioned with birth and death years required no audio.

Our first year of marriage flew by. We had successfully settled down as a family, and Linda now felt comfortable in accelerating her legal career. Making partner was out of the question, but there were plenty of cutting-edge opportunities beyond Brannon & Black and its seven offices around the globe. As she explored opportunities, I was put to the test as a step-parent. Ben's after-school routine required supervision, and he also led an active social life. I worked really hard to fit in with the New York private school "helicopter" parent set, but it was just not me. I always felt like a fraud. For Linda and Ben's sake, I played nice and managed to fake my way through it for years.

Before she made a career change, Linda and I thought it would be a good idea to take a trip with the boys after school let out for the summer. The four of us had all traveled abroad, but not yet as a family. Linda and I had had wonderful experiences with our own sons, and we wanted to make travel a high priority for this blended family. Coming up with someplace new was the goal, but building consensus among four people proved more difficult than we imagined.

I came forward with a rather novel, albeit self-indulgent, idea. The summer of 1998 would mark the twenty-fifth anniversary of my first setting foot on Icelandic soil. As risky as it may have been to propose a camping trip for novices, Linda and the boys approved. We got busy putting together a ten-day itinerary. Four city slickers were determined to rough it in the land of fire and ice.

Sam and Ben were very different in many ways. This was common enough in blood siblings—Nicky and I were proof of that—let alone in steptwins. (I loved using that moniker because they were just three weeks apart in age.) Their palates were radically different; Ben was an Iowa-corn-fed, beef-and-potatoes kind of guy, while Sam preferred more exotic cuisine like dim sum and curries. In Iceland, they'd both have to adjust. I gave them a sneak preview based upon my past experiences. The thought of hot dogs made from horsemeat and whale steaks marinated overnight in cold milk repulsed them almost to the point of reneging on the trip. So I changed the subject, took them downtown to the local backpacking outfitter on Park

Place, and had them pick out the latest in tents, sleeping bags, and other gear we needed for the trip. Retail therapy reeled them back in.

We arrived at the international airport in Keflavík with open and in- quisitive minds. I had warned everyone that the airport was in the bleak- est part of the country. We loaded up a rented station wagon and headed straight to the Blue Lagoon, a natural outdoor spa powered by Iceland's geothermal energy. We spent the day bathing in water full of minerals, silica, and algae. The water's aroma was far from pleasing, especially for the boys, but it was such a different experience and created so much en- ergy—the best tonic for jet lag I've ever found—that the trip started off on a high note.

The majority of our time was spent on the western part of the island. We visited a whale factory and some geothermal fields, sped up to the top of a glacier on snowmobiles, and took cold showers under waterfalls. Tourists are allowed to roam freely in Iceland, meaning we could camp on private property as long as we didn't disturb the owners. Since there is perpetual daylight in the summer, it was easy—from the standpoint of visibility and energy—to keep driving until we found an idyllic pan- orama worth waking up to the following morning.

On Sam's birthday—June 22—we encountered cold and windy weath- er such that camping outside might have resulted in severe cases of hypo- thermia. Given that we were literally in the middle of nowhere, finding a nearby bed-and-breakfast or motel was unlikely. We were lucky, though, and stumbled upon an unlocked and vacant shelter with four wooden bunk beds framed into the walls. It served us well, and sheltered from the wind, Sam was able to enjoy a birthday cake with candles.

The next night, however, we weren't so fortunate. We headed for the western *fjörds*, expecting calmer and warmer weather. It sure started out that way. We had no trouble pitching our tents and settling in for the evening. A few hours into the early morning—it was still light out—I was awakened by the sound of our tent fly being blown off. I took a peek outside, and the *helvítis rok* I'd experienced as a younger man was showing me its teeth again. I knew enough to get out and find something to weigh down both tents.

Airlines always encourage adults, in the event of an emergency, to attach oxygen masks to their own faces before dealing with their kids. That's what I was trying to do at this juncture. Get our tent weighted down first, then help the boys with theirs. Unfortunately, by the time I'd finished with our tent, the boys and their tent had been lifted off the ground like a magic carpet and were headed for the *fjörd*. I tried grabbing a guyline to stop the tent's progress, but it was fruitless. Sam and Ben soon found themselves wide-awake in shallow water. Only then was I able to trawl them like a pod of dolphins and dry them off.

Everyone moved into high gear at this point. We stuffed everything in the back of the car and got a move on. Finding no break in the wind for hours, we decided to just continue all the way back to Reykjavík. There, we could stay at a large and impervious campsite near the city center and adjacent to Iceland's largest geothermal swimming pool. Once there, we were cozy compared with the previous evening, and we ended our vacation on an up note.

This trip was beyond memorable. It proved to be the one and only time the four of us took an international trip together. In the future, Linda and I would let too many things—most of all our careers—get in the way of family adventure. No sooner had we returned from Iceland than Linda was closing in on a new job with the white-shoe New York law firm of Sterner, Klein & Trelease. They needed someone to work in the firm's London office on their thriving emerging-markets practice. Linda had mixed blessings about this opportunity. No doubt it would be good for her career, but what about Ben and me?

Ben could join us and enroll in a new school in London that fall or stay stateside and continue at his present school, provided he live full-time with his dad and stepmom across the Hudson in New Jersey. Rather than offer Ben that choice, we considered a number of factors and tried to decide what was best for him.

He had already been put through considerable change, and if this move to London was not going to be permanent, for whatever reason, then it wasn't fair to make him start at a new school and make new friends. But without any guarantees about when or if the move would happen, Linda decided to proceed with caution. She gave her ex-husband temporary custody of Ben while we tested the waters in London.

I would try to find a new job in London—perhaps even get a transfer within Time Inc.—and I was forthcoming with my current boss about our plans. The company accommodated my move to London in surprisingly generous fashion. I was allowed to keep my current job and rotate cities every two weeks. My experiment in telecommuting from London was long before the era of mobile devices, but I did pretty well by phone and the company "packet"—express delivery of hard-copy documents. Three times a year, I'd stay in New York City for an entire month to work on extended financial projects such as the annual budget and the year-end close. Other than that, I could delegate from afar.

I loved being back in London, thrilled to once more experience the people, the culture, the food, and oh yes, the pubs. Linda was nailing her job and adding another gold star to her resume. She was taming the short, mercurial, and often insecure Lebanese boss who scared the shit out of everyone else in the office. She was traveling to exotic countries like China and Egypt to teach local structured-finance gurus new tricks.

Ultimately though, after nine months, Linda made the gut-wrenching decision to pull the plug on London and transfer to Sterner's New York office. She missed her son terribly and was rattled by my commuting between New York and London. Ben, it turned out, was doing just fine. He was wrapping up sixth grade and looking forward to spending the summer in the 'burbs.

But Linda wanted Ben back under our roof. We agreed that we'd all be well served by upgrading our housing situation in Manhattan and starting over in a place of our own. Ben would get the larger bedroom he needed, as he was now a growing teenager, and Sam wouldn't be banished to the living room anymore. The market was heating up, and the inventory of pre–World War II apartments—one of the great prizes in Manhattan real estate—was shrinking every day. As supply went down, prices went up. It was not a good time to procrastinate.

I put my apartment on the market and had multiple offers within a week. I accepted one immediately, fully aware of the pressure it would put on us to find a new place to live. We wanted to stay in our current neighborhood, but after two weeks of intense shopping, we realized that was a pipe dream. We couldn't afford a larger apartment anywhere between 72nd Street and 96th Street on the Upper West Side. We would have to become pioneers and head uptown. Ironically, moving farther north meant being back on my old Columbia University stomping grounds.

Our broker had studied our tastes closely and called me at my office one afternoon. "There's a place you *have* to see," she said. "Trust me. I'm at the apartment now; please get here in half an hour."

"But, Laurie," I said, "it's so far—" I wasn't able to finish. She'd hung up.

Funny, I thought I was the client and called the shots. That's just the way property was bought and sold at the beginning of the US housing bubble. I met our agent at a building at 108th Street and Riverside Drive. The moment I set foot in the apartment, I knew that it was the perfect place *and* a steal. I'd never seen anything, even at twice the price being asked, with such character and views.

I immediately called Linda at her office. "Do whatever you have to do to clear your schedule and get up here. You won't believe the size of this place and the views of the river. And you won't believe the price!"

I didn't add that the apartment was in "mint condition," even though that selling point was obvious to me and plastered all over the sales sheets. I had already learned from shopping with Linda that any new home we'd purchase together would require some additional investment to give it a touch of her own personality.

We didn't debate at all. We called our broker and made an offer on the apartment that very night. We weren't worried about finding a mortgage, but we did fret over getting approval from the new building's board of directors. Our main worry was Linda's fairly recent bankruptcy filing, the only thing that could give them concern. With some New York City housing boards, the quality and character of their future neighbors is more important than their money. But she was frank with them, detailing her divorce and the circumstances of her bankruptcy, and we were "in."

After we closed on the new apartment, Linda and her army of semi-professional, Upper East Side "ladies who do it for pin money" decorators surveyed the property. She was rightfully insistent that Ben have some additions and modifications made to his room, but I'm still vexed by the new crown molding in the living room being replaced with something more "tasteful." I wasn't *that* architecturally challenged!

Since the contractors needed time to burn through our money—proceeds from Time Inc. stock options I exercised—we needed a temporary place to live during this rather indefinite period of renovation. We rented a modest one-bedroom apartment in the Prospect Heights neighborhood of Brooklyn on a month-to-month basis. It wasn't a bad place, nor was it cozy. But it definitely necessitated a longer and more stressful commute than the walks within Manhattan I so revered. But we made the most of it and ended up staying in Brooklyn for three months.

Ben and Sam stayed with us one weekend during our furlough in Brooklyn. We thought they'd enjoy "roughing it." After all, they'd quite enjoyed the wilds of Iceland. We were so wrong. Both belittled the apartment and its Brooklyn neighborhood, calling the combined real estate an "armpit." They refused to ever go back.

Linda and I had been fantasizing the past two years about having our own baby, a little girl. We'd already named her Charlotte. Hoping for instant gratification, we stopped using birth control. Linda's fortieth birthday was less than a month away, and there weren't many ticks left on the clock. We crammed all the sex we could into three cycles, striking out each time. So we decided to consult a fertility specialist.

That additional stress and expense opened up a huge can of worms. We started to argue and blame each other. "Cherished" was being reduced to just plain old "married."

CHAPTER 13

David Versus Goliath

TALK ABOUT BEING consumed by stress! By the end of the summer, I was hanging upside down by moon boots during intercourse; living in disarray between two apartments; supporting Linda as she navigated her way through Sterner's New York culture; visiting Ben in New Jersey and Sam in Washington, DC, during their Brooklyn boycotts; and, most of all, anxiously awaiting news about a job promotion. Dan Gitman had left the company—way back in June—and the position of president at TIHE was still open after three months.

I knew and they knew—hell, *everyone* knew—I was the best candidate for the job, but no one had whispered a word to me about it. I had no clue as to why the company was dragging its feet. The longer it took, however, the more paranoid I became that Time Inc. management was looking past me for Dan's replacement. I could taste this job like no other I'd ever wanted before. I'd been the corporate underdog for quite some time and come a long way out of nowhere. I wanted to roll up my sleeves and get to work.

TIHE had grown meteorically into a $200-million mail order, retail, and licensing enterprise and was now on the corporate radar. During my earlier tenure at TIHE, I had played a significant role in laying the foundations for this growth. I wanted it to succeed. The indecision in naming a new leader was causing the division to hemorrhage human capital. And an even bigger problem faced TIHE and the rest of Time Inc.

The US Congress and several state attorneys general were applying pressure on Time Inc. to tone down our sweepstakes sales promotions—those ubiquitous "*YOU HAVE WON A MILLION DOLLARS!*" mailings to many wishful thinkers and a few honest-to-God readers. Companies like Time Inc. successfully used sweepstakes to entice people to buy more magazines and ancillary products. However, the headlines in the promotions were much too aggressive. The matter reached a boiling point when it was revealed that a good number of customers were actually paying to fly to Time Inc.'s data processing center in Tampa, Florida, to hand deliver their sweepstakes entries and collect their winnings.

Too many entrants had missed the disclaimer lines printed in mouse type above the main headline. As the current executive creative director, I was an integral part of the team working overtime with our legal department and senior management to tone down our sweepstakes promotions with new and more transparent copy to replace the time-honored but now-banned approach.

TIHE was no different from its parent. It relied so heavily on sweepstakes that I questioned whether it could survive with a watered-down version. So did Time Inc. management. This may have been the perfect time to fold TIHE into the other mail order book divisions of Time Inc.— Book-of-the-Month Club and Time-Life Books—both of which were immune to sweepstakes.

Finally, on the Friday before Labor Day weekend, the decision was made to install a new president at TIHE—and management wanted it done immediately. After drifting in the wind all these months, I was suddenly the most popular guy on campus. Here was my shot at the big time. I'd spent almost two decades preparing myself for this calling.

I was fully aware of the time and energy it would take for anyone to focus on a business in TIHE's current condition. I also knew that I'd have to perform at a very high level while under stress outside of work. When asked about my interest in the job, I "tested positive," but I also tempered my enthusiasm with some well-founded reservations. I didn't mean to sound like a doomsayer, but I brought forward my concerns about the sustainability of the current business model.

I wanted to make sure everyone knew what I'd known for months: TIHE was in need of a major overhaul. Not only was the future of sweepstakes in doubt, there was also a finite amount of new product that could be launched. *TIME Magazine* content was converted into TIME Books, and the same was true for all the other magazines published out of New York. Despite having its own profit goals, TIHE had essentially limited itself to the role of an agent of the magazine group. The original business model and current strategic plan just weren't going to work much longer.

I shared these concerns while I interviewed for the job and made it clear that if the business model didn't change, I wouldn't want to stay in the job for more than a year. I was happy to hire new troops and rebuild morale, but I also wanted to build a better mousetrap. I wasn't sure if anyone was listening to all this ambitious talk, because the initial financial offer from management included a lockstep increase in compensation.

I felt underwhelmed enough that I turned it down.

Throughout my discussions about the position, I kept Linda in the loop. After all, she had been there for me when I worked at TIHE under Dan and nearly had a nervous breakdown. But even more to the point, for gosh sakes, she was my wife. I valued no one's opinion more. The negotiations, however, took place when Linda was in Costa Rica and virtually impossible to contact. She asked me to put any further discussions on hold until she returned. But Time expected a quick response, especially from an insider like me. I understood the company's culture, having been a part of it for seventeen years, in a way that Linda, as an outsider, couldn't.

I couldn't exactly put my finger on what was gnawing at her about the job. Perhaps it was the bad "smell" of sweepstakes. More likely, I thought, it was the prospect of my rise in rank and income. Up to now, we'd been financial equals, though she maintained complete control over how money was spent regarding Ben's welfare. A sudden spike in my income might change my behavior, make me a bit domineering. Linda would resist that like the plague, I knew.

There was yet another possibility: that my new and improved title would subject me to an evil temptress like Doreen. Linda was horribly insecure—even jealous—about my past wives. I had all these hunches but nothing definitive from Linda's lips.

Within a matter of days, Time Inc. doled out enough money for me to be satisfied on that front. They also *encouraged* me to come up with a new strategic plan for the business. All that was left to nail down for Linda was the issue of job security. I made it clear that I wanted a way out of the job in a year's time if I wasn't happy. And if it should come to that, I wanted to be placed in a comparable job somewhere else in the company. As far as I was concerned, I was a Time Incer for life.

Linda, being an attorney, insisted I get everything in writing. But Time Inc. was an at-will employer and did not offer contracts to most of its senior managers. I agreed to take the job and received e-mails from the two managers with whom I'd negotiated the deal, affirming what I thought to be my job security. I don't remember the exact words they used, but the sentiment was on point. That was all I needed. I was a handshake guy and preferred it that way.

When I told Linda that I had accepted the position, she was, well, let's just say extremely ticked off.

"I thought I told you not to accept this job until I got back and we had a chance to discuss it," she barked.

"I had to give them an answer before you came home," I answered defensively.

"They couldn't wait a couple of days?" she asked in a more respectful tone.

"Linda, you didn't want me to hold them off for a couple of days—you wanted a whole week!" I countered.

"So what? The job was open for three months!" Her point was valid but too late.

We went back and forth like this. As far as Linda was concerned, I was a jerk for making a unilateral decision and stupid to boot for taking the job. They would work me to death, she said, and our personal life would suffer.

The powers that be at Time Inc. knew I'd had trouble selling the wife. To see me flex my own muscles and prove that I had a mind of my own pleased them. They wanted a leader in their ranks, not a follower. So all things being equal, I thought I had made the right career decision and handled it the best way possible under the circumstances.

I started my new job right away—even before Linda returned home—and discovered that the business and company morale were far more broken than I had imagined. That served as a motivator and, in very short order, I was able to hire new managers and avoid having my head count reduced. These weren't just warm bodies but people who sat through my new vision speech in interviews and felt like they were getting in on the ground floor of something big.

I also saw the public relations value of throwing a "New and Improved TIHE" party, once we were fully staffed again, and inviting people from both inside and outside the Time Inc. flock. This wasn't just some small "pour" in our offices in the Time & Life Building, but a proper soirée at The University Club of New York. I wanted to project to everyone who had ever heard of TIHE that this little upstart division was a viable business with great talent and a new mission. The evening was a huge success.

I dove into drafting a new strategic plan for the company with an explosion of new product. Under the new plan, within five years, TIHE would exit the "agency" relationship it had with the New York magazine group and finally publish its own books, videos, and ancillary products. TIHE would expand into rich and previously untapped markets such as travel, health, and religion.

Writing the plan and getting input from my immediate superiors as well as key colleagues at the magazines was exhausting, but it helped crystallize my vision. Putting together the final deck—Time Inc. speak for a paper document used in a presentation—and getting five or six increasingly higher levels of approval to implement my new plan took as long, if not longer, than writing the darned thing. All that was left was a dog-and-pony show before Lawrence Fitzgerald, then president and CEO of Time Inc.

This final presentation took place about ten months into my tenure. To be honest, I didn't think Larry really gave a rat's ass about my plan. The fact that he interrupted my presentation to allow his assistant to bring him a package from a mail order company in the middle of the meeting added credence to that observation. While at first I waited, he told me to carry on as he directed his attention and his energies into opening up his parcel and pulling out new fly-fishing gear. As I continued to talk, he carefully studied his new toys. Even though I wanted him to take in what I was saying, he nonetheless approved my new plan. "Just do it," he said. Like the Nike slogan.

I was ready to start implementing the plan immediately, but the following week something far more critical caught everyone at Time Inc. off guard. It would completely change our future. On January 10, Time Warner, the parent company of Time Inc., announced its merger with AOL. This huge development consumed everyone's attention. In the subsequent days and weeks, a variety of confusing memos came out about future developments with Time Inc. One memo, however, was very relevant as far as I was concerned, and signed by Larry Fitzgerald. The line that caught my attention said: "All new initiatives approved in the second quarter are to be placed on hold until further notice."

I was crushed. All that heavy lifting my staff and I had done over the past six months was for naught. They'd worked such long hours and postponed vacations to help build TIHE into a dynamic company that would be more profitable than ever before. Purposeful change, it now seemed, was out the window.

Linda was also going through an exceedingly difficult time outside of work. Her ex-husband filed suit in New Jersey to claim full custody of their son. True, Ben had spent nearly a year living exclusively with his father while his mother was in London, and true again that he was spending more time with his father as our new apartment was being refurbished. But once we were in our new home—far removed from the "armpit" of Brooklyn—Ben remained in New Jersey. Whatever the father's motivations—and in my opinion they were suspect—he now wanted his son to live with him full-time.

No way would Linda agree to give up custody of her son. This was their own "World War II," the first one being the divorce. Ben's father had never abided by court orders regarding child support and was always pimping Linda around with money. Now, suddenly, he'd found the resources to hire one of the best family law attorneys in New Jersey? Linda's funds were limited, to say the least, but she came up with enough money to retain legal counsel. But as the case wore on, she couldn't continue to pay her attorney. She was now in this fight up to her eyeballs and all alone.

With or without a lawyer, this was going to be a difficult custody case for Linda to win, one involving a male child seeking to live with his male parent. Ben testified to all the court-appointed experts that he wanted to live with his father at this stage of his life. Forget about who did what, or said what, or paid for what, or did not pay for what, over the years. If a teenage boy wants to live with his father, the game's over.

As for me, I would never place my child in the position of having to choose between parents. Obviously Ben's father did not share this sentiment. As many of us expected, the judge decided in the dad's favor. To make matters worse, after he read his verdict, the judge tried to comfort my sobbing wife with this bonehead comment: "Mrs. Hotchkiss, get over it. Your son is old enough now and doesn't need you anymore. You need him more than he needs you."

To describe my wife's reaction as a meltdown would not only be accurate but quite justified, given the judge's decision and his macho behavior throughout the trial. Linda was, to all who knew her then as well as now, a devoted and dedicated mother. But reconciling herself to this new set of conditions would take a great deal of time and healing. Hence, my home and work situations were creating the perfect storm.

In the final analysis, my job was not what I'd signed up for. I'd been hired to first plug the hole in the dyke, which I'd done, and then revamp the business, which was now off the table for the foreseeable future. These things obviously happen in the business world; I got that. All the same, I thought I knew how to proceed if I wasn't willing to stick it out at TIHE. As devoted as I was to my staff and as loyal as I was to Time Inc., the best decision for me—and my family—was to resign from TIHE and ask for another job in the company.

Eager to smooth the waters, I offered to resign in a time frame that worked best for everyone. I was happy to help recruit and train my replacement and work with him or her in transition into the job. I thought I was going about things the right way. But I was wrong. I can't remember the exact details of the moment-of-truth conversation I had with my immediate supervisor, Justin Knowles, when he asked, "Are you sure you won't change your mind?"

I was sure, but something was said—or perhaps it was the way he said it—that made me realize we weren't on the same page about my job security.

After sharing this concern with Linda, she strongly urged me to speak with an attorney before I had any further dialogue with the company. I did, and the attorney advised me not to attend a multiday TIHE offsite meeting in Newport, Rhode Island, without a written guarantee of future employment. It seemed like bad advice to me, given that the meeting was due to start the *next day*! And I was the host. But I planned to follow the opinion I'd been given, and I told Justin I wouldn't be at the meeting. Not surprisingly, he took it as a threat.

I had just let years of goodwill fly out the window. Not to mention any indirect benefit I had or would derive from Justin being a graduate of The Hotchkiss School.

Without so much as skipping a beat, he told me, in no uncertain terms, that I wouldn't stand a chance of getting another job at Time Inc. unless I attended this offsite. In fact, he added in for good measure, "You'll never work in this *industry* again if you don't go."

Ominous words to say the least.

He was as mad with Linda as he was with me. He remembered how much of a distraction she had been in my negotiations to take the job. "She's putting you up to this, isn't she?" he asked me before I turned and left his office. I didn't reply. My loyalty to my wife was unwavering. But he was spot on.

I actually wanted to attend the offsite meeting, and I did. Justin's decree helped me put Linda and the lawyer in their places—for now. I felt a deep sense of loyalty to my staff. My senior managers had help put together a dynamite agenda, and we had hired professional facilitators to make the meetings fun and engaging. There was even a competitive scavenger hunt planned throughout the streets of Newport. It felt right to pack my bags and board the team bus. I'm still glad I went; it was the right thing to do.

Back from the offsite, I thought I had earned enough political capital to enter into productive conversations about my future. To Justin's credit, he made sure discussions with the relevant parties took place in a timely manner. However, their ideas were not what I wanted or expected to hear. They'd found a qualified candidate for my job while I was attending the offsite, and they determined a date for my departure based on the candidate's anticipated acceptance of their offer. The party line was they simply wanted to cash me out. No one recalled any promises made about a comparable job within the company. I'd saved and reread the e-mails the two hiring managers—one of whom was Justin—had sent me earlier, but their interpretations about what they *really* meant were diametrically opposed to mine.

In response to these new developments, I went up the ladder and met with more senior executives at Time Inc., trying to explain in polite terms that there had been a misunderstanding. I even went as far as writing to Donald Lindstrom, then president of Time Warner and Larry Fitzgerald's boss—all to no avail. The company's position was hard and fast—I had voluntarily resigned, and they had offered me a reasonable severance package. Happens all the time; good luck with your new career.

I didn't want to leave Time Inc., and I knew I hadn't made that sort of deal.

What was I going to do? Sue Time Inc.? Of course it was an option, but the thought of litigation seemed like such a no-win proposition. First of all, if I were lucky enough to win a lawsuit, how long would it take before they exhausted all appeals and I actually saw any money? Second, at my age, would it be worth the risk to be labeled as litigious while I was looking for another job within the industry?

Linda reminded me—over and over and over again—that I should never have taken this job in the first place. She kept at it until she coerced a guilty plea out of me. She felt Time Inc. had been dishonorable, and she certainly resented Justin's inference about her being a legal bulldog. She consulted some colleagues about the matter and, apparently, they all thought if I sued I could win. It was also unanimous that the firm of Vladeck, Waldman, Elias & Engelhard should represent me if I decided to do so.

I had no choice but to proceed. After all, the person I *cherished* and who happened to be a well-respected lawyer in her own right was also my wife. She was advising me to go down this road. If I didn't trust her, whom could I trust? I had already ignored her on the front end of this fiasco; I could now make amends by listening to her on the back end, I figured. My speculation—that she was looking for some kind of a legal win to offset her recent loss in family court—was irrelevant. We were finally on the same page, and I came around to accepting *our* decision.

My initial consultation took place with Judith Vladeck, a fiery, chain-smoking, raspy-voiced labor lawyer and pioneer for justice in the workplace. She described her firm, which she still headed at age seventy-seven, as the last socialist law firm in America. Five minutes with Ms. Vladeck and I felt as though Time Inc. was in for a real ass kicking. However, she wouldn't handle the case on contingency. Ding ding. Wake up, you two invincible yuppies with four college degrees between you. *That* was the sign to shake hands and walk away.

But persist I did. A small amount of savings might get me somewhere—perhaps far enough to get a better settlement offer—but not all the way to trial. Any additional outlays would have to come from refinancing our apartment, which had appreciated very little in the eighteen months since we'd bought it. Linda and I both had our limits—the apartment was the sacred cow that we would tap for emergencies, and only as a last resort. So, for all practical purposes, I was bluffing.

I plopped down a large first retainer and charged solo into battle. I worked with the lawyers to draw up a two-count complaint against my Fortune 100 employer. After the legal spit and polish was applied, *Hotchkiss vs. Time Inc.* was on. Thus began an eighteen-month litigation nightmare; I was in over my head the entire time.

I had totally underestimated the emotional drain of legal discovery and depositions. It became a full-time job without pay. The longer it went on, the more I realized I *had* to win. I'd be going into debt by the time the case was finished, and I was already considered radioactive in the marketplace.

I interviewed in earnest for a new job during the lawsuit, and I was honest about the reasons for my departure. No one bought them. Why would a guy at the pinnacle of his career, running a division of a Fortune 100 company, decide to leave voluntarily? And not for a comparable or better job? Prospective employers and headhunters surely thought I was trying to cover up the fact that I was fired. The industry was also small enough that once the lawsuit was public knowledge, everyone made up their own version of the facts anyway.

Ms. Vladeck assigned my case to an attorney in her firm named Julian Birnbaum, who had earned his JD from the University of Chicago and an AB from Harvard. His character could not have been more unlike Ms. Vladeck's. The more I got to know him, the more he seemed to me like a psychology professor rather than a plaintiff's attorney. Though he was dedicated to my case, the fiery passion of the firm's leader was missing.

Time Inc. decided to represent itself internally with Miles Brugerman, deputy general counsel, as the lead lawyer. Miles was very much a gentleman and had the credentials to match: Amherst College and the University of Michigan Law School. He and I had never met before, but we had work colleagues in common. When he deposed me and put a face to a name, he realized and acknowledged that I would make a formidable opponent in court. At the end of his three-day deposition, Miles offered to settle the case. After consulting with Julian and my wife, I declined. Strike two.

The journey from filing suit in November 2000 to jury selection on a Monday in May 2002 was exceedingly nerve-racking. Over this year-and-a-half-long period, I suffered mood swings like never before. The night after the terrorist attacks on the World Trade Center, I walked down from my apartment to the West Side Highway and along the unprotected footpath that paralleled this always-busy six-lane thoroughfare. I stared into oncoming traffic, trying to imagine if I'd experience any pain by taking two steps to my right. The slightest imbalance on my part could have ended the lawsuit.

I must have made that same five-minute walk at least five other times during the lawsuit. Each adventure occurred during the evening, when it was nearly impossible to judge the speed of oncoming traffic. Sometimes I ran across the full six lanes just to dodge traffic. It wasn't Russian roulette, but it was a potentially lethal game of chance.

Time Inc. made four separate motions to have the case dismissed for insufficient evidence. They were all denied, but the longer the case dragged on, the larger my legal bills grew, and the more I realized that Time Inc. was never going to agree to settle on terms acceptable to me. I finally saw that I could end up with a lost case, a six-figure debt and, worst of all, a lien on our apartment. The sacred cow was close to being sacrificed.

As I was preparing for trial on the Friday before the following Monday's jury selection, I received an unexpected call from Julian. Time Inc. was making one last-ditch motion to dismiss the case, and the judge assigned to the case wanted to meet with us. This couldn't be happening, could it? We were about to go all the way down to 60 Centre Street in Manhattan so the judge could tell us in person that's he's granting this final, eleventh-hour motion?

Ira Gammerman was a highly respected jurist on the Supreme Court of the State of New York—the highest trial court in the Empire State. As a judge who oversaw commercial disputes in Manhattan, he had heard his share of celebrity cases, including those involving Woody Allen, Rosie O'Donnell, Leona Helmsley, and Dan Rather. Justice Gammerman has been described to me as a hands-on judge who might empanel multiple juries if the case required it and, if the mood suited him, question witnesses himself if he felt that the lawyers before him were inept.

My heart was pounding hard and fast as I walked into Justice Gammerman's chambers that afternoon with my wife and Julian. The judge was every bit the legend I've just described. He was frank and very direct.

"Mr. Hotchkiss," he said. "I'd love to hear your case. I think you've got an excellent chance of winning. And I would be much happier to preside over your case rather than a typical 'slip and fall' matter. But let me ask you a personal question," he continued, "are you independently wealthy?"

I replied that I wasn't. He then began a short and private counseling session.

"Mr. Hotchkiss, you have no idea who you are up against. These guys will never give up. Even if they lose the case, they will appeal this thing until they have bled you dry. You could win a five-million-dollar verdict from the jury, and I'll predict you'll never see a dime of it after you've paid Mr. Birnbaum his legal fees. Time Inc. is willing to place their most recent offer back on the table, and I suggest that you take it and run."

I was speechless, but I somehow managed to get out, "Thank you, Your Honor," as we left his chambers to digest what we'd just heard. Julian pointed out the obvious—I was already in arrears with his firm, and Ms. Vladeck would only agree to go to trial if I gave the firm a guarantee of payment, meaning put the apartment or some other security up as collateral. My wife and I excused ourselves to chat alone. The conversation lasted only a minute or so. Once utterly adamant that I should not surrender, Linda now became conciliatory and told me everything would be fine if we settled. I remember thinking at the time how out of character this mood swing was! In retrospect, I realize it was most likely the prospect of using the apartment to finance further legal battles that made her buckle.

It was the most pitiful moment of my life. I'd never before run a race and quit a few yards shy of the finish line. But what else could I do? What would possess me to fly in the face of free advice from a distinguished jurist like Ira Gammerman?

I took it up the ass and settled. The agreement signed between Time Inc. and me is protected by confidentiality, so I can't go into any particulars, but suffice it to say that the only winners were the lawyers.

When I went to Ms. Vladeck's office to collect the net proceeds from the settlement, she sat back in her chair to reflect a moment on the case. She took a long, final drag from her cigarette and pushed the filter and the few remaining cuts of tobacco hard into an ashtray full of dark butts on her desk. She immediately lit another one, sucked it like a vacuum cleaner and, as noxious smoke poured from her mouth, she delivered what would be her final message to me.

It was short and sweet. She had trouble getting the words out, as she coughed and laughed at herself simultaneously. "Mr. Hotchkiss, here's what I tell all my clients after a case: All's well that ends."

I repeated her words, "All's well that ends," then I added the word "well" at the end, since it's the only way I'd heard that phrase.

"No," she said. "All's well that *ends.*"

She was right. It was over. I'd not spend another minute or another dime on this case. I could pay my bills, move on with my life, and focus on starting a new career.

That was the positive way to look at it. However, Justin Knowles's threat about my "never working in this industry again" still lingered in my mind. I had just walked away from a mid-six-figure income and thrown financial security out the window.

The things we do for love.

CHAPTER 14

Underemployed

NOT HAVING A job was both financially ruinous and enervating. I was faced with the ebb and flow of not having any money coming in and too much time on my hands—time when all I seemed to do was think about the fact that I didn't have any money coming in. I had to get over this supremely stupid lawsuit, and I had to find a job.

It had been two full years since the start of my falling out with Time Inc. Everyone seemed to know that my career there had an ugly ending, but no one wanted to discuss it. As time marched on, no one wanted to talk with me at all. I was being treated as though I were radioactive.

I wanted to tell someone my side of the story, but setting aside confidentiality, I wasn't ready to admit blame and take ownership for the mess I'd made. I was still in finger-pointing mode. Linda certainly got in my face to pursue justice, but the truth of the matter was, *I* had decided to sue Time Inc. and *I* had signed the retainer agreement with Vladeck, Waldman, Elias & Engelhard, not *her.*

I was feeling more than a little sorry for myself. My network of friends and former colleagues offered encouragement but very few job leads. But there were plenty of opinions, both public and private. Some were presumptuous: my wife had a good job, so why did I need to work? Some were insulting: I was lazy and didn't want to work. And some were misguided: I had made out like a bandit in the lawsuit settlement and was set for life. Ha!

I had never planned to live off of my hardworking wife. I'd never in my life been lazy and had survived enough stressful bosses and jobs over the years to prove that point. But my financial situation was desperate. Aside from joint ownership of the New York apartment—most of which the bank owned—my only other liquid assets were flimsy at best. My 401(k) had lost 90 percent of its original value from the implosion of my Time Warner, Enron, and WorldCom holdings. I wanted—and needed—a job as badly as anyone in America, and the longer I remained out of work, the harder it would be to find another employer.

I thought I had found a lifeline in late 2002. Korn Ferry, an international executive recruitment firm, pursued me for the position of president of Visual Bible International (VBI). This Toronto-based, publicly traded company was the mastermind of legendary theatrical producers and entrepreneurs Garth Drabinsky and Myron Gottlieb. VBI planned to produce feature-length films based on several books of the New Testament. The main channel of distribution would be mail order, not movie theaters, and would rely heavily upon the continuity marketing model I knew so well.

To save the company from legal and public relations nightmares, Garth and Myron were on record as consultants to VBI at the time. They were under investigation by the US Attorney for the Southern District of New York and the US Securities and Exchange Commission for defrauding investors in their most recent company, The Live Entertainment Corporation of Canada (Livent). Without question, they were talented guys—their productions had won nineteen Tony Awards and included Broadway hits like *Showboat* and *Ragtime*. But Livent had gone bankrupt in 1998, and once their books were investigated, the shit hit the fan. Facing the prospect of years in prison and millions of dollars in fines—and fearing they wouldn't get a fair trial in America—Garth and Myron became fugitives from the US justice system. They were trapped in Canada.

Therefore, Korn Ferry was working with VBI to find a president in title only. They needed someone like me—a presentable spokesperson for the company who could do the quarterly tap dance on Wall Street. What they were willing to pay in base salary and bonuses was higher than my final Time Inc. compensation, and I could have made lots more from the stock options. With this chance of becoming wealthy, Linda and I quickly came to grips with the obvious issue of my working in Toronto and coming home to New York on the weekends. What spooked us about the opportunity was the uncertainty of getting caught up in Garth and Myron's shenanigans.

Before accepting VBI's offer, I consulted lawyers from the firm of Frankfurt Kurnit Klein & Selz in New York. They were pros in entertainment law. I hired them to review the employment contract I'd been presented. It easily passed the smell test, but my lawyers felt a sense of obligation to go beyond their brief. They warned against taking the job. The risks far outweighed the rewards, they said; Garth and Myron were no two-bit criminals. When they gave me a "for instance"—my potentially being met at a New York airport by federal agents and hauled away as a material witness—I became unsettled. In the blink of an eye, the job I thought would solve my financial worries and make amends for my throwing away a promising career at Time Inc. was starting to curdle.

With the offer on life support, I asked to meet with the company chairman, Dr. Steven Small, also a Toronto dentist. I made one final demand, asking him to add a provision to the existing employment contract that would give me the authority to fire Garth and Myron for any sort of misconduct. Dr. Small was taken aback by this new stipulation.

"What on earth makes you think this would ever become necessary?" he asked.

"If Garth and Myron are merely consultants, then why would such a thing bother you?" I answered.

The diminutive Dr. Small pushed back his chair to stand up and gave me a dirty look. "I thought you truly believed in this business," he pontificated.

I did believe in the business model, but not in the designers. Before I had the chance to reply, however, he withdrew the company's offer.

Man, had I dodged a bullet! Garth Drabinsky and Myron Gottlieb were both tried and found guilty of fraud and forgery in Ontario Superior

Court in 2009. The business headed into receivership only a few years after my interviews. The stock options I once imagined as a money tree now wouldn't buy a cup of coffee.

After this opportunity dissolved, Linda tried to both support and encourage my ongoing search for employment. For the first time, we began discussing ways of starting a business. The plan for me to wait for something that paid six figures was abandoned. I was tapping into the lines of credit I had on credit cards every month to help with household carrying costs and to meet my child support obligations. At some point, this strategy was going to bite me in the ass. I knew it.

So it was the occasion of my forty-eighth birthday that I finally felt a bond with my father. Underemployed. I was fast evolving from top dog to dog walker.

Linda took me out to celebrate my birthday and take my mind off the subject. I knew we were in for a night of fine dining—Linda was more than generous in that regard. But I didn't expect any surprises.

She insisted I meet her first for a quick beer at Heartland Brewery, a convenient spot across 51st Street from the Time & Life Building. But it was a Friday night, and the place would be loud and packed with thirty-somethings trying to get loaded in a hurry.

"Can't we go somewhere else that's not so noisy?" I bargained. "How about Limoncello?" This popular restaurant had a great basement-level bar below Seventh Avenue and was only a block west of Heartland. It also offered a complete range of drinks and a less frantic ambiance.

"Please, let's just stop in Heartland for *one*," she pleaded. "I have an old colleague who might be there, and I'd love to say hello."

One drink for Linda's benefit was more than fair. The rest of the night would be devoted to me. Besides, after one beer at *any* bar, I tended to mellow out to crowds and noise. We stepped inside Heartland and, oh boy, was it packed. I claimed what was, at best, a square yard of standing-room-only space a few feet away from the bar while Linda snaked her way over to an available bartender and brought us back a couple of pints. Sure enough, that first one mellowed me out, and I stopped complaining.

We continued inching our way closer to the bar, certainly within earshot of conservations people were having in our immediate vicinity. One couple seemed oddly out of style. Their hair was long and on the wild side, and they both wore makeup that made them look like dated rockers. They also spoke with British accents. Linda joined in their conversation and beckoned me over. Perhaps they were celebrities—Linda had a knack for rubbing elbows with the rich and famous. I joined the repartee and made direct eye contact with the couple. But I still couldn't figure out who they were.

As is often the case when the "sauce" kicks in, I started a new conversation. The still unidentified duo listened intently and, when given the opportunity, asked relevant questions. Then, as though something I said had tripped a switch, one of them asked, "Are you Stuart Hotchkiss?"

I was stunned and didn't answer at first. I was not the least bit famous, not even at this once-frequented watering hole. So he asked again—"Are you *the* Stuart Hotchkiss?"—presuming I hadn't heard him the first time.

Suddenly, I became suspicious. "Who are *you*?" I asked.

The sleazy world of process serving had yet to engulf my world and jaundice my view of strangers, but I was picking up a bad vibe.

"I'm Martin Hubbard," revealed the first imposter as he removed his wig.

"And I'm Cathy Hubbard," revealed the second as she removed her disguise.

What relief! Martin and Cathy were two old friends from my first tour of London—and now friends of Linda, too, from our most recent tour. After their practical joke, we all had a huge laugh and more libations. Then we dined fabulously well at The Terrace, a charming restaurant located on the top floor of Columbia University's Butler Hall and one of the best-kept secrets in Manhattan.

Martin had just come into some family money, and Cathy and he were about to emigrate to Canada to start a new chapter in their lives. Linda had tracked them down in London and invited them to New York to help celebrate my birthday weekend. We caught up on one another's lives before Martin shared his big news.

A serial entrepreneur during the late '90s tech bubble, Martin was preparing to launch a new business in Canada, qualifying Cathy and him to live there. His father had recently died, and Martin spent a great deal of time tying up many loose ends of his dad's life. With all that he had been through, he had come to see the need for people like his father to have a smart and useful end-of-life planning tool—not just to create a legal will, but to organize and disseminate important personal information as well. He decided to try me on for size.

"Who's your favorite golfing buddy?" Martin asked.

I had three current favorites, actually—the "Hibernians" with whom I'd traveled to Ireland back in 1995. I selected Walter the Storyteller, an ocularist, who was the best one-eyed ball finder in the heather, ever!

"Imagine leaving instructions for Walter to receive your golf clubs and then writing him an e-mail message with a personal note that could be delivered after you die," Martin illustrated. I lit up when I heard that. Walter always made a fuss over my Spalding Top Flite persimmon woods, the very first clubs given to me by Papa when I took up the game.

Martin had me now. He was speaking my language. "Just think," he continued, "if you could plan *all* your final choices and wishes online. I liken it to emotional life insurance, and it says a lot more about a person than money ever can." He lamented the fact that his father hadn't taken time to say proper good-byes to family and friends and provide anyone with details about his prized World War II medals and extensive book collection.

As our conversations about his business plan continued during our weekend together, Martin reached a climax that I never saw coming. I thought he had just been using me as a sounding board, not trying to sell me on working with him. "Stuart, why don't you join me? I'd be willing to offer you a share of the business if you commit to the project."

I'd already bought into what Martin was saying. And I had no money to invest in a new business of my own. So Martin and I discussed my putting in sweat equity along with his cash. The only thing I'd front was the cost of airfare back and forth to their soon-to-be new home in Victoria, British

Columbia. He purposely chose the "Queen City of the West" because it was a technology hotbed, full of smart and cost-effective web developers. We figured that in order to launch the business in a year's time, I'd need to spend ten days each month in Victoria. I would stay in their home to cut down on expenses. It was an intimate proposition, to say the least.

In exchange, I'd receive a 25-percent stake in the business, with the possibility of it rising to a third if I turned out to be the principal rainmaker. Linda didn't hesitate to give her stamp of approval. I was elated to be working with a friend whom I trusted, rather than another corporation. A simple handshake with Martin sealed the deal.

I had not been in Canada since passing through its Maritime provinces as a young man on my first attempt to get to Iceland. The Hubbards' new oceanfront home on southern Vancouver Island—just miles from downtown Victoria—offered breathtaking views and a tranquil work environment.

We worked well, and efficiently, together. We fleshed out the business plan, designed a website interface with our developers, and worked with a local attorney to ensure that everything the site offered consumers would stand up in court. Martin and I had loads of fun working from early morning until mid-evening. After hours, Martin, Cathy, and I would go into town for drinks and a meal, and Martin and I would gloat over our progress.

Our individual contributions and diverse skills complemented one another. Things were going smoothly until we realized that we couldn't agree on a name for the business. We'd go back and forth daily, but each time we thought we'd found a compromise, either the domain name was not available or Cathy would nix it. I began to wonder why her opinion was so valuable all of a sudden.

My suspicions should have been aroused, but they weren't. Martin and I had worked over a year as a twosome. Three was going to be a crowd as far as I was concerned. When I found the right time to confront Martin about it, he broke the news to me gently. Cathy was now a shareholder in the business. Burning through capital much faster than he'd expected, Martin had persuaded his angel to invest.

I needed some clarity on how Cathy's participation would impact me. Martin and I were in his car, driving from a brief trip to the store, when I raised the issue. He was a classic shoot-from-the-hip kind of guy, but at this moment, Martin made a statement as prepared as McDonald's french fries. "You know, Stuart, I've ended up spending a lot more money on the business than anticipated. I really think this business is going to work and generate a lot of profit, but we need to rethink how we divvy up the shares."

The idea of revisiting ownership percentages after more information about the business is available and what people are actually contributing is a valid one. I also empathized with the stress Martin was under, having put his money on the line. I expected some sort of negotiation to follow, but I feared he would try to postpone such a debate as long as possible. So I dove right in.

"By 'rethink,' are you saying that you want to *change* the shares?" I asked.

"Well, I think we need to go back to square one and reevaluate everything. Cathy and I believe that if the business works, you should definitely benefit."

They were so worried about the size of the investment they were making, and so uncertain about the viability of the business, that I had become expendable. The malignity of his intention shocked me to my core.

"Are you shittin' me? I've spent more than a year working on this project and haven't earned bupkes." *Now he wants to squeeze me out?* I thought. "Who the fuck are you kidding?" He'd dropped this bomb on me from so far out of left field that I couldn't help but get steamed about it.

The rest of that day and evening were ghostly quiet. The spooks at neighboring Ross Bay Cemetery made more noise than we did.

I returned home to New York the next day, as scheduled, and spent a few random moments to reflect about what had just transpired. Perhaps I should have taken their own worries into account, stayed the course, and waited patiently for a level-headed decision to be made. After all, I had no other prospects at the time. But once feeling screwed, I knew I wouldn't be able to work on the business as hard as I had the past year and that I'd always be looking over my shoulder, expecting Martin to backtrack on something else.

I just gave up. I didn't feel like arguing over umpteen percent of *nothing*. I e-mailed Martin with the news that I was walking away—from the business as well as the friendship. He tried desperately to reel me back in by phone and e-mail, but I simply got rip-roaring drunk and ignored him. Done was done. I cut Martin and Cathy out of my life and moved on. We've not communicated since.

I felt foolish and used. I'd just given away a year's worth of free consulting and racked up more debt courtesy of Air Canada. Whom could I trust now? Time Inc. had let me down, and, now, so had two people I once considered close friends. I could pound the proverbial pavement again to find a corporate job, but I knew it was a waste of time. No reputable business was going to hire me now. My resume had become nothing more than a faded and dog-eared romance novel, worthless sheets of paper not even suited for the bargain bin.

Looking back, this was a unique moment in time when so many wonderful things could have happened for us as a family. Time was a precious commodity, far more important than money, and I had lots of it.

Linda and I had spent four years trying to have our own baby. She'd stopped the fertility treatments. The remaining option—a wonderful one, in my opinion—was to adopt. Working-mom, stay-at-home dad couples were succeeding in a nontraditional division of roles and responsibilities within the family, so why couldn't we? Ask Linda.

Ben was a senior in high school and floundering. It was a two-person job to help him stay on the straight and narrow, and I desperately wanted to help. I believed in tough love, a commodity sorely lacking in his upbringing. When given the chance, I'd proved my style of parenting worked. So why wasn't I acknowledged as a partner in this effort? Was she ever going to stop undermining my efforts? Ask Linda.

By default, then, I decided to go back to work as an entrepreneur. I had to create a business that would be quick to market, require very little capital, and turn profitable in six months or less. Somehow, it dawned on me that five thousand or more Republicans were coming to New York that summer for the second coronation of President George W. Bush as their standard-bearer. The four-day Republican Convention was a tightly scripted political rally, sure to generate millions of dollars in merchandise sales. While President Bush was a polarizing figure, he was also a marketer's wet dream. I decided to capitalize on the man and his nickname, Dubya.

Linda liked my idea. Since the business would be registered as a sole proprietorship, she insisted that we protect ourselves from any unplanned liability and financial loss. She scheduled a meeting with Brian Compton, the New York bankruptcy attorney who had represented her previously. Consulting with an attorney of my own never crossed my cluttered mind.

When the meeting ended, I had been persuaded to transfer my interest in the apartment to Linda. Since there was nothing left to borrow against my credit cards, my wife's ability and willingness to support me was offered as due consideration for my "gift." In reality, they said, I would always be recognized as half owner of the apartment by the New York courts. Seemed kosher to me. And I certainly trusted Linda to have my back.

I designed and manufactured a small line of ball caps, T-shirts, polo shirts, and neckties—promoted under the assumed business name Dubya Duds. I sold retail through my own e-commerce website and a booth at the private GOP Marketplace that was housed inside the New York Hilton. I enjoyed one last hurrah as a vendor at the Black Tie and Boots Inaugural Ball, hosted by the Texas State Society at the Woodley Park Hotel in Washington, DC. Since native son Dubya had won reelection, it was the toughest ticket of all the balls in town. Ben even came down to help me work the booth. There was so much business people refused to wait in line to pay. They just threw money at us.

I dissected the business to determine if any part of it could become a full-time scalable business. There was no question that I could sell neckties in high volume and with large profit margins. I wanted to continue to design and manufacture whimsical silk neckties, sewn in America and sold to educated rich men for sixty-five dollars. "Poor man's Hermes" was an apt and shorter description. I took an even closer look.

Vineyard Vines was the market leader. Started in 1998 on Martha's Vineyard by brothers Shep and Ian Murray, the company grew meteorically during the long 2004 presidential campaign. Major players of both political parties wore their ties. Mainstream media gave them millions of dollars in free ink. The word on the street was that Vineyard Vines was approaching $10 million a year in sales. There appeared to be room for copycats.

As I developed my new business plan, I spoke with a few wholesale accounts that had sold my Dubya ties. Yes, they would carry my line, but most suggested that I simply go to work for Vineyard Vines rather than compete with them. They knew the company's owners and offered to make introductions. But after my experiences with Time Inc. and the Hubbards, I had serious trust issues. I was also a risk taker. So I unplugged my debt clock and steamrolled an untested brand, Capital Ties, into the marketplace.

The initial line was heavy in designs paying tribute to famous personalities, like Lance Armstrong, Fred Astaire, wine critic Robert Parker, and the "Golf Animals"—Tiger Woods, Golden Bear Nicklaus, Great White Shark Norman, and Bantam Ben Hogan. I knocked those out of the park. But I also treaded on unfriendly toes and received far too many cease and desist letters. That forced a transition to designs with cute icons like martini glasses, daffodils, and hedgehogs, and that helped attract some well-known personalities to give the business some buzz. But there just weren't enough of them to turn Capital Ties into a public relations darling. To build a successful business, you first have to know your industry ice freaking cold. Then you have to be well funded. I had flunked on both fronts.

To add insult to injury, Vineyard Vines expanded quickly, beyond its neckwear origins, into clothing and accessories. They were moving into competition with Lands' End and becoming a real lifestyle brand. I watched them grow, one fancier and larger catalog after another. They were opening retail stores in partnership with leading haberdashers in cities along the East Coast and slowly squeezing the life out of competitors like me.

I hung in a bit longer by producing custom ties and formal wear for clubs and organizations and selling off existing inventory. But survival mode simply wasn't good enough. Not even for a household with a mid-six-figure income. My status as an underachiever had become a source of embarrassment for Linda. She'd grown tired of being my sugar mama.

On top of my anxiety and depression, I was now having a self-esteem meltdown. The only thing that got me out of bed in the morning was our issues-laden beagle-and-border-collie mixed breed, Lucy. We'd rescued her right after the September 11 attacks from a shelter a hundred miles north of the city, in the town of Glen Wild. Demand for pet adoption had more than tripled after 9/11, and fence sitters like us were quickly transformed into customers.

In the five years since we'd found Lucy, she and I had bonded like glue. On days when I was working from home, she helped relieve my stress just by lying at my feet or cuddling up for an afternoon nap. When I wasn't busy, I took her to neighboring Riverside Park for long walks and visits to the 105th Street Dog Run. She gave me a purpose and made me feel useful. And loved.

Linda's focus became her career. She'd already left Sterner to become in-house counsel at an international trade association for the bond market industry. It would be the first job she'd ever had with "regular" hours. But it was fraught with politics, and no sooner had she mastered that nonsense than a merger with a similar organization ensued. Linda knew it was time to start looking around. She would not survive with so many bosses in the new matrix management structure.

A quasigovernmental agency created by Congress in 1979 to provide oversight of firms engaged in the municipal securities market—a regulator—was looking for a new executive director. By the time Linda heard about the job, the search was almost over. Korn Ferry—yes, them again—and the agency had already interviewed over a hundred candidates, ranging from state treasurers to bankers to Wall Street execs.

Linda almost didn't apply for the job. "Why bother?" she said. It seemed obvious that the right person would have to have a penis. But she went for it anyway, and this smarty wowed the pants off the search committee and was offered the job. With my help and advice, she negotiated a very lucrative compensation package. The job was based in Arlington, Virginia, just outside Washington, DC. Even though I loathed the thought of leaving New York, I insisted we move. I was her biggest cheerleader, because I still *cherished* her. This was a "Hillary Clinton" moment for Linda and, indirectly, all women in the financial services industry.

In 2007, the New York City real estate market had peaked—yes, I acknowledge this with the benefit of hindsight—and our apartment had a theoretical market value of $3 million. Linda wanted to hold on to the apartment since we had not otherwise saved for retirement. I wanted to cash out at what turned out to be the ideal time. Not only would that have been the smart investment decision, it would also have provided the funds I needed to pay Sam's college tuition expenses. Even the real estate broker we consulted suggested selling, but Linda wasn't giving in. With the title now in her name, she had control.

So we rented out the apartment in New York as an investment property and leased a house for ourselves in the posh and pricey Georgetown neighborhood of Washington, DC. My job was to oversee the winding down of one home and starting up of another, which made me feel like I was working—and contributing. But I needed hard money.

I took my remaining Capital Ties inventory along to DC, just in case. There were a few new bright spots, but it didn't take long to realize that both the business—and I—were still a distraction and a load. It was terribly lonesome being stuck in the basement of a Georgetown row house during the day. I came in contact with only nannies, housekeepers, and deliverymen—not to mention the sporadic mischief of rodents.

Linda and I both agreed I'd be much happier looking outside the home for employment. I had a small professional network left over from my first stint in the Washington area, and I tried to build on it. I reached out to professional societies, trade associations, and membership organizations.

John Fahey, my old boss at Time-Life Books, was now president of the National Geographic Society, and he offered to serve as my lone Time Inc. reference. I'd lost all the others after the lawsuit.

I found what I thought to be the perfect job opening at Smithsonian Enterprises, the for-profit arm of the institution. They were looking for a director of new business development and licensing. The head of the operation, Tom Ott, was a former Time Inc. employee and a friend of Fahey's. I was highly qualified for the job and had the right temperament to work within a matrix-management environment like Smithsonian.

Tom didn't doubt my suitability for the position. He just couldn't figure out how to sell me to his boss, the head of the institution. Tom looked at me with a straight face and laid it on the line, exactly the way I would have done it, had I been the hiring manager. "Tell me how I'm supposed to explain to Cristián Samper that I want to hire a tie guy for this position."

I responded with the truth, not blarney. "Look at the whole picture," I argued. "I believe my blend of corporate and entrepreneurial experience makes me more well rounded than any other candidate."

It was a solid answer—Tom smiled when he heard it—but not enough for him to go out on a limb for me. I didn't even qualify as a finalist for the job.

Perhaps there was another reason I didn't make Tom's short list. Smithsonian likely did a background check and found the growing financial and legal baggage I was carrying around. My credit card balances were in collection and had escalated with interest, fees, and missed payments. Admittedly, I was paranoid. Wasn't all of corporate America going to judge me negatively because of my FICO score?

Like it or not, I had to aim lower and, therefore, targeted small, privately owned businesses. If I could help someone make money, they might view my checkered past as a healable black eye rather than a chronic disease.

It took nearly a year, but I finally found a job through Craigslist. My new employer, Jim Warlick, had gone from making and selling campaign buttons supporting Jimmy Carter in 1976 to owning a political memorabilia shop in Washington, as well as a traveling exhibition that showcased replicas of the Oval Office, *Air Force One*, presidential desks, and similar items.

Jim wasn't hiring for his current businesses. Rather, he was days away from signing a lease for five thousand square feet of prime commercial space across the street from the treasury department. Jim planned to erect an inaugural souvenir store to capitalize on president-elect Barack Obama's immense popularity and the millions of people expected to visit the nation's capital to celebrate the swearing in of our new chief executive.

After signing the lease, Jim expected the space to be rehabbed and the store stocked and ready to open for business by the first of December 2008. I was to hire and train the store's employees as well as manage the store. I'd be working *eighty* hours a week on a $700 weekly salary. I desperately needed a job. When it was offered, I had no choice but to grab it.

I was exhausted from the long hours and lost fifteen pounds in two months. Drinking two milk shakes a day from a nearby Potbelly Sandwich Shop couldn't put the weight back on. As crazy as the pace was at the store, I did meet interesting shoppers from all over the world—lots of Australians, for some inexplicable reason. On occasion, I was allowed to pinch hit for Jim and do radio and television interviews with both national and foreign press. I was especially touched when an Armenia 1 TV reporter dropped off a copy of our interview and a sculpted national emblem as a gift.

Good help was hard to find...and keep. I was hiring and firing every week. The weekly staffing schedule became a moving target. I was burning out before I barely started. After a month, I asked Jim for a raise, and he bumped me to $900 a week. That bought my loyalty until January 20, 2009, and not a day more. It was a prudent decision. Business dwindled dramatically after the inauguration, and there were massive layoffs.

Surprisingly, I found another job—albeit seasonal—rather quickly. The National Cherry Blossom Festival wanted to expand its merchandising efforts that spring, and they asked me to help them set up and manage a new boutique. Through a special arrangement with the city, they received free space inside the DC Visitors Center, located at the Ronald

Reagan Building and International Trade Center. Lots of people went to the store to shop, and lots more went to the center for information about tourist attractions. Essentially, I worked two jobs for the price of one.

The part-time job hits just kept on coming. In fact, the next one was actually waiting for me after the Cherry Blossom Festival ended. I became a brand ambassador for World of Grains, a new line of healthy snacks by Mars, Incorporated. I went around to a variety of Whole Foods Markets in the metropolitan DC area to inform consumers about the company's new cookie product and hand out samples. I rehearsed my lines well but rarely had time to recite them. Customers scarfed up my samples, preferring to eat and run rather than chat about the health benefits of ancient grains like quinoa and amaranth. Most shoppers mistook me for a Whole Foods employee and pestered me with questions about organic produce, the company's green mission, wild rabbits—everything *but* World of Grains cookies.

This string of jobs, in addition to dear Lucy, put some skip in my step, but I was also developing a bad rap for not staying long in a position. I was the quintessential executive migrant worker.

There was just enough money coming in to pay Sam's monthly "child" support—he was now twenty-two years old and a senior in college—but nothing left over to stem the onslaught of envelopes marked "Overdue" from collection agents. And the fiercest creditor of all was Patty Beekman. She had paid Sam's college tuition and engaged her lawyer to force me to reimburse her.

There was only one thing I could do to stay sane during this time—ignore it all. All but my dying mother.

For the past ten years, Peg had lived a rather healthy and insouciant life at the finest continuing-care retirement community in Richmond. She'd outlived her savings, but this wonderful, faith-based organization, Westminster Canterbury, provided fellowship grants to many residents, like my mother, who faced financial predicaments. No one ever got kicked out of "The Home."

Now, at the age of ninety-one, Peg was experiencing frequent fainting spells, the result of aortic stenosis, a life-threatening disease that can only be remedied through open-heart surgery. Given her age and rather delicate constitution, she was in mortal limbo. But she was strong willed and begged her doctors to replace the bum part with a healthy pig valve. One of her favorite public figures, former first lady Barbara Bush, had just received a successful implant a month earlier. That got my mother oinking.

"I'm just as strong as Barbara Bush," Peg told her doctors and me. "And even if I don't make it, I'd rather die on the operating table than continue to live like this."

I knew no one was going to operate. Peg had suffered a mild stroke during a fairly routine carotid artery stent procedure in February. Rather than offer straight talk, the surgeon told her she had to get stronger before they could operate again. Decoding this "doctor speak," I realized that modern medicine could keep her alive during the actual surgery, but the chances of her leading a healthy life postsurgery were grim. He wasn't going to operate.

Peg held out hope for a medical miracle. And she was also holding out for me. She didn't want to leave this world until my life had rebounded. It took a long, long time for me to appreciate the fact that my mother loved the career success I once enjoyed because of the rewards it brought *me*, not *her*. But now I finally got it.

With Peg confined to either health care or assisted living, I visited her weekly, camped out in her studio apartment, boned up on some card games, loaded up the liquor cabinet, and started filling up my dance card with numerous invitations from her wonderful friends and neighbors. Peg and I were both readying for a proper sendoff.

CHAPTER 15

Best Interests of the Child

ACCORDING TO THE terms of my property settlement agreement with Patty Beekman, all decisions regarding the welfare of our son, Sam, should have been made in the spirit of what American courts refer to as "the best interests of the child." But they weren't. They were made in the best interests of the Beekman family.

I took the responsibility of supporting my son quite seriously. Each and every month, I sent Patty a four-figure child support check. That was my duty as his father, and I gladly obliged. Most lawyer-advised dads agree to an eighteen-year plan. I had agreed to a super-extended plan because our "shared" lawyer had played favorites and sold me out.

Although I was an "egit" for signing such an agreement, I didn't have any remorse at the time. I couldn't imagine any scenario down the road that would prevent me from honoring it wholly and in perpetuity. And for the first thirteen years of the agreement, that's exactly how I continued to feel. I was gainfully employed, and everything was going to be just tickety-boo.

My complacency ended during Sam's junior year of high school. The two of us had several conversations then about his college choices. Although I didn't share with Sam every last detail of my financial pickle, he was well aware that I had been going through a rough patch. At the very least, he knew it had been quite some time since I had collected a paycheck. But he was also quick to point out that I owned a nice, big apartment in Manhattan. He must have wondered to himself just how hard up I could really be—his thoughts fueled, no doubt, by Patty and her father.

I suggested to Sam that he apply to a couple of state colleges and universities like William & Mary and the University of Virginia—not shabby choices by anyone's definition—in addition to any private ones already on his list. Surely, I thought, he would understand that parents and children have to reason these things out.

"I'll have to consult with my mother," Sam said to me, as if Patty were his lawyer.

I had already communicated with Patty, by letter, about Sam's college plans, asking her to please be rational about the application process. I explained that I was tapped out financially and would prefer for Sam to stay in state. Perhaps, I continued, she could use funds from the trust if Sam had his heart set on going elsewhere.

Patty called me on the phone shortly afterward to follow up. She made it crystal clear: "Sam will go wherever he wants, and *you* will pay for it."

They really rubbed it in, too. They submitted ten college applications, and not a single packet bore a commonwealth address. In the end, Sam chose Davidson College in Salisbury, North Carolina. No question about it, this highly selective liberal arts college was the bomb. But it was also going to be a four-year, $160,000 nut after all was said and done. This was, of course, in addition to the monthly child support. I was getting screwed, but only Patty was getting off.

I asked Sam why he'd chosen Davidson. I was being genuine.

"I really hit it off with the director of admissions. She's gay, too," was his answer.

Sam had come out at fifteen. I was the last family member he told. He was absolutely sure I'd go ballistic. He waited and waited for what he thought would be the perfect moment, but one never came. So he just got it off his chest it at some run-of-the-mill pause in a conversation.

To everyone's surprise, I acted nonchalant. "Good to know," I said. "That's all you wanted to tell me?"

Surely there was an academic reason why Sam had chosen Davidson.

"They provide a free central laundry service. I just drop off my clothes, and they wash, dry, fold, and iron them," said the proud new Wildcat.

I'm no math whiz—Dan Gitman will testify—but I think that works out to over $1,000 per load, not including books. What else did they offer, room service?

Patty wrote the checks out to Davidson herself. She cleverly borrowed the money to try and prove undue hardship. As her father had warned years before, she hired a prestigious legal bully to come after me. I was served with a subpoena to appear before Judge R. Terrence Ney of Fairfax County Circuit Court on December 3, 2004. I was ordered to show cause why I hadn't reimbursed Patty for Sam's tuition expenses.

I had no lawyer, no money to hire one, and no sympathy or empathy from Linda to finance one. Who could blame her? I'd brought this legal debt into our marriage. She had her own son and financial responsibilities to him. Most of all, she refused to subsidize a family as wealthy as the Beekmans.

Rather than appear before Judge Ney, I remained in New York and filed an affidavit of defense with the Virginia court. I prepared a thoughtful and respectful three-page written explanation as to why I couldn't pay for Sam's tuition or afford to travel south to attend the court-ordered hearing. Why are courts such hypocrites? If I *did* have money, shouldn't I first use it to pay Sam's tuition rather hire a lawyer? Wasn't this case about the *best interests of the child*?

At the conclusion of my affidavit, I asked the judge for permission to use the county's teleconference facility as a way to participate in the hearing. I wasn't trying to hide from anyone. Three times before the day of the hearing, I called and left messages with Judge Ney's law clerk to confirm receipt of my affidavit and learn his decision about the teleconference. I received no response of any kind.

On the morning of December 3, an hour or so after the hearing was scheduled, I called the law clerk once again. This time, I wanted to know the judge's ruling. Still no response. I went about my daily business for days, weeks, and even a few months, before I would find out the horrible truth.

Ross Hotchkiss, a purported "kissing" cousin, offered to help as best he could. For starters, he asked a lawyer friend in Northern Virginia to run by the Fairfax County courthouse and look up my case. She came back with the alarming news that Judge Ney had cited me for contempt and issued a bench warrant for my arrest. I doubt he even saw my affidavit, much less read it.

I felt protected from the long arm of the law while living in New York. But each visit to my mother was a huge risk and yet another expense to ask Linda to pay. Sooner rather than later, I knew there would be a funeral to attend, and that's when I'd be hauled away in handcuffs in front of all the mourners. Would Patty stoop that low? Yes, and she made that point with action, not words.

Easter came early in 2005, March 27 to be exact. My mother was alone in her apartment watching television when she heard a knock on her door. Two uniformed deputy sheriffs greeted her. "May we speak with Stuart Hotchkiss, please?" one of them asked.

Peg was stunned for a moment. Perhaps they were bringing news of my death.

"Stuart isn't here," she replied. "Is something wrong?"

"No, ma'am," one answered. "We just need to speak with Mr. Hotchkiss."

"Why are you looking for him *here*?"

They produced paperwork signed by Michael Fish, Patty's lawyer, stating that my permanent residence was the same as my mother's, a retirement community with a minimum age requirement of sixty-five. I'd just turned fifty in January.

"He doesn't live here; he lives in New York!" my mother snapped at them.

Patty *and* her attorney knew full well that I didn't live with Peg. My feelings for my former wife had now shifted from indifference to utter disgust. What would possess this woman to harass the aged grandmother of her own son?

My mother was mortified and, of course, worried that some of her neighbors might have witnessed this visit from Henrico County's finest. Similarly, she wondered about my well-being. Peg called me right away.

Saddened and confused, she fought back the tears as she pleaded, "Stuart, you've got to do something about this, please. I know you can figure it out."

She and I both knew what "figure it out" meant. It was code for "get Linda to give you the money."

Peg continued to get caught up in my mess. Collection agents repeatedly called to shake her down for money on my behalf. These were intimidating sons of bitches. She told them to call me, not her, but obviously not forcefully enough. The calls continued, and no one was spared. Linda got them. So, too, did Linda's parents in Des Moines. Even Patty Beekman got them. At least she learned I wasn't bluffing about my indebtedness.

I had two pipers to pay—Patty and my creditors—and neither was giving an inch. Patty was an infinitely higher priority. Landing in jail was a lot different from having a lender put a lien on my assets—the few assets I had after Linda, for all intents and purposes, took my share of the apartment.

Since I couldn't reason with Patty, I thought I'd try doing so with Sam. He was old enough now to have an open and frank conversation about the mess I was in. He might actually take pity on me and speak with his mother.

I gave him a penetrating look and asked, "Are you aware of the measures your mother has taken to try and land me in jail?" There was no verbal reply or use of body language. So I continued to dig for answers. "Is this what you want, too?"

Sam snapped out of his trance. "Daddy, I'm sorry. We all just want this to be over." I thought Sam was ready to pour his heart out, but he remained calm and businesslike. "Michael and I believe you can find the money."

Michael? My nineteen-year-old son was on a first-name basis with his mother's lawyer?

Sam was exceedingly clear about his thoughts on the matter. He'd done his homework on the estimated value of the New York City apartment—$2,195,000—and proffered it as evidence to his mother and new friend Michael. I tried to explain about title transfers, mortgages, and other such things. Poor Sam, he just couldn't look beyond those seven figures.

One month, two months, then several more months—nearly two years in total—passed without any more frontal attacks by Patty or her attorney. Despite this period of relative calm, I still lived in alternating states of unattainable wishes and fear. Staying in physical contact with my mother was the only gift I had left to give her, and I tried my level best to please her. She nagged, of course, about my not visiting enough yet never knew the consequences of my being careless in my travels. It was a high-wire act from which I could never retire.

Once Linda and I made the move south, the issue of the bench warrant in Virginia was rarely discussed. Fortunately, we both wanted to live in the District, so our day-to-day lives would not force me into harm's way. But I continued to make those trips back and forth to Richmond and, now, driving there became the practical option. Each time I got behind the wheel of the car and crossed into the commonwealth, my anxiety crept up like ivy on red-brick walls of a three story mansion.

After settling into our new home in Georgetown, I received a letter from the Fairfax County Circuit Court, forwarded from my New York address. It contained a whole lot of legalese that I didn't understand. So I called the clerk of the court and asked her to please decipher it. She put me on hold to pull my file. When she returned, she told me to simply disregard the letter; that it was the result of a computer error. My case had been inactive for over two years, she said, so I had nothing to worry about.

Not wanting to risk any miscommunication, I leveled with her about the bench warrant. I asked if it was still in effect.

"No," she told me. "Warrants attached to inactive cases automatically expire."

I breathed a huge sigh of relief. I could now visit the commonwealth as a free man. Sam may have held a grudge regarding the tuition, but he, too, was relieved that I could now drive him down to Richmond to visit his grandmother. Being able to parade us around the Westminster Canterbury campus meant the world to her. In the coming year, she would turn ninety, and Sam would graduate from Davidson. The future held a lot of uncertainty.

I stepped up my professional networking in Virginia. My old pal Nigel Homer, now back in London, kindly connected me with the principal owner of a direct marketing agency in Arlington, Virginia. Years earlier, I had loaned my New York City apartment to the two of them when they came to visit Manhattan. I'd completely forgotten this gesture, but Jim Hussey, the Southern gentleman and businessman, hadn't. It was the first thing he mentioned when we met, and it served as a great icebreaker.

Jim's agency had a fine reputation on a number of fronts, and they'd built up a significant competitive advantage in direct mail print production. Jim was looking for a rainmaker who'd be willing to work as an independent contractor. He was prepared to pay a nice commission based on performance. We hit it off right away and decided to give each other a try. He drew up a contract, which I liked even more; I gladly signed.

It felt great to be working again. One of the agency's senior executives was assigned to authorize my sales plan, some promotional materials, and my list of prospects. The first three weeks or so went very smoothly. I was given new business cards and hit the ground running. News about my new gig went viral through social media like LinkedIn and Facebook. I'd be officially working from home, but I also had an office in Arlington whenever I needed it. This fit my lifestyle—and Lucy's—perfectly.

Less than a month after I joined the agency, I received a call from the head of human resources. She'd been covering for the receptionist during his lunch break and happened to be at the front desk when Deputy Sheriff O'Hagan from Arlington County came looking for me. Fortunately, I was working from home that day, and no one else from the agency saw the sheriff. She discreetly passed his message on to me. I was instructed to call him about an urgent personal matter.

O'Hagan answered my call, not some switchboard operator. I had taken the bait and could almost see him grinning like a Cheshire cat.

"How long do you think you can keep hiding from us?" He pumped me two or three times before I said anything.

I first wanted to ensure that he had a valid arrest warrant. He said he did—that they *never* expire. The clerk of the court had duped me. Maybe I was the target of a sting operation.

"Why don't you walk across Key Bridge, and we'll pick you up on the other side?" the sheriff suggested.

It was a daunting thought. That's exactly the way I walked from home to Jim's office in Arlington every time I went there—even the day before O'Hagan's surprise visit. I asked the sheriff if he would please listen to my side of the story for a moment.

"Mr. Hotchkiss, I'm not paid to listen. My job is to just pick you up. The quicker you surrender, the easier it'll be for the both of us."

I told O'Hagan I'd think about it and get back to him. It wasn't the last time I'd speak with him.

First things first. I tracked down Jim Hussey and told him, without getting into the details, that it would be best to put our arrangement on hold. "Jim, I can't say a lot at the moment, so please trust me. Your agency's reputation is way too important."

It was the appropriate thing to do. And as a result, I was rewarded. If I hadn't put Jim's interests ahead of mine, the door to Jim Warlick would never have opened.

The second thing I did was plead with Linda to open up her checkbook. I couldn't keep living like a fugitive. I'd fallen so far down the slippery slope of self-esteem that I would do just about anything to get my money-grubbing ex-wife to leave me the fuck alone. Linda's professional reputation was also at stake. What if I appeared at her office one day, only to find Sheriff O'Hagan waiting for me in the lobby? I wanted Linda to avoid any guilt by association.

I thought back to the transfer we had made on our New York apartment. Could we not transfer it back into joint ownership so that I could have access to some of the equity? Failing that, couldn't Linda *lend* me the money?

We could make it all legal. I didn't mind if she took the money off the top in a settlement down the road if, God forbid, our marriage should fail.

I was willing to sign any sort of promissory note to end my nightmare in Virginia.

Linda balked at first. That apartment was *her* Holy Grail, *her* retirement nest egg. So I upped my ante considerably. "Let's just pay Patty off, and I'll give you my entire interest in the apartment. I'll put it all in writing," I promised in desperation.

I was willing to take this risk of conveyance because it beat my other option—lazy days in the Fairfax County Detention Center. Furthermore, as Linda herself advised me, such a promise probably wouldn't hold up in court if we ever got divorced. I was stunned; that was the first time the word *divorce* had come up in serious conversation between us.

With my autographed, one-page, unwitnessed promise on paper, Linda took charge. She called Michael Fish and offered to negotiate directly with him. She wasn't going to play nice unless he agreed to a discounted, lump-sum payoff and specific language in a new consent order. Linda wanted to be certain Patty could never again threaten me with legal action.

She struck a deal with Fish and then hired an attorney to smooth out some language in the proposed new order before letting me sign it. Linda had acted as the dealmaker and banker, but, once again, this was my agreement and mine alone.

The plan was for Linda to pay Patty a total of $120,000, in four installments, over a six-month period. Patty would also *recommend* to the court that the bench warrant for my arrest be lifted. But there were no guarantees. The judge could still slap me with a fine or a token amount of jail time, or both, as punishment for my contemptuous behavior.

It took only minutes for the judge handling that Friday's civil motions to sign the new consent order. Mercifully, he withdrew the bench warrant and didn't punish me or even ask me to come into his courtroom. I was officially reclassified as a regular dad! To keep me honest, a compliance hearing was scheduled ten days after the final installment payment date.

The first two checks were hard for Linda to write, but she did so in a kind and loving manner. A huge burden had been lifted off my shoulders, and I felt really safe having Linda on my side. My promise regarding the apartment was well meant, but it also seemed moot. As far as I was concerned, Linda was stuck with me until one of us died; I *cherished* her.

Then something abruptly changed. Linda began to act distant. After a normal Christmas together, she was readying herself for a combined business trip and a visit with Ben over the New Year holiday. She'd be gone while the third installment was due, so I asked her to please write that check and leave it with me before she left.

Linda didn't give me a straight answer. She was having a bad case of buyer's remorse. My industrious and self-made wife didn't feel comfortable sending "Trust Fund Patty" more money. Why should *she* make the crown prince, Sam, and his millionaire mother even wealthier? The prospect made her feel downright queasy.

I could easily relate to her frustration. But why was she reaching this tipping point in the middle of the payment stream? She had to know there would be consequences if she stopped writing checks.

"I want to invest this money for *our* future," Linda agonized. "Instead, I'm sending it to a bitch who's done nothing her entire life but live fat and happy."

Without a doubt, this was a stressful time for Linda. She deserved better from me, that's for damned sure. I had to beg, plead, and yes, even grovel for another check. The court would be unforgiving and throw me in jail, I told her. Something I said—or perhaps even threatened—resonated with Linda. She finally broke down and wrote the check before her departure.

What a relief! One more check, and I'd never see the inside of a Fairfax County courtroom again.

Linda returned from her trip, and she was all business. She must've made a slew of New Year's resolutions, one of them being to never send Patty Beekman another red cent. She made that abundantly clear. "I'm done," she exclaimed. She had the look of a badgered philanthropist.

I tried to reason with her. The $90,000 she'd already forked over to Patty was sunk, like buried treasure. Why add even more financial cost by reopening the case? Michael Fish was certain to ask for, and receive, additional attorney's fees if we went back to court. She didn't care. For the first time, I saw poison, not sparkle, in my wife's exotic green eyes. I told Linda that her pertinacity was tearing our marriage apart.

"What marriage?" Linda retaliated. "You're only in this for the money! I feel like I've been sleeping in the same bed with you and Patty Beekman since our wedding. All of the dreams I've had of growing old with you were nothing but bullshit."

To be sure, I was grossed out by the threesome analogy. But it *killed* me to be envisioned as a money-grubbing scumbag. No matter how far I'd fallen, I knew I was better than that.

In order to consider paying the final installment by its due date, Linda proposed having a lawyer draft a postmarital agreement. *Fine*, I thought, and I didn't view this as a totally hostile act either. Why not be prepared for an endgame? I told her I'd sign any agreement that was fair and reasonable, and she promised to write one final check to Patty if I did.

Emboldened by my reaction, she hired an attorney. I didn't expect the process—a first draft, for starters—or my review to take long. But days turned into weeks, and worry turned into anguish. The last day of March—final installment D day—came and went, and Linda still hadn't written the check. I contacted Michael Fish's office, asking if we could move the date of the compliance back a couple of weeks. Professional courtesy, they call it. My request was gruffly declined. He was ready to ask the judge to fry me if that payment was late.

Linda finally presented me with a document from her lawyer on April 8, two days before the compliance hearing. It was conspicuously missing the word "Draft" on all thirteen pages. I carefully read it through several times, looking for some meat on the bone. In a nutshell, Linda was proposing that we remain married and share a residence, but if and when *she* was ready to call it quits, I'd get nothing—absolutely nothing. She wanted, in essence, for me to waive all interests in our marital estate for the final $30,000 payment!

"It took you a month to come up with *this*?" I exclaimed, slamming it down on the kitchen table.

She was calm and defended her offer, suggesting the first couple of drafts were too harsh. She claimed to have arm wrestled her lawyer into toning down the demands.

Too harsh? Was she kidding me? What in the world was left to tone down? I told her the document, in its current form, was nothing short of extortion. I refused to sign it.

What would I tell the judge? Fortunately, I received the gift of time to prepare my argument. Michael Fish's calendar suddenly, and divinely, became cluttered, and a new hearing date was set for May 8.

That extra month afforded me the opportunity of a lifetime. My mother was quickly slipping away. She'd been moved to assisted living at Westminster Canterbury. Her spirits were still high, but her body was frail and her breathing labored. We both knew she was dying, even though she'd never admit it out loud. She needed me, certainly. But, oh, how I needed her.

I was still a free man and no longer in Virginia's Most Wanted database, at least until May 8. I drove back and forth to Richmond as often as possible. Peg and I tried to keep our conversations light—even staring at heaven's gate, she wanted to avoid the unbearable heaviness of truth. At every opportunity, she kept reminding me how lucky I was to be married to Linda: "Everything's going to work out fine. She's not going to let you go to jail."

I kept my mouth shut. I didn't want Peg near my marital emesis.

In the middle of what I thought was a calm period, I received an e-mail from Jim Hussey. The subject line read, "Personal." It was dated April 23. We'd long since made our disengagement permanent, but he had some important news to share:

A man appeared in our office yesterday afternoon looking for you. Our receptionist thought the person was seeking to serve you with legal papers. The receptionist let him know you are no longer affiliated with the firm. I'm letting you know as a favor, but also to confirm that this has nothing to do with our firm. Whatever it is…good luck.

Michael Fish—part litigator and part collection agent—had been up to his old tricks. The court had acknowledged our new hearing date in writing. His office had already called me with the news, so he could have simply dropped a copy of the paperwork in the mail. Instead, he chose the more expensive route of hiring a process server. And he had taken one more jab at my career. This time he had missed.

Friday, May 8, came in a hurry. I appeared lawyerless before the Honorable Michael P. McWeeny. Fish had punted the case to a young associate in his firm. Perhaps the senior counselor couldn't stand the sight of me either. I came right out with the truth—Linda had broken her promise. Unfortunately, the judge couldn't have cared less. He focused only on the arguments from the plaintiff's attorney, the same recycled bull from one of Fish's earlier playbooks. I'd get charged twice for the same work, too.

"Your Honor, Mr. Hotchkiss has done everything in his power *not* to pay the tuition that he owes, and we ask the court to incarcerate him. As you know, incarceration has a funny way of freeing up money," bandied the young bulldog.

I tried to explain to the judge that it was Linda being difficult, not me. She'd orchestrated the whole deal and written the first three checks. I needed just a little more time to produce that final payment. Judge McWeeny refused to hear the third-wife alibi again. He gave me two weeks to come up with a plan to pay off my debt. He wrote the date of May 22 into the court calendar.

"Mr. Hotchkiss, the plan you bring back to this court better not have anything to do with your wife." Wise man, that judge. He'd seen couples take years to settle their affairs.

I shared this news with "cousin" Ross, who insisted on helping again. He reached out to an old college friend, a retired judge who knew McWeeny quite well. The three of us sat down over lunch and discussed my options.

Ross's friend got down to brass tacks. "McWeeny will want you to pay this thing off in two years or less. That's almost two thousand dollars a month. How close can you come to that number?"

I did the excruciating math. From my life insurance policy, $8,000 in cash value; $7,000 from my 401(k); starting the following February, $1,300 a month from my Time Inc. pension if I elected early withdrawal. Adding it all up, I concluded that I could pay off my debt to Patty in twenty months. How I'd stay afloat myself in the ensuing financial quicksand was a whole other matter. But right now, staying out of jail to be with my dying mother was my sole objective. And forking over everything I had was my only option. The chance of Linda writing a fourth and final check was now utter fantasy.

A midweek visit with Peg on May 13 was a pivotal day. We ate lunch together, played cards all afternoon, and had supper before I was to turn around and head home. The next day, I was supposed to do a World of Grains product demo in Bethesda, Maryland. Peg had been coughing since the time I got there, but she refused to have the doctor drop by on his evening rounds. She kept offering the excuse of an unshakable cold. God forbid she interrupt the rubber of a card game I'd just dealt. She had her priorities, after all. But after playing a few more hands, she started coughing again, and this time couldn't stop. I called a nurse in to listen to her heart. She detected a lot of fluid. Peg was taken immediately by ambulance to the emergency room of Henrico Doctors' Hospital.

Doctors there detected right away that Peg was suffering from congestive heart failure. They strapped her head into a shockingly loud breathing apparatus, something with the look and weight of an outdated M17 gas mask. Mist started to appear inside the mask, which startled my mother. I could see her tired red eyes peeking out. She was—pardon my choice of words—a dead ringer for Darth Vader with a cigarette addiction. That damn insistent noise muffled her seeming cries for help. I was as lost as she. Poor thing must have thought this was the end, and she wanted to tell me good-bye. So I just held her hand and tried to get her to read my lips. I kept it slow and lip synced, "I love you." Again and again. The mask needed to stay on. I knew she heard me because she squeezed my hand and nodded. Peg was stubborn and independent, but in rare times like this, she hung on every word I said.

After what seemed like an eternity and was, in fact, several hours, they removed the mask. When the doctor stopped by to examine her in the morning, he noticed she'd lost the use of her right arm. The loss of oxygen had apparently caused another stroke. Even with slurred speech, she made it clear she wasn't giving up.

"When are you going to give me that new pig valve?" she asked the doctor in a tone that held no hint of Southern charm.

In fact, she was nothing close to the woman who'd raised me, who in times of crisis would panic and ask others what to do. She'd become a survivor. After all my years of bitching about her Southern belle persona, I had nothing of which to be ashamed. And I never discovered her Sacramento secret.

I asked her doctor how long she had left.

"She could live a couple of weeks or a couple of months. It's really hard to tell," he replied, not going out on a limb.

I explained to him that I would not leave Peg's side. The two of us were going to cross the finish line together. I asked him to write a letter to Judge McWeeny to excuse me from the May 22 hearing. I'd serve time in jail for failing to appear in court if I had to, but only after I bid my mother adieu.

The judge had no choice but to reschedule the hearing for June 19.

I was staying in Richmond until the bitter end. I contacted Linda and enlisted her help in tracking down Sam. Having graduated from Davidson the previous summer, he was now living and working in the Vendée region of France, teaching English to *les jeunes* with no more of a care in the world than himself. It had been quite some time since Sam had checked in with me, and even longer since he'd corresponded with Peg. Sad to think that he held a grudge against either one of us, but to completely blow Peg off for six months was inexcusable.

Peg had loved her only grandchild unconditionally his entire life. She kept asking me why Sam was punishing *her*, and I had no rational answer.

Perhaps he'd soon tell her himself. Having been found in France, he was about to call the hospital. When his call came through, I first spoke with him briefly, in code, of course, since Peg was there by the phone and quite lucid. I handed her the phone, and, without any of the usual niceties, she laid into Sam. Instead of saying good-bye to her grandson, she chose instead to lay it on the line. She put him in his place for not standing up to his evil mother. Peg had maintained a cordial relationship with Patty for quite some time—for Sam's benefit—but they'd gone their separate ways by the time we all convened at Davidson for Sam's graduation ceremonies.

Sam seemed to take it like a man. I wasn't sure because I couldn't hear his voice and Peg did all the talking. But I can't forget the moment. The emotional force of Peg's dying words sent Sam reeling. I haven't heard from him since.

Bless Peg's failing valve. She didn't suffer long. I was right there at her bedside, holding her hand, just past midnight in the new day of May 23. I hadn't seen anyone die since Jed lay still in my arms those many years ago. Peg's death scene was straight out of the Bible. Her body rose up, she developed a worried look on her face, and her hand reached out like she was receiving a personal escort to heaven. I called the nurse, not to try and revive her, but to share this divine moment with another human being.

Peg took one last breath and then slowly lowered back down into her bed with a peaceful look on her face. A true lady to the end, she had considered the best interests of her child.

CHAPTER 16

Floor W

PATTY BEEKMAN SENT a compassionate message via e-mail to me two days after my mother died:

> I am so very sorry about Peg's passing. Just the other day I was telling a friend a story Peg told me about speaking with veterans at the Civil War home when she was a young girl. Though Peg and I did not always see eye to eye, I have always valued the things she taught me, most of all, how to be a good Virginia cook. She was one of the best I have ever met. I live for shad roe and asparagus every spring because of her.

Was this the beginning of a truce? Her way of saying, "Forget the last payment; Here's a little Christian charity?"

Yeah, right. When pigs fly. I believe she was greasing the skids for a smoother transition of one of the two assets from Peg's estate. I'd made it a priority to distribute her only remaining treasures, an English walnut writing desk and a diamond pendant, to those whom she'd designated in her will. I admit, it was tempting to sell those items—they would have fetched good prices—but a promise is a promise. The sooner I got them to their rightful owners, the better. I didn't want to give into temptation.

The desk—a real stunner my parents had purchased as an antique in England during World War II—was meant for Sam. Since he was in France, Patty agreed to stage it for him at her home in Springfield.

The pendant had been promised to Linda. In our marital heyday, Linda had been financially generous to my mother and a loving, agreeable daughter-in-law. Had Peg known that Linda had me by the short and curlies, I'd have hoped the pendant would have followed the same path as the Hotchkiss heirloom silver and other fine antiques that ended up at the pawnshop.

On the occasion of our twelfth wedding anniversary, Peg had mailed an envelope addressed only to *me*—a precedent worth noting because of her obsession with good manners—with fifty dollars cash and the following admonition, handwritten on a small, partially torn sheet of yellow lined paper:

> Happy Anniversary! Keep your marriage going. If you don't, you will regret it. Give and forgive.
>
> I love you, Peg

For a person with less than $200 to her name, to give me such a large share of it meant she knew that I was broke and she was dying. Mercifully, she couldn't imagine what was about to happen to my third marriage. I'd have followed every word of her advice if given the chance.

Ray Inscoe, head of pastoral care at Westminster Canterbury, was the only one who knew the intensity of my emotional free fall. We'd gotten to know each other quite well over the past month, and he frequently ministered to my needs, as well as my mother's. We planned Peg's memorial service together and made it a fitting tribute to a well-loved member of the community. Peg was repeatedly eulogized—by Ray, several of her friends, and me—as the life of the party and a great friend. She'd been living proof that you don't need money to be happy.

Linda traveled to Richmond for the funeral and once again to help clean out Peg's apartment. Other than the few keepsakes Linda wanted, I donated Peg's expansive and tasteful Chico's wardrobe—purchased entirely with credit she couldn't repay—and modest furniture to Westminster's two secondhand shops. Recycling was a small and visible way to help repay the grand amount of fellowship allocated to my impoverished mother. However, it was much harder to decide what to do with the hordes of photographs, letters, and diaries that documented her life. After a day's pleasant journey down old and new roads alike, I tossed it all. As a man on the move, I couldn't bring myself to start hoarding again.

Moreover, if I was offering Patty and Linda everything I owned to reach closure on dual fronts, I wanted it to be 100 percent of *nothing*.

One last time, before turning in Peg's keys, I scanned my memories of the fourteen years Peg and Linda knew each other and couldn't help but remember the good times. They had given each other so much of themselves. Maybe I felt the pain deeper. Maybe I had to live with the hole in my heart longer. But I gave Linda her due—she most certainly lost a good friend in the process, too.

Back in Georgetown, I took stock of what lay before me: a house divided, with Linda living on a different floor, a looming court date, irresolvable financial pressure, and the anxiety of everyday life. The thought of losing Linda and that cherished love she'd once promised was gut-wrenching. But the tone of our marriage was so far off-key that it wasn't worth the commitment of counseling to try and retune it. Deep down, I knew Linda had a new plan, and when she announced it a few days after I returned from Richmond, I was prepared:

"I've given notice that I'm not renewing the lease on the house. I've started looking around Georgetown for a new place to live starting in August, and you won't be coming with me."

Unmistakably, she wanted to remove the shackle of a distressed husband. There was no discussion or opportunity for negotiation. She was kicking me to the curb, and her timing stunk. She said nothing about a divorce or legal separation, not even a revival of her dormant postmarital agreement proposal. Just adios.

Linda was exhausted from having three Hotchkisses, as well as a grown son, on her sizable payroll. Even with Peg gone and Sam's tuition mostly paid for, she felt my expenses and debts were denying her the well-deserved pleasures of an income inching close to the seven-figure mark.

Linda had struggled growing up and experienced firsthand the dark side of poverty. Back in her formative years, when her family was on welfare, her father had helped himself to extravagant things like cashmere socks before turning over what was left of the monthly dole to his wife for food and utilities. Why should she continue to enable a guy from the *right* side of the tracks? Enough charity. Enough "for richer or poorer." It was time for her to cut her losses, and too bad about the timing.

While I understood Linda's utter frustration, I could not understand her vengeance. She didn't have to leave me high and dry. We were a couple, and her money, I thought, was *our* money. But she had redrawn those boundaries so that I had no resources to draw upon, no means to hire a divorce attorney, and absolutely no idea how I'd be able to live separate and apart from her during an eighteen-month-or-so trial, should it come to that. I was completely vulnerable.

I admit my post–Time Inc. life was mercurial and rained on Linda's parade, but, hell, we'd both contributed to my downfall! I deserved *something* out of the marital estate—certainly a few crumbs to pay off Patty and start a new life. Could Linda really be so cold and calculating? All at once, I was puzzled, sad, and worried. I needed a lawyer, for starters, but apparently, no one had any money to lend me, or so they said. Who wanted to take a chance on someone like me? And who really believed I was flat broke?

An old Richmond buddy pulled me aside at Peg's funeral. He'd overheard talk between mutual friends of some "issues" I'd been having. When I gave him a snapshot of my predicament, he chuckled, "It's probably not the right time to say this, but hey, at least you'll be coming into some dough from your mom."

He was right. At some point I'd have access to the $159 in her checking account.

It was no use obsessing about my current predicament. The glory days were over, the mistakes made. It was now 2009, and time for me to pay the piper. All I wanted, without any acrimony or lawyer intervention, if possible, was a fair shake.

Thus far, Linda was intractable on the issue. She wouldn't offer anything beyond what was presented in that ridiculously worded postmarital agreement. In her mind, everything she had provided for me—and my family—over the past several years made us square.

Faced with an immovable wife, a dead mother, and an estranged son—not to mention financial ruin—I decided to give up trying. I saw nothing but total darkness. I couldn't run anymore. The burdens of life had me trapped in a hole like Saddam Hussein and, sooner or later, my enemies would capture me.

As fate would have it, I had a routine appointment with my primary care physician, Dr. Jennifer Beach, just when I felt I'd hit rock bottom. She'd been treating me for things like high cholesterol, anxiety, and sleep deprivation. Now, having absolutely nothing to lose, I was ready to admit that I had another malady, one that first surfaced in Mrs. Kimbrough's car, intensified after Nicky died, and was long shielded from the world ever since. I admitted that after nearly forty years, depression was still ruling my life.

Dr. Beach knew instinctively at the time that I was in a very bad place. She may have only been in her midthirties, but she had a tenured mind and an inviting personality. She sat back in her chair and closed the laptop she used for note-taking.

"Doctor, I should let you know that I've reached the end of my rope. My life is such a mess, I'd rather be dead. Even if I have to do it myself."

"Do you have a plan?" Dr. Beach asked me with enormous concern.

"Yes, I do. I know exactly how and where I want to do it," I said with nerves of titanium.

"Would you let me try and help you? We have a great hospital here, and I can arrange for you to receive treatment."

I thanked her but said, "No." I didn't want to go near a "hospital." That sounded like code for "cuckoo's nest" to me.

I shared with her the main reasons that had driven me to this point of despair—my broken relationships, my debts, my underemployment, and my mother's death.

"Dr. Beach, no one can help me. I have too many demons; they are killing me."

But she wasn't giving up easily on my life. "I'm so sorry that you're going through all this. But we *can* help you."

We went back and forth like a long McEnroe-Borg tennis volley until finding a mutually acceptable compromise. She scheduled another appointment in two weeks, and I promised to keep it. Until that time, I agreed that I would not try to harm myself without first calling her or going to a hospital emergency room. I didn't owe Dr. Beach a thing, but she was the only person who seemed to give a damn about me, even if it was in her job description.

Those two weeks weren't spent idly waiting. Linda was moving full steam ahead and had retained the best family lawyer in the District that money could buy. While a few friends offered advice, no one offered bucks, dinero, greenbacks, moola, scratch, or whatever you want to call money. I was left to my own devices, and that made finding a loaded gun the priority. *That might not be so easy*, I realized, but I wouldn't burden any true friend with the enduring guilt of assisting my suicide. I couldn't survive on my own, but I'd figure out how to die that way.

Who better to ask than a casual drinking buddy in the repossession business? Aware of the dangers he faced in his line of work, I assumed he either had a spare gun for sale or could easily find one. I dropped into our local watering hole, the 51st State Tavern, and found him there during happy hour. We had one or two pints before I popped the question. He thought a moment, then came up with a plan.

Time was of the essence. He told me to meet him back at the tavern on Sunday afternoon. "Bring three hundred bucks," he ordered. That gave me a couple of days to scrape together an amount my highly compensated wife made in an hour.

Sadly, I'd already taken the remaining cash value from my life insurance policy and sent it to Patty. I'd been advised by Ross's friend—the retired judge—to do so. The court would see it as a sign of proactivity and good faith, he said. The only liquid asset I had left to sell was that damn collection of Civil War books I'd been dragging around with me since Papa died—no one else in the family cared much about them. I took a couple down to show the folks at The Antiquarian Book Shop in Georgetown. Not interested. So I scanned a few covers and listed the entire collection on eBay, using the fixed-price option. They sold right away to a collector in Maryland. I drove the books to him on Saturday, and he paid me in cash. On and on he went, praising Jedediah Hotchkiss and my uncle's famous maps of the Shenandoah Valley. All I could do was stand there and just "grin fuck" the poor guy. My head wasn't in the game.

I could now pay for the gun, with a little left over for gas money to Richmond and a few final pints of my favorite brew, a beer appropriately called Wacko from the Magic Hat Brewery in Vermont. I'd always found drinking beer invigorating. As it flowed down my throat, the taste of this liquid song of summer refreshed me. This was one thing I looked forward to each day and did all too well.

My man arrived on schedule with the Glock and removed it from a black gym bag. I held the gun briefly under the bar and then stashed it away. *Christ, the thing weighs a ton!* He quickly explained how to use it, and I gave him the money. He didn't pry into my business, and I didn't volunteer any information. He'd probably read about me soon enough in the *Washington Post*, I figured.

I planned to drive south to Richmond, Virginia, in the morning. My destination was Hollywood Cemetery, a living history in stone, iron, and landscape. Ironically, it was also the final resting spot of twenty-two Confederate generals! Sitting on the main family plot overlooking the James River is where I'd planned to end my pitiful life. My great grandfather had purchased the plot in 1903, after the early death of a daughter from tuberculosis. A serene granite angel was commissioned to watch over her, as well as those who followed.

But first, I had the appointment to keep with Dr. Beach. Normally, I'd walk over to her practice at Georgetown University Hospital, but today I drove. I wedged my car into a residential parking space on Reservoir Road and stashed the gun under the front seat. As I got out, I couldn't help but realize what a beautiful and sunny day I had picked to be my last.

I entered the medical center and took a seat in the packed waiting room. Dr. Beach emerged, a mere seven minutes behind schedule. I rose and met her, one foot inside the "Patients Only" area.

"Thank you so much for coming back to see me," she said in a caring, compassionate voice. I forced a token smile.

As she looked at me, there was a powerful message in her eyes. So powerful, in fact, that I realized God was pumping her full of good advice. It was the beginning of an epiphany, and I continued to listen. My plan to kill myself later that day was neutralized, at least temporarily.

"If you're set on this, then I'm obliged to help," she confessed, not merely as a professional disclaimer, but for my own reassurance. Announcing a code yellow and summoning a bunch of muscle-bound orderlies in short-sleeved white shirts to physically restrain me was the last thing Dr. Beach wanted. She much preferred that I work with her.

I could have lied about being suicidal and walked away, but I was tired of pretending. That's all I'd done my entire life.

Instead, I chose to hear her out. She reasoned that a brief stay in the psychiatric ward of the Georgetown University Hospital would provide a safe and secure environment.

"Does that mean I can refuse visitors?" I asked, thinking of current and ex-wives, lawyers, police, bill collectors, and all the other vermin in my life.

"Yes, you'll only be known as 'Henry,' and no one will ever be told you're here, not without your consent."

I was certain if I appeared in court in four days, as scheduled, the judge would have me locked up. Dr. Beach informed me that if I was taken away to Floor W—the Psych Ward—I'd be out of harm's way. I'd never been incarcerated before. Actually, I take that back. I was "arrested" once, in Iceland. Drunk and disorderly. Got thrown into the pokey in Reykjavík with a bunch of other rowdies for the night. Like Otis Campbell, the town drunk in Mayberry, we let ourselves out in the morning. No mug shots or fingerprints.

I allowed one of Dr. Beach's assistants to escort me to the hospital emergency room, where a staff psychiatrist did an extensive evaluation. I asked that Linda be notified of my whereabouts—but not allowed anywhere near me. She came right over to the hospital and made it her business to peek inside my cubicle. She looked a bit bewildered—and betrayed. She asked why it had come to *this*—at the same time I told the nearest attendant to get Linda outta my face. He understood the inherent risk of two dueling spouses meeting face-to-face at this crucial time and asked her to leave.

After check-in, I was taken in a wheelchair to the psych ward. I took umbrage at this, but the nurse explained it was a security precaution. Every once in a while, she told me, they'd lose walk-ins. When we reached the entryway, I quickly learned why someone would run. Looking out at me through a small window in the door was the face of a man bronzed by the hot Libyan sun—his head wrapped entirely in checkered turban cloth. If I was crazy, what did that make him?

When we got inside the unit, the nurse parked my wheelchair and me at a makeshift processing station. As soon as she left, patients seemingly came crawling out of the woodwork to check me out. Each exhibited some form of mannerism similar to the characters in *One Flew Over the Cuckoo's Nest*, although this Washington, DC, cast was more culturally diverse and multilingual. They demonstrated a great deal of angst over the most minor things; I thought they were totally deranged and a bunch of whiners. What had I gotten myself into?

My blood pressure rose to a level of 200 over 110, and I felt every millimeter pounding through my arms and chest. Turban Man—Hosni Ben Saad, a Tunisian, as it turned out—came back. He hovered over me and just stared, stiff as a mime. He appeared to be in a depressed state. But when I started to talk with the registrar, he became manic and started ranting in Arabic—then broke into uncontrollable laughter as he walked away.

"Am I rooming with him?" I asked. She didn't know. Barely looked up to answer me. I suppose we were all a bit crazy on Floor W.

Once officially admitted, I got up and wandered around, peeking into open doorways for telltale signs of room assignments.

I hadn't gotten far before I was reprimanded. "Henry, take a seat," came a voice, seemingly out of nowhere. Rule number one on the floor was to obey, and I did. The only available chair was in the group living room. A black girl in her late teens had control of the lone television. She was wearing pajamas and sucking her thumb while watching a cartoon show.

"Do you mind if we watch something else?" I politely asked.

The girl was catatonic. My body could have been engulfed in flames, and she wouldn't have flinched. I asked another time. Still no reply. I got up and changed the channel using the button on the television itself. As I did so, I asked the girl if the station I'd settled on suited her. Rather than talk, she got up and left the room.

In came a short and wiry black man, full of pain in his face, with both hands pressed into his lower back. He'd had a couple of rough days since jumping from a building and landing on his tailbone. This wasn't the first time he'd failed to kill himself. Nor his first time on Floor W. In fact, he'd stayed at least once at all the DC psych hospitals. He wanted me to know I'd come to the best "house" in town.

He spoke—and looked—like a man who was worn out by life. Half of it had been spent in Leavenworth, the largest maximum-security federal prison in the country. Gil had been found guilty on three counts of first-degree murder. And would do it all over again, he claimed: "Dem no good sons of bitches were better off dead." He survived Leavenworth, and only once did anyone ever try and fuck with him. He knifed that guy in the neck. From then on, the other inmates stayed away from Gil. A self-taught man, he'd developed a passion for philosophy during his incarceration.

Perhaps someone observed our compatibility, because, suitably, I was assigned as Gil's roommate. After turning in my belt, razor, and the yoga strap I used for stretching—all things I could use to hurt myself—at the front desk, I was taken to the shared bedroom. It had a definite "lived in" stench, but the smell of life was as fragrant as roses that night. My only fear of dying was Gil slitting my throat. I soon learned from listening to the "philosopher" that he meant me no harm. He was done with "the killin'." He'd been consumed with rage as a young man, partly due to his upbringing in a fatherless home and partly due to his drug and alcohol addictions. Now, in his later years, he was resigned to battle what he called "confuse-yun."

Listening to Gil squirm his way through a mattress minefield to ease his back pain made my first night a sleepless one. His being a "frequent flyer," the staff disregarded my roommate as a monopolizing hypochondriac. I knew from my own experience with lower back pain that he wasn't faking a thing. In fact, considering that he had a confirmed fracture, I thought the hospital's reaction was negligent and irresponsible.

So I became Gil's advocate. Yes, I had a vested interest—sleep—but even more so, a burning desire to see my roommate treated like a human being and not like an animal. I fought on until the hospital yielded. All it took was a back support brace one could buy at Walmart for less than twenty bucks, and Gil's world was righted. Two days later, he was discharged.

Each morning, I'd meet briefly with a team of psychiatrists, including my assigned doctor. I believe his name was Cummings. As a group, these young docs were cold and clinical, not the least bit like Gerald Laufer, the fatherly shrink I'd seen back in New York. Walking into their conference room struck me as odd—and cruelly ironic—like I was walking into a courtroom full of judges.

As I expected, they tried to treat me by pumping me full of meds and taking me down the same unworkable path Dr. Laufer had veered from years ago. Fortunately, when I invoked the psychiatrist's name into the conversation during a protest, they groveled and asked me what I wanted to take. Why second-guess one of the most highly regarded mental health professionals in the country?

The doctors could also tell I was adjusting well to my new environment. I tried extremely hard to get to know all the patients, not just Gil. I participated in group therapy. I never sat by myself during a meal. I listened more than I talked, and I never walked away from a conversation with anyone, even if he or she had been rude to me.

Although we all suffered one thing in common—insanity—our unique personalities made an interesting village. Even Hosni. Turns out this rather intellectual fellow was enrolled at Georgetown, pursuing a master's degree in international relations. Never mind if his stories as a former lieutenant in the Libyan army and helping squelch an assassination attempt on Gaddafi may not have been true. After all, I told people that I once ran a division of Time Inc.

Despite coping in this strange environment, being inside a locked facility was coarse. I desperately missed my daily walks with Lucy, almost as much as she herself missed them. But I found a way to adapt. Floor W had one long hallway, stretching from the locked front door to the locked back door. It was exactly thirty-three paces. I measured it over and over. Assuming a pace to be a yard, it took fifty-two "laps" to walk a mile. I walked that distance in the morning, afternoon, and late evening. Slowly but surely patients came out of seclusion to walk with me.

I was also able to pull the couch potatoes away from the addiction of television and bring out the playing cards. I was now the only guy left on the floor. Gil and Hosni were history. The ladies—a car mechanic, a medical technician, and an executive recruiter—and I played a few hands of games like spades and hearts, minor league stuff, but something inside their comfort zones. Like mine, their brains had been fried with meds.

After some small talk, flirting, and a knock-knock joke, I started to reminisce about my mother. Being surrounded by women, I felt unselfish doing so. You never know how far to go with conversations about family around strangers. Everyone's past is more delicate than the other's. That being said, my new pals seemed to enjoy my stories about party girl Peg. Naturally, it wasn't long before I revealed her favorite pastime.

"Want to learn a game my mom and I played all the time?"

This was a bold move. Forty-Five was a tough game to teach to sane people. But they sensed how badly I wanted to play and tried especially hard to please me. By their own reckoning, I was the "mayor" of Floor W and could name my poison. Slowly but surely we went from practice games to real games. Then we got into a rhythm, which turned into an addiction. Yes, a healthy addition. And to add just a bit more balance to their lives, I made them do a few simple yoga poses with me before going to bed.

I was allowed to make outbound calls from a communal landline phone. My friends expressed shock and awe, but they congratulated me on my decision. One of them, Jeff Litt, was a longtime buddy whom I'd helped through two divorces; now it was my turn to do the leaning. Jeff made it his business to lecture me about the practical matters I faced once back in the real world. He was the sharpest tack in my dwindling box of allies and annoyed at the thought of my going toe-to-toe with Linda and her fancy attorney without a lawyer of my own. He told me he'd front me as much money as I needed so I could retain counsel as soon as I was released.

"Stu, I don't blame Linda for being tired of carrying the financial load all these years, but you've got to have something to live on. I'm not going to let you get hosed," he insisted.

I'd never borrowed money from anyone before. The few times I'd lent it, I was burned. Jeff's friendship was worth more to me than money, but he was the only one offering a blank check. I reluctantly accepted his offer and promised, as soon as I was released, to find a competent attorney and finish the business of divorce.

Soon after receiving phone privileges, I earned the right to accept visitors. I was reluctant to invite anybody into a place like this, but my first visitor was all-too familiar with psych wards. I had called Ray Inscoe upon my arrival and left him a message regarding my status. When he called back and learned where I was, he dropped everything he had planned for that Saturday and drove north, on insanely congested Interstate 95, to the hospital. In a steady downpour. What sort of person, other than a priest, would do that?

We laughed, we cried, we prayed, and we planned. Ray had known I was in deep shit, but, man, my ending up here was beyond his wildest expectations. Between the time he'd left Richmond and arrived on the floor,

I'd compiled a list of reasons to live. It was my way of rewarding him for such an undertaking. In return, this blessed man left me with the gift of the Holy Spirit.

One day at a time. The next one happened to be Father's Day. I knew I wouldn't be getting a call from Sam, still in France—not after the tongue-lashing he'd received from his grandmother on her deathbed. So, I called Linda and asked if she could bring my other "child" for a visit. We could meet outside the hospital for twenty minutes or so with supervision. Linda was in a bit of a time crunch, but to her credit, she agreed to bring Lucy for a visit if we made it quick.

I sat and chatted with my chaperone until I saw Lucy's fluffy white tail—spinning like an old Fokker propeller blade—in my peripheral vision. What a pretty sight that was. She jumped into my lap, and I ran my fingers through her soft tricolor fur. Linda parked herself on the opposite end of the slab where I'd been sitting—a respectable distance away, safe enough for light conversation. I was too wounded to delve into anything material, but we each admitted to the same fantasy: it would be nice, someday, to try and become friends again.

When the three of us parted ways, I was reasonably content to return to the ward. My interactions with fellow patients were certainly as good, if not better, than the one I'd just had with Linda. A new me was emerging, or perhaps it's better to say, the old me was making a comeback. I no longer saw dark clouds, just the bright light of new days. I couldn't wait to tell the doctors in the morning. They needed to hear that before releasing me.

But sharks still circled in the waters. A young man in civvies came through the front door on Monday afternoon, claiming to be a hospital employee. He went room to room, examining the single-digit numbers affixed to the walls. The on-duty nurse approached him and asked him the nature of his business. He was slick, this kid. He told her he was from the billing office downstairs and needed to discuss some outstanding charges with one of the patients.

"You're not supposed to be on this floor!" she exclaimed. "Let me see what you have."

She grabbed the paperwork out of his hand, did a quick scan, and then pointed at me. "If you're looking for Stuart Hotchkiss, he's standing right there."

That's right, she actually pointed at *Stuart* and not Henry. The paperwork said *Stuart* and I was only to be known as *Henry*. Hospital rule. That should have been a red flag for her to do something other than shrug her shoulders.

The young man quickly retrieved his paperwork and shoved it in my hands, saying, "Stuart Hotchkiss, you've just been served." Then he bolted for the exit and escaped with nary a wound.

Could this really be happening? Team Patty had hired a process server to penetrate the privacy and security of the psych ward in order to lay more court documents in my lap? How much hate was in Michael Fish? First he intruded upon my mother's life on an Easter Sunday with utter vindictiveness and now he'd broken my balls while I was trying to repair my mental wellbeing. Even someone as venal as Fish should have been able to realize that his client wouldn't see another penny if I were dead.

I was livid with that trouble-making scumbag and the hospital, too. The nurse—our sole line of defense from the cruel, outside world—buzzed the kid onto the floor without asking for credentials. She'd never seen him before. He didn't state his business *outside* the locked door. The hospital was beyond negligent. I fought with myself to not let their shoddy security create a personal setback. However, the thought of retaining an "ambulance chaser" to sue MedStar Health, the hospital's parent, was inviting.

We were all done with one another after that, and I was discharged the next day, June 22. I was truly safer outside than inside. As I walked home from the hospital, I bumped into two different neighbors. Both acted as though they were happy to see me and wanted to know how I felt after my "operation." Linda was both too private and embarrassed to share the truth with anyone. But I wasn't. I was done faking it. The truth came out, but my words didn't convince them. These poor Georgetowners couldn't envision Stuart Hotchkiss, that happy guy on Cambridge Place, with a hair out of place.

I gingerly unlocked the door to our "home." Linda was on yet another business trip, working hard to pay the rent. It hit me the moment I walked in just how excessive our lifestyle had become. Yes, I once enjoyed all the toys—the safari vacations, cordovan leather shoes, spa treatments, and hundred-dollar bottles of wine. I had even asked for them, but not anymore. I was trying to rid myself from a decade of "affluenza," that unfulfilled feeling that results from trying so hard to keep up with the Joneses. The party was over.

What I wanted more than anything at that moment was to be with Lucy. A dog walker was caring for her full-time until further notice. We had spent many a night alone together in that empty, cavernous house, and the familiarity of doing so again would have been especially comforting on this, my first night back. I wasn't worried about a visit from the boogeyman, but I was still a bit wobbly from all the meds as well as my reentry into Georgetown society. I kept dialing but couldn't connect with the dog walker until the following morning. I made it through the night; let's leave it at that.

With Lucy's unconditional love, Jeff Litt's financial assistance, and Ray Inscoe's spiritual guidance, I was armed and ready to duke it out with Linda as well as check Patty off my list. The numbers may not have shown it, but I felt like a wealthy man.

CHAPTER 17

Go West, New Man

I KNEW THE legal battle would be lopsided from the get-go. Linda's lawyer, Marsha Traxel, was Washington's divorce diva. I had first contacted Ms. Traxel on April 28, asking her to represent *me*. Just like the other good lawyers in town—Sandy Ain, Deborah Luxenberg, and Ronald Ogens—she wouldn't say, "Boo," without a five-figure retainer. Money talks. By June 10, five days before I entered Georgetown University Hospital, Marsha was already in Linda's corner. She was waiting to trounce me.

By virtue of spilling my guts to sympathizers in super dog-friendly Montrose Park, I was put in touch with an attorney who offered to size up my situation in an hour or so—for free. That was a good omen. After meeting, he agreed to represent me for a flat fee. That made us an even better match, because Jeff wasn't offering unlimited charity. This was no young buck looking to undercut the competition in order to make a name for himself. No sir, Doug Hagerman was an experienced, multipractice lawyer with an undergraduate degree from Harvard and a JD from the University of Pennsylvania. His touchstone was negotiation—collaborative law—not litigation. Doug had crossed swords with Marsha Traxel many times and, coincidentally, represented her ex in her own divorce. Knowing the enemy the way he did had to help, I figured. And it would certainly provide good theater.

I made my position regarding a reasonable settlement crystal clear: I had acted lovingly, but irrationally, and under tremendous stress, in signing over the title to the New York apartment to Linda. Now I simply wanted a fair share of the equity we had in it—nothing else, no other real property, none of her cash or tax-deferred assets, not even a monthly assist from one of the most highly compensated executives—man or woman—in the area.

Unlike me, Linda was a meticulous record keeper and had sent her lawyer copies of every written promise I'd made to her. I couldn't remember exactly what I had or hadn't sacrificed, so Doug presumed a modest amount. When he met with opposing counsel and saw the evidence laid out on the table, he was stunned. I'd given away the store. After their meeting, he called and ordered me down to his office right away.

"What the hell did you do?" he screamed at me. Fair question—I had screwed up. "Are you crazy?" That was being insensitive.

He could not believe a person of my supposed intelligence would do something so utterly self-destructive.

"Who told you that your creditors could come after the apartment if it was held in joint name?" asked my interrogator.

I explained it was the handiwork of Brian Compton, and I gave Doug a quick summary of the meeting Linda and I had had with her bankruptcy attorney.

"Whose idea was it to go see him? Who paid for the consultation?" I knew where Doug was going with these questions, but the truth was complicated. So I kept my response short and on point.

When you love someone as much as I loved Linda, and she also happens to be an attorney, you accept her actions and advice at face value. She was my wife; we were partners. It wouldn't in a million years have occurred to me that she, or Brian Compton, had any other motive. After two failed marriages, I'd decided my third—and final—union would be based upon love and humility rather than force and exaction. I had stuck to this belief till the bitter end.

Doug felt like he'd been undermined by his own client. My promissory notes had blown any negotiating leverage he might have had. Further complicating matters was my debt load. I was going to have to exorcise my financial ghosts before Linda would budge. Although this tactic was perfectly legal, I was ashamed to have to go down a path no other Hotchkiss had gone before.

I had already contacted a bankruptcy attorney, Christopher Porco, who was merged into the Traxel-Hagerman loop. The three agreed that Linda needed to buy me out of the apartment with a combination of cash and alimony. The cash portion would be minimal and fixed—just enough to pay that final installment owed to Patty and my lawyers. Alimony—the portion that needed to be negotiated—would be exempt from bankruptcy and give Linda a tax break.

By July 24—the day of my hearing with Judge McWeeny—numbers had been exchanged but no deal struck. It looked grim—Linda and I were too far apart. So I presented my payoff plan to the judge, promising only what I could control. I didn't go to court alone. John Daly, a long-time Washington public relations and marketing executive I'd first met at Washington's Direct Marketing Day in the late 1970s, wouldn't allow it. My octogenarian friend was a colorful and gregarious figure and a holy man, a devout Catholic, schooled in the District at both St. Anselm's Abbey School and Georgetown University. Despite convalescing from surgery—the same pig valve replacement my mother had so dearly wanted—John was adamant about meeting McWeeny and personally backing up a letter he'd sent to the judge on May 11:

> I can assure you Stuart has been actively seeking full-time employ-
> ment lo these many months, but I also know as one who has oper-
> ated his own communications business for more than three decades
> (and was an employee before that for a quarter century) that when
> someone reaches Stuart's age the pickings are slim indeed. This is
> mostly due to "the cost of benefits" so employers are more apt to
> hire younger, i.e., less-expensive (albeit less-experienced), employ-
> ees. As one who hired employees since '76 until my recent retire-
> ment, I understand the rationale.

Slim pickings, indeed. And it wasn't just an age thing. I'd been out of the management loop much too long. My resume had more holes than Swiss cheese, as he pointed out:

Consider also, how—in an effort to at least get some money coming in—Stuart operated the "Obama Store" in the heart of DC before, during, and after the inaugural, and also how he's even semidemeaned himself to "talk up" healthy snacks at selected Whole Foods locations. His Capital Ties operation, while not full-time or financially viable, showed he tried to use his considerable business skills to land a full-time spot, in marketing or a related activity.

John hit the nail on the head with "semidemeaned himself." I loathed my twelve-dollar-an-hour job as a brand ambassador. Why are Whole Foods shoppers such vultures? He concluded:

In sum, Your Honor, given the considerable pressures being exerted from many sides on this fine gentleman, I hope you will find it in your heart to grant Stuart adequate time to pay the remaining amount that's owed.

Judge McWeeny had no other choice but to accept my plan, but not before tacking on another four thousand dollars in plaintiff's legal fees to my tab. Still, it was a victory, and one worth celebrating over lunch. That's when I learned John had brought his checkbook along to bail me out of jail, just in case.

John's work was done, but we stayed in touch weekly via telephone. I had come to see him as a surrogate father as much as a friend. He made me feel protected, someone in my corner besides a hired gun. The main fight was still ahead. Linda and Marsha were formidable women and opponents, and I certainly wouldn't add to the mistakes I'd already made by underestimating either of them. They'd made two offers, both of which I turned down, despite Doug's recommendation to accept the second one. The pressure to get one more, and better, offer in less than a week was wearing, to put it mildly. Why is marriage such serious business and divorce such a game?

Doug had instructed me that under no circumstances was I to move out of the marital home until the ink was dry on a deal. My leaving could appear, from a legal standpoint, as abandonment. If we went to trial, I wouldn't want the fact that Linda was leaving me to get twisted. If the lease on our house expired and we had no agreement, I was further instructed by Doug to continue to reside there and force the landlord to evict me. While I didn't care to drag our landlord—a member of the prominent Shriver family—into our marital woes, I promised that I would do as I was told.

Linda had scheduled movers to come a few days early and crate some of the more delicate items such as oil paintings and marble tops to furniture. She was jumping the gun. The antique furniture we'd purchased over the years at considerable expense was not hers until we had a deal. I decided to temporarily render these items less desirable and valuable by removing an odd door here and a drawer there on a couple of marquee pieces and hide them in my car. While I didn't become "clumsy" like I had during my divorce with Doreen, my motives were entirely the same—to move the needle in my favor.

We met on July 30 and struck a deal. Linda opened her checkbook and starting signing. Her ability to help me financially was now binding but finite. If I hadn't realized she wanted to move forward with divorce, conversations overheard between the lawyers that a filing was imminent made that abundantly clear. They were finessing the date of our physical separation and fast-tracking the process.

As soon as Linda's checks cleared, I called junior Fish and asked if his client would accept a reduced amount if immediately paid in full. He was livid and threatened to call Judge McWeeny. I then threatened to write a letter to the Virginia State Bar, citing his boss for unprofessional conduct on that memorable Easter Sunday in Richmond and then later in the psych ward. What in the world was I doing? I was d-o-n-e, done, and getting myself right back into a fight. I came to my senses and satisfied my debt.

With a month's worth of alimony in my pocket, I applied for a studio apartment in a building at the corner of 24th Street and Pennsylvania Avenue, in the Foggy Bottom neighborhood. I had a long talk with the building manager, explaining, among other things, that I was a financial wreck. She wasn't the least bit fazed. Recently divorced and broke herself, she told me not to fret over her company's mandatory credit screening. As usual, cash was king, and a second month's rent paid in advance would seal the deal and make her owners smile. Plus, the copy of my property settlement agreement proved that I had a steady income. She promised a quick answer—and delivered. I was sleeping in my new apartment the next night.

Clearing out my belongings from the spacious marital home brought the greatest freedom I'd ever experienced. As one of the beatitudes teaches, "How happy are those who claim nothing, for the whole earth will belong to them!" The massive purge that everyone dreams about doing one day became a reality for me because, well, I didn't have anyone to talk me out of it.

While the apartment worked for me, it didn't for Lucy. Despite the "No Pets" house rule, I could sneak her in for sleepovers, most easily on Saturday nights. Whether it was the early morning noise coming from the college bar across the street, or there being no real bed to crawl into, Lucy didn't enjoy herself a bit. She was much happier in Linda's new house, and I didn't try to force the matter. I loved that dog too much to put her through more upset.

Christopher Porco and I worked diligently on my Chapter 7 bankruptcy petition. It was a chore to locate all the paperwork required, but I had sufficient incentive: stopping my creditors in their tracks. Over $200,000 in unsecured debt was going to be legally forgiven. Once Christopher had the necessary documents and signatures he needed, I completed a mandatory online credit counseling and debtor education course, and my petition was filed. Thus began a three-month waiting period. Other than needing to be in court for a meeting with my creditors and the bankruptcy trustee, I was free to roam about the country.

I had lots of time to research and explore my next abode, but my first instinct was to reach out to family—what remained of it. My closest—and only male—cousin and I had a distant yet ever-ready relationship, based on both lifestyle and blood. And we had an unbreakable link with the past: his mother had broken the news to me about Nicky that unforgettable Sunday evening in 1971. If there was but one wise person who could respectfully and intelligently address my situation, it was John Day.

John and his wife, Judy, had long ago abandoned their unfulfilling suburban life in West Hartford, Connecticut, for the wilds of northern New Hampshire. They enjoyed living in a remote area, and, from the pictures I saw, their white colonial farmhouse and four-acre retreat in the White Mountains was charmingly secluded. They'd added on a small, modern apartment to the side of their home to accommodate Judy's frail parents in their declining years. Both parents having passed away, the apartment was vacant.

John reached out and encouraged me to find a way to begin again. He admitted that this was so easy to say and so hard to do. But rather than suggest how I might reinvent myself, he simply opened a door to freedom. If I wanted the apartment, it was mine. There wasn't an ounce of reticence in his offer.

Nearly sixty years old, John had become a crusty, old New Hampshire guy who didn't care a whole lot about much except his garden and his grandkids. Both John and Judy had years of experience as social workers, counseling people in crisis from all walks of life. They knew the idea of starting over was scary as hell. Cousin Stuart, as tough as he thought he might be, could benefit from their compassion.

Moving to a town like Easton, a third of the sparsely populated Franconia–Easton–Sugar Hill triangle, was the epitome of radical downsizing. Even if you counted in all the squirrels and chipmunks, you still wouldn't get to five thousand. Yet there was one saving grace: as tucked away as the area was, only one hundred and fifty miles in different directions separated Easton from Boston, Montreal, and the Atlantic Ocean.

Within a few weeks, after topping out on morning coffee with mountain views from the farmer's porch, I surmised that living in Easton was downright lonely. I'd spent far too many years living a stone's throw from restaurants, bars, bookstores, and brew pubs. I missed walking on crowded sidewalks. As charming as it was to live on Sugar Hill Road, I was six miles away from the simple conveniences of grocery stores and a library with Internet access.

My body was in the Granite State, but my heart longed for something else. Fortunately, I'd done some homework before going to New Hampshire and booked a trip out west. No worries if I didn't like the High Desert or Pacific Northwest, and not much expense, either. I had lots of frequent flyer miles and hotel points to burn.

I narrowed down my selection to seven diverse locales that ranked highly on at least two best-places-to-live lists. All but one—Santa Fe, New Mexico—were north of the 43rd parallel. I didn't expect to add that one outlier to this trip, but I certainly planned to visit the other six: Portland, Oregon; Bend, Oregon; Seattle, Washington; Bozeman, Montana; Jackson, Wyoming; and Boise, Idaho.

I flew to Salt Lake City, Utah, the most centrally located venue, to rent a car and start traveling north and west. My first stop was Boise. A recent article in the *New York Times* had described Idaho's capital as the "Up and Coming Portland, Oregon." It had experienced substantial growth in the late 1990s when Californians plundered the real estate market. Still, the city's population was only two hundred thousand—the same size as my hometown of Richmond, back when I left. And the majority of Boiseans lived in the outlying suburbs, not in the close-in, older neighborhoods.

Once inside the city limits, I took the first exit indicating "Downtown," passing the famous Boise State University football stadium and its blue turf. I'd grown accustomed to living smack-dab in the middle of cities, and I couldn't bear the thought of altering my lifestyle. Easton had confirmed my angst. Using the state capitol building as my beacon, I soon found a humongous parking space—large enough for two cars in New York or Washington—and started wandering on foot. Immediately, the city center's modest scale yet vibrant feel impressed me. A Saturday street market was in full swing, and every café and restaurant was chockablock with patrons. The locals were approachable and gave me their best Chamber of Commerce pitches. They raved about the hipness of the city, its street activities, its outdoor lifestyle, its culture, and the beauty of its surroundings. Talking to them confirmed that what I saw was real.

The city's nightlife was also jumping, at least that Saturday night. The pedestrian zone on 8th Street was teeming with revelers streaming in and out of bars and restaurants. The sun set late, around nine o'clock, in late August, and when it did, the temperature dropped perhaps twenty degrees by midnight. A place so cool and dry in late August? I was sold on the high plains desert climate and wondered how I had managed to live through unrelenting summer heat and humidity most of my life.

Finding Boise so perfect in climate and lifestyle, I realized there was no point in visiting the other cities on my list. I already knew Portland and Seattle would be stretches for me financially, and I preferred a dry climate over a wet one. Jackson and Bozeman would be far too cold and windy in the wintertime. That left Bend, about half the size of Boise and more of a retirement destination, and Santa Fe, a chic town full of overpriced art galleries. Someday, these six cities might warrant closer looks, but not now, not in 2009. I was fifty-four years old, saturated with feelings of "been there, done that," and cured of my affluenza. I hungered for a new beginning in an unpretentious and community-focused city, not too cold, not too hot, with good health care, and plenty of culture and recreation—all at a price that would keep me out of debt. Before discovering Boise, I'd thought a place like that was pure fantasy.

Having blown off the rest of my planned visits, I remained in southwest Idaho an extra week. I played a few rounds of golf; took day trips to nearby towns like Horseshoe Bend, Emmett, and Weiser; and sampled some wines from Idaho's one and only American Viticultural Area (AVA) in the Snake River Valley. My nightcaps were pints of tonsil-choking, hoppy brews from each of the four local microbreweries and countless other guest beers from the region.

I was feeling quite slap happy when my plane landed at Reagan National Airport on August 31. I was still on Idaho time, and the last thing I expected was a buzzkill. How could there be any more bad news? My affairs were in order, and the loss of loved ones was history. But when I retrieved a voice message from my cell phone that had been left in-flight, my mood swung fiercely to melancholy.

I played and replayed the message, hoping against hope that I'd misheard it. But the truth was inescapable. John Daly, after suddenly developing a rare blood infection stemming, somehow, from his aortic valve replacement, had passed away four days earlier. He was the first person I wanted to share the scoop with on Boise. Not being able to do so left me filled with a heavy heart. And guilt ridden. I tearfully confessed to his widow that I'd allowed John, in the midst of his recovery from surgery, to exert himself and join me in the showdown with Judge McWeeny. This compassionate woman not only forgave me but also helped me bear the loss by revealing John's attempt to reach me from his deathbed to say good-bye.

I returned to New Hampshire, breathing a lot easier. Still, I yearned for company and appealed to Linda to let me have Lucy for the remainder of my stay. She'd be in the country for three or four weeks and have a play-mate—John and Judy's dog, Sadie, an elderly golden retriever. I thought it would be a no-brainer, but Linda thought otherwise.

"I'd rather keep Lucy in DC as I have a few weekend things planned with her already. Perhaps another time," she proposed.

Another time? There would be no other time, unless I stayed longer in Easton or made a home elsewhere in similar range of DC. Taking Lucy twenty-four hundred miles across country in a car and permanently away from Linda would have been cruel to both. That's the way it had to be.

I second-guessed my choice of Boise several times. Was I giving up too much to move so far away? Not just Lucy, but friends, too? Maybe it was best to stay closer to my eastern roots. New England had suited me in the past, in large part because it did not appeal to affected people.

To make absolutely sure, I looked at a few cities outside of Easton, no more than one or two hundred miles away. Cities like Burlington, Vermont; Portsmouth, New Hampshire; and Portland, Maine, had all received high accolades, and once I got there, I couldn't argue with their boosters. But I couldn't help recounting that quixotic trip I'd made to L.L. Bean in the winter of 1983, which framed New England's worst liability—winter weather. Locals confirmed that the humidity contributed to bone chilling temperatures in winter and constant snowfalls, as early as October and as late as May.

This could not be good for my mental health. For people like me, gray weather was a big risk. Sudden weeks or fortnights of unseasonably mild temperatures were virtually nonexistent in the North Country. That was Winterland, the home of bum sliding, pond hockey and snow safaris. Couldn't do it. My decision was made; I was heading to the high desert. Bada bing, bada boom.

I announced my decision to friends and family, and they just didn't get Boise, let alone Idaho. They confused it with Iowa, they thought the iconic resort Sun Valley was in California, and worst of all, they believed all Idahoans were potato farmers. Even the *New York Times* portrayed the capital city as being behind the times: "Boise, once ruled by the bait-and-bullet crowd, has come to embrace the Lycra lifestyle…while remaining a mining and farming town at heart." I hadn't seen any of that and realized that it can be dangerous to rely too heavily on the *Times*.

My comeback was as simple as Boise itself. I had lived in many large and thriving cities, and quite comfortably, too. But I'd never lived in such a small and compact city at the crossroads of civilization and nature as Idaho's capital. It was all an emotionally weathered easterner like me needed.

During my drive back to DC, I thought about where I might live in Boise. My emotions were stuck on the downtown area, 8th Street in particular, and wouldn't it be divine if I could find a place to live that had some antiquity and character? If I could keep one thing constant in my life, as a reminder of the East, it would be that—a New York-prewar-style apartment replicated in Boise.

Style still mattered. In fact, I looked like quite the dandy for my meeting the next day with the creditors, but not a single one showed up. Wasn't I worth an hour of anyone's time? Didn't Bank of America want a piece of the $35,000 I owed them in credit card debt? American Express absent? They had lawyers up the wazoo. I'd spent all these years agonizing about the size of my overall debt when, in fact, the big boys seemingly couldn't have cared less. At any rate, my bankruptcy petition would now sail through the system. By mid-December, my financial nightmare would be over.

And, in less than two weeks, I'd also be divorced.

The October 27 hearing, in front of Judge Linda Kay Davis, was designed to be uneventful. My Linda's lawyer had initiated the necessary paperwork the day after our legal separation. My wife not only wanted out of the marriage but had also requested a formal order from the judge to restore her surname to Murphy. Even though Doug Hagerman would not be present at the hearing, he promised it would be quick and pro forma. All I had to do was answer, "Yes," to each of the judge's questions.

Despite it being all teed up, I managed to throw a spanner in the works.

We had not addressed custody of Lucy in our separation agreement. Knowing how much Linda and I both loved her, the lawyers had decided to dodge the issue. Otherwise, our negotiations would have bogged down to the point of a stalemate. So when Judge Davis asked if all matters had been settled, I said, "No." It was an honest answer. I thought if I explained to the judge that we had planned to sort it out later, she'd appreciate my candor.

I couldn't have been more wrong.

Judge Davis ruled that our heretofore uncontested divorce was, in fact, now a contested one. This case no longer fell under her jurisdiction—it belonged on a different calendar, in front of a trial judge. What the hell just happened? Panic set in. I had just created one big clusterfuck for everyone.

Later that evening, Doug Hagerman, having just been advised of the situation by Linda's lawyer, called and ripped me a new asshole. "What've you done?" he shouted. "Why couldn't you keep your damn mouth shut? Do you realize that your separation agreement is now worthless? You've just thrown the whole thing out the window!"

I wanted to annihilate the person who'd first said honesty was the best policy. Oh Lord, help me. When was I *ever* going to learn to play the game? A contested divorce could run into six figures against a lawyer like Marsha Traxel. And guess what? With a worthless separation agreement, Linda no longer had an obligation to pay me alimony.

Thankfully, everyone regrouped for damage control. No one wanted the agreement to unravel, especially the lawyers. They could have been disbarred for lying to the court. Oh, how I wished I was independently wealthy, Judge Gammerman, and could watch them grovel. They devised a plan for me to reappear before Judge Davis and admit to a momentary lapse in judgment. I would also cede custody of Lucy to Linda. My signed affidavit was submitted to the court and the case was restored to the uncontested calendar for November 23.

My "scoutly" deed permanently separated Lucy and me. Yes, it was unfair that Linda could provide her with a cozy new home in Georgetown, but hadn't I learned by now that life wasn't fair? There was certainly no need to clash over her. It's the sort of sacrifice I was willing to make for my "best friend." Remembering the way Linda and her first ex-husband fought over their son left no doubt. Lucy would be fine. And, in due time, so would I.

The end of my tenure in DC was drawing near. And I had a several more weeks to kill. Why not go back to Boise in a different season and size it up from the perspective of a resident rather than a tourist? Could I truly afford to live there? If so, were there apartments for rent downtown? Would landlords rent to me after a bankruptcy? I wasn't rethinking my decision about Boise—not one bit—but I wanted to address these questions before committing time and money to a cross-country move.

So I hopped on a plane to Portland, Oregon, and rented a car there. I resisted the temptation to poke around the city because I'd mentally scratched it off my list. The drive through Oregon and along the Columbia River was much more scenic than the one I'd made in August through Utah and eastern Idaho. The beer trail was impressive as well. Both good omens in my book.

I arrived in Boise on a Friday. The preponderance of people had moved indoors, but they seemed as warm and friendly as the ones I'd met in August, so there was no letdown. During happy hour, I chose to revisit TableRock BrewPub—I remembered their Friday night feature, a small keg of something new served on NitroTap, meaning the beer was pushed from the keg to the tap with nitrogen rather than CO2. Beer geeks love it! That night, they were offering an imperial stout infused with Jameson whiskey. By six o'clock, the two brewers and their flock had bellied up to the bar, and soon there were no strangers in my midst.

A woman, probably in her early forties, sat next to me, on my left. She'd overheard me talking to others about Washington, DC, prompting her to cut in. She introduced herself and proceeded to regale us with a bit of her past in Charlottesville, Virginia, and Baltimore, Maryland. The two of us shared some similar tales about the East and that was all. No pick up lines, no phone numbers exchanged, nothing more than a few laughs and firm good-byes.

Caution now agreed with me. Healthy relationships with women obviously weren't my forte. For someone with my history, a lustful spark might lead to a love storm, and then, by gosh, the possibly of a romantic union. No thanks. I'd put my hand on the hot stove of matrimony one too many times. No way was I going to succumb to another fatal attraction. From here on, I only wanted one friend with benefits—my daily dose of Lexapro.

From the time I was eleven—that day in Mrs. Kimbrough's car—to this moment, I had always thought that antidepressants were no more effective than a placebo. Forty-three years later, I couldn't live without my "little white pill"—full of a libido-sabotaging chemical known generically as escitalopram. A few unwanted side effects paled in comparison to a life riddled with anxiety, unexplainable panic attacks, and chronic depression, hands down!

The next three days were consumed with searching for a place to call home. I found plenty of single-family homes and apartments for rent within a three-mile radius of 8th Street, but nothing in the core downtown area. So, as backup, I met with the owner of a small bungalow in the historic Warm Springs neighborhood, about a mile from the city center. He and his family were moving up and keeping this house as investment property. He had to play it loose as far as a start date. That suited me fine. I gave him a postdated check in the amount of $1,200—a month's rent— with the understanding that he not cash it until we drew up a lease. Both our plans could change. He didn't even bother to check my credit, probably assuming it was a waste of money to investigate a prosperous-looking dude like me. *It's a wrap!* I realized. *Time to get my little chicken arse back to DC and start packing.*

This time, my return to DC was uneventful. Not a single voice message.

I made my final appearance before Judge Davis in late November. This time, I followed my script line by line. She granted Linda her two wishes. Fourteen years spent with one of the most vivacious, shrewd, and passionate ladies in the world were now but a memory. What she took from me was much more than the money and the vow of a lifetime together. She took away my confidence to fall in love like that again.

Christopher Porco advised me to "head west, new man." He was certain my bankruptcy discharge would occur on schedule. Besides, he said, I could always fly back to DC if the judge requested my presence. He gave me a book to read on my journey, something that helped reduce the stigma of my financial blunders. Turns out my situation was far from unique; pretty intelligent guys like Abraham Lincoln, Mark Twain, Henry Ford, Milton Hershey, Walt Disney, and Stuart Hotchkiss would soon be brethren in bankruptcy. Not the fifteen minutes of fame I'd always wanted, but a jolt of reassurance, to say the least.

It took me three weeks to get myself ready to move, a fatuous waste of time for someone with so few possessions. Eager as I was to hit the road, I found myself procrastinating. Being so free was utterly freaking cool, and yet, so alien. Movers came to pick up and store my desktop computer system, my kitchen gear, and my premarital furniture. I loaded the essentials — mostly clothes and a few irreplaceable family photos—into my car, trusting my always-reliable Toyota RAV4 could make the cross-country trek. Once done with the movers, my newfound independence left me feeling like that teenager back in New Orleans. I had one key to my name—my car key—and holding on to it was my only responsibility.

I was free to explore. I had no concept of time. I was the ultimate bachelor. Best of all, I could stop anywhere en route to Boise and make it my new home—the ultimate audible, for you football fans. There I was, day after day, cruising through middle Tennessee, the Arkansas wine region, downtown Memphis and Oklahoma City, Amarillo, and Albuquerque. Nothing caught my fancy for more than a few hours. I kept on truckin'.

When I arrived in Moab, Utah, I ran into the first snowstorm of my trip and wound up having to spend three nights in this out-of-season tourist mecca. It was charming and loaded with sights: Arches and Canyonlands national parks! Dead Horse Point State Park! Grand County Public Library, the best small library in America! Moab Brewery! What was there not to like about Moab? There was even a downtown apartment for rent. I didn't take the bait. It wasn't even remotely close to Boise in city amenities.

Moab's snowstorm had quickly become a blizzard, reminding me why I preferred the high plains. I bolted for Idaho, trusting my hoopty to handle the icy roads and driving snow with all-season radials. Chevy Suburbans and tractor trailers whizzed by and threw up more snow and ice onto my windshield than my wipers could handle. I was driving on US Highway 191 in a whiteout, and there was no way to pull onto the shoulder of the road because it wasn't plowed and I couldn't see where I was going. All I could do was keep moving, and pray.

Once past Price, Utah, I was on the downslope of a mountain pass and nearing Interstate 15. The weather mellowed, restoring visibility. I stopped to assess the damage to my car and found only two ice chips on the windshield. I got the message: forge ahead and trust the process. My wandering days were almost over.

I'd grown up in Richmond, Virginia, and run away to New Orleans as a teenager. I'd lived in Iceland, London, New York, and Washington, DC. I'd buried my brother, Nicky; Papa; Lizzie; my son, Jed; Bunks; and

Peg. I'd been married and divorced three times. I'd faced the premature end to a brilliant career and the stigma of bankruptcy. Added to this, I was at an impasse with my estranged adult son, Sam. I'd endured so many demons—including a carefully planned suicide. But on Christmas Day, in the year of our Lord 2009, I pulled into Boise, Idaho, ready for a fresh start, excited to begin anew. For better or worse, this was my new slice of paradise.

I'd long ago ended my fear of dying. Finally, I was no longer afraid of living.

Acknowledgments

Sometimes, a project as deeply personal as this memoir needs a champion. Without the help of Glenn Mason, a former colleague at Time Inc. and current New York City public school teacher, the process of exploring my life would have never started or finished. For two years, Glenn served in numerous capacities as my writing mentor, editor, and muse. Thank you, dear friend, for helping me draw out my revealing and unconventional journey onto these pages.

Once my memoir was completed, I then needed financial help to publish it. I put together a rather basic Kickstarter campaign, and the money rolled in. Special thanks go to these people who had the ability and desire to go above and beyond:

Anonymous (7)
Amie and Brad Bruggeman
Bruce C. Cann
John and Marilyn Cottingham
Anthony Del Broccolo
Peter Dubner
Randolph F. Harrison
Bill Henry
Sir Walter Johnson

Elizabeth Kerrigan
Lud Kimbrough
RV Lardon
Edward "Uncle Rusty" Lehman
Rick Miller
Steve Ports and Joy Crandlemire
John Sandklev
Donna Baier Stein
W. Corey Trench

I've saved the best for last. I offer my love and admiration to my fiancée, Lisa, for having the courage to read—and critique—my manuscript
in advance of its publication. Despite all my past mistakes and imper-
fections, I hope you'll still marry me on July 11, 2015, at St. Michael's
Cathedral in Boise.

photo by Jeff Beaman

Stuart Hotchkiss is a former publishing chief who served as executive creative director of Time Inc. and as president of Time Inc. Home Entertainment. He is also a past president of the Direct Marketing Association of Washington.

A native of Richmond, Virginia, Hotchkiss now lives in Boise, Idaho, where he serves as vice president of the Episcopal Diocese of Idaho's Executive Council.

41606902R00183

Made in the USA
Lexington, KY
19 May 2015